KITCH

ANTHONY JOSEPH

KITCH

A FICTIONAL BIOGRAPHY

OF A CALYPSO ICON

PEEPAL TREE

First published in Great Britain in 2018
Peepal Tree Press Ltd
17 King's Avenue
Leeds LS6 1QS
England

Printed and bound by CPI Group (UK) Ltd, Croydon CR0 4YY

ISBN13: 9781845234195

Supported using public funding by
ARTS COUNCIL
ENGLAND

CONTENTS

Part One: Bean   7

Part Two: Lord Kitchener   85

Part Three: The Grandmaster   185

Epilogue   255

Afterword   264

For my father
Albert Hugh Joseph
1943 - 2017
who was human, after all

KITCH

PART ONE: 'BEAN'
1941-1947

He have melody like peas grain. — Lord Pretender

Everybody know 'Kitch' but few know 'Bean'. Is he sister give him that name, because as a boy he was so tall and thin. She used to call him 'String Bean', 'Bean'. Then some people, where he was living in Arima would call him 'Bean Pamp', because Daddy Pamp was he deceased father name. I used to call him it sometime, quietly, and he would laugh because he know that name dig far, the name is 'Bean'. But I never prostitute it or let everybody know.

— Russell Henderson

GREEN FIG

THE STABLE HAND in his rubber boots throws a bucket of disinfectant into the pig pen. Then he brush it down. Sun coming up slow on the market now, but a faint moon still in the sky. Black back crapaud still weeping in the gullies, corn bird flying from vine to river vine. Is Saturday. Donkey cart and wagon wheel coming down the main road from Valencia and Toco, leaning in the potholes and the lumps in the road, coming to the market, heavy with purple dasheen and pumpkin, plump with green christophene and lettuce by the basket, long brown cassava and breadfruit, mauby bark, yamatuta. The knock-kneed dougla woman sets her stall by the market side, near where the road slopes down into tracks and rickety cratewood stalls. She stirs her cauldron of cowheel soup and hums holiness hymns. She has been there since dew-wet morning, from the first glimpse of light burst. Her pot bubbles and spits and the scent of wild thyme and congo pepper drifts through the market like a spell. Soon, in the damp woody spaces of the covered market stall, chickens will be swung by their feet, to flutter against the grip of the abattoir man, with his cutlass hand and his hot water boiling on a fireside, to dip and pluck them beating, from wing and narrow bone. Morning opening like a promise above Arima.

Miss Daphne sits on an overturned iron bucket shelling pigeon peas in the market yard, with rose mangoes and speckled breadfruit laid out on a crocus sack before her. She speaks to the full woman selling navel orange in the stall beside her – reels her head back, laughs – and peas fall from her crotch. Down the aisle, Ma Yvette selling bottles of black-strap molasses, Ma Pearl selling saltfish, smoked herring, pigtail and garlic, Madame Hoyte have nutmeg and mauby bark, Mr Chambers selling lamp oil, Picton have corn. Customers walk now among the stalls, choosing okra and sweet peppers, cow-foot, tripe and live crabs for Sunday callaloo.

Later, in that afternoon time, after the market has been deserted, when only the stink of fowl-gut and rotten fruit remains in the gutters, and the traders are packing their unsold goods, a team of long cars will roll slowly across the ragged field behind the market. The dry season has parched the ground there till the earth is veined with fissures. Dust. Buicks, Austins and bullet-shaped Chryslers are taking French Creoles to the Santa Rosa race track for that afternoon's races.

⇒Up hill to the north, young Bean sit down on the worn wood of his front step with his head between his knees, making rhythm beat with a guava stick against the splintering edge and humming upright bass in the throat, comping with the high notes. Eileen, his sister, frying fish in batches in the outside kitchen behind the house. Bean could smell the flour and oil burning in the skillet. A bee start to inveigle the stick. Bean get up, dust off the seat of his pants, catch a vaps just so and walk down St Joseph Street, whistling, his slipper slapping the gravel. He wave to the hornerman Deacon sanding cedar crooksticks in his shed, he say hello to the black-tongued soucouyant hanging white sheets on a line flung between her lime and barbadine tree, to Baboolal the one armed tailor, needle in his mouth.

Crossing the main road, by the dial, he passes the market vendors dragging their carts home, then he walks across the dusty field beyond the market to the old Samaan tree near the paddock. Its branches spread over the wild yard where horses roam. He sits among its raised roots where a rage of ti-marie bush waits with leaves that shut to the touch. From where he sits he can see the jockeys walk their horses from the paddock to the races. He can smell the horse dung, hear boots kick dust. With his head resting on his forearm, and his forearm across his knees, he takes a stick and starts interfering the poor ti-marie bush. But is bass for a tune what humming in his head. He watching how the ants and batchaks live in that little jungle down there, between the picka bush. Each frond he touch folds like a shy shutting fan. It take him right there by the paddock and he didn't even know it take him. One thing he thinking and another thing thinking behind, melody spring before the words reach the rim of his mouth, like something telling him each time what the next word or note would be, the song singing itself fully formed in his head, as if he had been working on this song even as he worked in the field that morning, even as he walked through the village at night and waved, stuttering to the hunters going uphill with flambeaux and lances, cocoa milk and cigarettes, black-back crapaud bleating in the bush.

He looks up through the diamond patterns of leaf and light, to see if the song has fallen from the saaman trees' canopy. His lips move to whisper, his ears shut out all sound but the song. And not even the thoroughbred gallop along the dirt track with its high ass pumping, the splash of dust it kicking, not the whip or the rustle of savannah breeze through the leaves, or the announcer on his megaphone, or the sky-blue Buick engine's roar can shift him from where he is.

> *Mary I am tired and disgust*
> *doh boil no more fig for me breakfast*

It come out whole. He never have to write it down. Gone back home now and have to keep it in his head, trap it in there, like a humming bird in a bottle, seal it in by repetition, stitch and tie it into creation.

1941: GASTON AUBREY

WHEN I FIRST SEE Kitchener is in Arima I see him.

My band used to play a lot in Arima and it had a dancehall upstairs the Portuguese laundry, right by the old racecourse, where they used to have christenings and wedding receptions. Was right there I used to play piano with Bertie Francis band, Castilians. We would play, a lil' Count Basie, Glen Miller, calypso music. And after we done play we go looking for Chinese restaurant, for cutters, or the souse woman by the market.

Right by the dial there was a tailor shop, an' sometimes, if you there in the day, you may see Kitch, always dressed well; he very tall, a good looking brown-skin fella, always with the open shirt an' the neck tie, an' he singing calypso.

The first tune I remember Kitchener singing was 'Green Fig'. I see him sing that right in Arima, one evening, Carnival season, when he stand up under the dial, light on him, an' he singing this song an' people start to gather round. *'Mary I am tired and disgust, doh boil no more fig for me breakfast.'*

People calling 'Kaiso! Kaiso!' So he sing a next verse.

An' when he finish he say, 'Gus boy, I feel I going down town. I going down Port of Spain to m-m-m- go make my name. Arima eh have n-n-nothing for me.'

I watch him. I say, 'Bean, town not easy, you feel you ready for town?' He wasn't Kitchener yet, he was 'Bean'.

He say, 'Yes, I ready.'

I say, 'Well, if you need a piano man, ask for me when you reach down; I living Belmont Valley Road.' An' you know when that man reach in town he really come up Belmont and look for me. And is so we start to play music, from then, for years.

TOWN SAY

BEAN STANDING IN THE MORNING YARD under the kitchen window where the earth was slippery with mud from washbasin water, scent of stale soap, swill, and cow dung and frangipani in the fields. He washes his face in the enamel rainwater bowl, wrings and flicks the water from his hands. In the bedroom he combs his hair in front of the mirror. He wears the white shirt he has starched and ironed himself, the brown trilby, pinched in the peak, the school blue suit his father left behind, the one with the pants a lighter blue because his mother once washed the thing with coal tar soap on the river rocks and it faded. The black shoe cracked across the axle of the instep from walking long and hilly places.

While dew still drying, he leaves the wooden house on St Joseph Road with his grip and box guitar in a burlap sack, grease from two fried bake oozing grease through brown paper in his inside jacket. His sister watches him from the front door, as he crosses between the fowl shit and the mud and onto the government road. Bean turns back to wave, sees the house leaning to one side like it want to fall, the wood corroded, termite in the ceiling, wood bug in the rickety balustrade, and his sister stand up there silent and proper, reserved. But is gone Bean gone.

When the people of the village see Bean walking along the gravel road with his suitcase, they come to their fences to wave. Sister Mag stops from sweeping her yard to smile broad and whisper a prayer for Bean. The Deacon stop bulling he craft, to watch the young man go, and Pundit, who old, turn from throwing his bowl of rancid urine on the breadfruit tree root. 'Bean boy, is you dress up like a hot boy so? This early morning, where you going? America?'

Bean grin like horse teeth, 'Is town, in town I going.'

Bean walking the slow incline, remembering down what Lord

Pretender tell him. 'Good as you is,' the younger veteran say, 'you not really a calypsonian till you sing in Port of Spain. That is where the angle does bend, me boy, that is where real calypsonian does get born. You could win all them country champion, but you *must*, you must come in town.'

Down from the east through rustling villages, brisk with raw country on either side, and the black wavering line of the main road stretching out in the bright morning. Bean sit on a smooth wooden bench in the back of the rickety Darmanie bus, and six cents to town he gone rocking in the bounce and swinging tug, with his long mango head leaning against the window watching the sun cast its buzz across so much wild countryside.

D'Abadie
> *Tacarigua*
> *Five Rivers*

over iron bridges, through pasture land with churches hid in bush, a pink orphanage beside a river, the mint and white minaret of a mosque...

> *Arouca*
> *Tunapuna*
> *St Augustine*
> *St Joseph*
> *Mt D'Or*

A wire-veined man sits in the seat across from Bean with reddened eyes that bulge in the leathered cage of his head. Two red fowl cocks caw and flutter in a wire cage between his knees. He wears raw brown linen trousers with frayed hems, a sky-blue shirt. His corns and mud-stained feet slip between rubber slippers. He shifts nervously, tapping his feet in some hidden rhythm. Bean lowers his gaze when the man turns towards him, then he catch the scar on the side of the man jaw. Entering the village of Champs Fleur, a song begin to compose itself in his head:

> *Pa pa dee, pa pa dee-o*
> *Ah come from the country*
> *Pa pa dee, pa pa dee-o*
> *cock fight in the country*

14

The man fowl cackle and cussing, but nobody will say anything. What you expect people to do? Bring complaint? And get cuss or badjohn beat them? But a middle-aged woman, sitting in the back, just wringing her wrinkled hands over the beaded purse on her knee. She wears a green lamé dress of her dry season menopause, patent leather court shoes, her feet shut at the ankles, church hat tilted on her head. When the chickens fuss and flutter and fowl shit start to funk up the bus, she put one dark gaze down heavy on the cock merchant, so he could feel the full weight of her stare, then she turn back, with the same pious gaze, suck her teeth to *steups* and summon a hymn.

Mt Lambert

Petit Bourg

Silver Mill

San Juan

The bus trembling, troubling the road. Bean, rocking between the fowl thief and the Adventist, leaning in the corner side the back seat with suitcase between his knees.

Barataria

Morvant

Laventille

These northern hills of Port of Spain, laden with wood-shacks and galvanize roofs, sparkle in the sun. Open sores of ghetto ravines. Slum wood. Hillside tenements where the heat burst like pepper in a pot. Driving down past the La Basse, on with its stinky sweet smell of black mud rotting in swamp land, and the rum and coconut oil factory, citrus scent, distilleries, and the sky extending out to brightness over Port of Spain, where human cargo spills out into the streets like ants from under a hessian sack of forgotten meat.

Policemen in white custodian helmets measure the traffic. Jay walkers and small-island market women stroll past carrying baskets on their heads. Walk a mile and a half. Bats in the garret of the big house, big men playing wappie there, slapping harsh cards down, and the drain in the abandoned land behind the barrack yard festering with thick black-blue love fly hissing, so the air there always have muscle. A dog licking salt from the edge of the world, in Marine Square where the tamarind trees

15

grow high and wide, and black dravidian beggars stew in heat and piss at the roots.

Bean puts down his grip on Henry Street, letting the city rock him in its river of flesh and concrete. He not sure what to do. Not sure how to move. Road running left, road running right, and he now come to town on the Darmanie bus. He step to cross the people road and a jitney near bounce him; was a Yankee Willys jeep that pass and splash a puddle on him; US Navy. One stink puddle, funk up with rancid water and genk that run 'way from the Syrian steam laundry, wash up on his foot, like baptism in the city.

'The Champion, boy!' The voice startles him. This man, Mr Gary, waving, crossing the road towards him. Bean notices his wide bandy gait, like the curving limbs of a calliper, the unlit cigarette between the fingers of his right hand, and his voice pitched high and almost girlish, to cut through the noise of the street. Mr G puffing from the exertion of running behind the calypsonian, but he is the kind of man who seems to wear a permanent grin. 'Where you going, Saga boy? I tell you wait for me by the bus depot and you walking like you know where you going?' Extending a hand for Bean to shake, patting the young man's shoulder at the same time. 'Ha, you walking like a drake, like you know Port of Spain, but you don't know town no arse.' Now he laughs, his head slung back.

'I just s-seeing what I could s-see. I thought maybe you did come and gone,' Bean says.

'If I say wait is to wait, man. How you mean? You feel you could just come from country and start perambulating up here? You want these vagabond rob you? Anyway…' He lights a cigarette, whipping the match shut, then flinging the wick to the ground. 'Come with me.' But it is this word 'perambulating' that Bean considers as he follows Mr Gary through the mess of black shack alleys and thoroughfares that is eastern Port of Spain. Unfinished wooden houses, barrack yards. The promoter stops grinning at the corner of Observatory Street. 'Now, champ, let me tell you from now,' he says, 'don't think because I bring you down from the country it mean I have hotel room for you, eh. You eh make a red cent yet, much less to pay rent. Once you start working in the tents, you can rent bungalow, but for now you could stay in the Harpe.'

Bean turn. 'La Cour Harpe? Is there you-you carrying me? I hear that place very terrible.'

Without turning to face Bean, Mr Gary says, 'Don't worry yourself, people does say it bad, but it not so bad in there.'

So they walk the slight incline up Observatory, cross a bridge, past the poor house and turn left into a yard, the entrance marked with a hand-painted wooden sign: *La Cour Harpe*. All this time Bean quiet, he just watching the yard; the Baptist flags in the far corner; the lush long zigar bush grown from the moist land near the latrines; the mud-walled bungalows; the sandy, snot-nosed children pitching marbles in the communal centre – *kax, pax, patax* – against their knuckles to punish; the young men knocking iron to music in the shade of a gru-gru bef tree; the laden belly of washing lines strung from shack to shack; the hot tin roofs and the rustling of leaves; the grief water stagnant and pungent in cess-pools; the women sitting on front steps scandalising, with their dresses drawn down between the valley of their thighs; the fisherman returning from the sea with a bottle of English gin; a cacophony of whores; rats in the attic and the soldier van passing; panty wash running in the ravine; moss like phlegm on the ravine bed like strands of something blown by water.

In the far right corner of the yard, just before the abandoned land and the dry river running under the silver bridge, by the palm tree in a tenement garden, a brown pot-hound barks and rolls in the rugged dirt to scratch mange from its back, and a big-headed boy runs out from behind a barrack house in khaki short pants; the fly undone, barefooted and barebacked in the government sun, to see the Arima champion coming his come with the grip and the guitar, just reach from country, smelling of earth and perspiration, laying his grip down. Watch how he pushes his hat back with the wrist, water pouring from his head. Bean 'fraid to stutter, but he somersaulting in his skin, and Mr Gary, standing there next to the country singer, hands on hip, his gut puffing out, clears his throat and spits,

'This a place they used to keep slave,' he says, 'and when the slave get free they stay living here. But these is good people here, is no problem if you live good with them, plenty calypsonian living here.'

Bean's eyes widen, 'It have calypsonian here? In this place…'

'How you mean man? Is here self they does live. Attila pass through here – you must know that – even Lion, Lord Snail, The Growler. It have plenty music here, plenty bacchanal too, and woman, lord. You playing stupid, man; you must know about the Harpe.'

But looking around at the bright-lit chaos of the tenement yard, all the young calypsonian can see is a whole heap of ketch-arse shack what breaking down. That night, Gary find him keep in the house of a gap-teeth woman who living in a corner house with a crop of rancid children, make him a pallet on the floor. Country boy used to that. He used to bathing from a pan cup, he used to poor-folk ways, and latrine and moist bush in the elbows of the land. But that night he ventures out into the city alone. He walks along the perimeter of a great savannah, past the oyster vendors with flambeaux and green-pepper sauces burning, then down Frederick Street, sees night clubs and American soldiers leaning on bonnets outside brothels. Creole Jazz. A band some-where, a cornet punching the dark; blue lights in lanterns in the Chinese restaurant.

The Arima Champion has entered Port of Spain.

Them days you couldn't just say you coming to Port of Spain to sing calypso. You had to be a certain level, and you had to have a certain pedigree, you had to be awarded. So unless you were the champion of Arima you couldn't come to Port of Spain. To sing calypso in Port of Spain you had to be the champ of Gasparillo, the champ of San Fernando, the champ of some place in Gran Cumuto and then they say, 'Well, he's Cumuto champ.' So Cumuto champ will now have to beat Arima champ, and when you win champion of Arima, *now* you could come into Port of Spain.

— The Mighty Chalkdust

EUGENE WARREN, 1943

I REMEMBER KITCHENER when he land in La Cour Harpe. I was living with my grandmother in an upstairs house right there in the barrack yard, what you call the garret, the attic. We used to stay up there, not because we was well off, but because my grandmother, resourceful as she was, used to wash clothes and cook for the landlord. So because I living up there on the top, I look like a big boy to them fellas down in the barrack yard. But is rat and woodslave up there, red ants, termite like nuts. And the old lady had to wash the landlord big flannel pants and his drawers on a jooking board in the yard, starch and iron his shirts till she catch dry cough and ague sometimes, so it wasn't nice. But even so we was better off than the people living in the yard; down there was pure ketch arse. The fellas used to call me Scholar because I could read and write, my head always in book, so them calypsonian who couldn't write or spell good, like Melody, used to sing and get me to write their words out for them.

La Cour Harpe was a big yard, a courtyard. It had a big house by the entrance, where the landlord living, and we living upstairs. Below had a big gate that used to close at night. On the other side of the entrance it have a little drugstore, a lady selling food, maybe a shop selling groceries. You walk through the gate and in front you, in the centre, was an open space, the yard, gravel, it hard, where people used to lime and skylark, and on both side it have barrack room around. Some room small but divide in two, a back door, a couple slat window, a bench where to cook. It had a long grass space in the back of them rooms, it had two-three standpipe there, some latrines that everybody using. Everybody washing clothes and doing their business right there in the back. Is sewage there, is dirty water; it squalid.

So you want to know how a lady and a man, or a lady who don't have no husband, living in one room with four and five children?

Or how from tanty to uncle and grandmother living in one barrack, or how fifteen, sixteen Chinaman living in one room, paying six cents a night? That was La Cour Harpe. And that is where Kitchener come to ketch his black arse, to live hand-to-mouth, sleeping where he could find a hole, where jamette stooping to piss and stick man bursting each other head, right there in the barrack yard with everybody. Kitchener get to know the life, he get to know town life.

When them calypsonians come down to town they always end up living in the Harpe. But when I say living, I mean they only changing their clothes. Because, remember, soon as calypsonian wake up they have to go and hustle, they bound to go sing by some corner for a lil' change or they never eat that day, they never pay rent. Unless, well, they have some woman minding them. So if something happen the night before, they sing about it the next day. Sometime they go by Lung Ting Lung shop on Henry Street to print lyrics so they could sell the copies on the street; penny a sheet.

When Kitchener come out he hole in the day – because he sleeping till 10 or 11 o'clock in the morning – he come and he take a bath, he change his clothes and he come out in the yard with his hand on his hip. He surveying Observatory Street like he build the road. But he have to hustle to eat that day, so he thinking what he could do, how he could get a few bob in his pocket, because he belly empty, rent must pay, he must maintain he image as a calypsonian. He would go by the corner of Henry and Prince Street. A Syrian fella name Moses had a bar there, and Moses would put out a plate with a few salt biscuits, a piece of roast saltfish and maybe a lil' flask of rum on the table for them calypsonian, and they would sing. Men like Spoiler, Melody, Sir Galba and The Mighty Viking used to go there to find out what mark play in wappie game or how the hustle looking that particular day. As a boy I would stand up in front by the bar and listen to them sing. But they used to run me! They used to say, 'Lil boy, move from here! What you doing here? You eh see is big men here. You mother know where you is?'

Because that's one thing, they very respectable, always dress sharp, they wearing necktie, suspenders, shoes shine up, always in suit. All the big bards used to wear suit and tie, felt hat, two-tone brogues. They looking good, but they broken to thief. Them days it had no real money in calypso, unless your name is Roaring Lion, Caresser or Attila the Hun.

Sometimes Kitch used to sing at the corner of Prince and Charlotte Street. There was a Chinese restaurant there and he used stand up in front the restaurant and play guitar and sing. People pass and maybe give him a penny or two, maybe he sell two or three music sheet. And if you call him, 'Ai Kitch,' he turn round and he answer you, whoever you is.

'Ai chief, wha' going on?'

Well, eventually the Chinee people run him from outside there. They say he was obstructing. Another time I see him quite down on the wharf, singing for them stevedores. All that time he struggling. Sometime not one black cent in the man pocket; he hungering, but you would never know his business, you would never know that is one good pair of leather shoes he have that he polish; the suit he will wipe it down when it dirty. Sometimes he wear just the jacket with a khaki pants. Sometime he wear the suit pants with a white shirt and a tie. When things brown he borrow a jacket. But Kitch would never ply you with prayers when he see you, he wouldn't moan. He hold his head high and he carry on, he make his kaiso and, joy or pain, he singing same way – white shirt and tie, he going up the road.

Up Frederick Street had a yard where tests used to go and lime, to listen to them bards old-talk and sing. I see Kitch there one, lean up under a tamarind tree, one foot up on the trunk, strumming his box guitar. He was composing 'Tie Tongue Mopsy', right there, in the dust blowing across from the savannah. And if you like it, maybe you give him a lil' change. Kitch wasn't no real hustler, he wouldn't lock your neck, he wouldn't thief, his whole intention was calypso – sun, rain, belly full or empty belly, is kaiso same way.

Is when he come Port of Spain, then everybody was saying this guy coming from Arima, the Arima Champion, the Green Fig man, and when we get to hear him, everybody say, 'Well, this man is a genius, boy'. The words he used to bring, and the things he used to use in the calypso, was unbelievable. And the way he rhyme is like a story, every verse is different – it tell a story. And the words, his diction, and the way he used to put his story together, was incredible, y'know. Anywhere you see Kitch, you see me, anywhere he goes, I there. When he make a calypso, even before he know it, I know it! Because I could retain, you know. And he sing it and say, 'This is a new one', and he have the guitar and he humming it under the big tree in the Harpe, and he'd sing it for me and within minutes I have it a'ready; I have it a'ready and I singing one of Kitch new ones. When I start to sing calypso, I call myself Young Kitch. We was very close. He live in my mother yard in La Cour Harpe for a while. In those days he had nothing, in the hard days. So Ma had an oven there, a mud oven in the yard, and for a while he used to sleep up there, on top the oven.

— Leonard 'Young Kitch' Joseph

STEEL BAND BLUES
Nights in the Jungles of La Cour Harpe

THE RIPPLE OF STEEL CAME to Bean's bed from the iron band beating there in the gap between wood shack and wire fence round Harpe yard. And the sound of the iron beating was Arima, and the sound of the beating was his father, Daddy Pamp, working the iron in the smitty, when iron red and melting till water make it rigid, and triplet notes would seep out from under the mallet and sing like a flute in his ear, and from the sound it making, everybody in the village would know that Pamp was in the fire-shed making iron bend.

Bean can't remember when he started singing calypso, but he sure he been singing since Pamp used to send him to fetch water from the river near, and he hear the bamboo creak, the parakeets whistle, the bull-cow bawl, the silver fisheries flitting. After a while, everything will sound like music, and when he start to hear it, he sing along, till now he reach town, as man, and he dreaming in the early dawn of the ragged yard, beneath the starch mango tree that hover, with leaves to trouble him where he sleeping, quite on top of Ma Holder's oven.

The sound from the iron band is not flung far from the blacksmith's treble, nor the stick from the steel, nor the wrist from the rubber, or the palm from the goat skin. Bean, in dream sleep, composing melodies for iron band to play; rugged polyrhythms of call and response, lavways, belairs, toumblack and yanvalou – all the l's. In this dream he walks a simple mile from the yard down town to Tamarind Square and by the time he reach there he done orchestrate the whole damn thing.

But Daddy Pamp son, the Arima Champion, can't afford even a six-cents room in the yard, so he begging pallet on floor and couch, and his real zeal strain from singing on the corner of Park and Charlotte Street every afternoon for two cents and three – a little meal. Yes lord, life in the barrack yard hard-hard like banga seed heart, and his bed so bogus and crumple, and the holes he wrap in have tarpaulin, and his perspiration pungent like cat piss in his armpit. He pick a bad time to come to Port of Spain. War in Europe, Carnival ban, people getting lick with cat-o-nine tail for playing mas. But maintain. You have to sing your kaiso in the tents, and the tent full of people. And he young still. So he hold still in the darkness, with the chirp of crickets and the hoot-hoot of toads in the ravine, where sewer cream and panty wash staining the edges of the world, until his heart becomes heavy in his chest, and he shuts his eyes tight against despondency, so that only the sound of the young men beating their iron drums penetrates his sleep. The sound is sweet, and beat by beat it expanding; it grow so wide until within it he can hear the whole village bluesing in the steel, the whip-waist man, the long-stones man, the children crying, the rag-and-bottle man who smelling of lizard shit, the Grenadian mother so protective of her daughter she walking five miles from the Harpe to Cocorite with the young girl beside her, to work domestic for the doctor. He hear how she rock back her head and laugh through sorrow. He hearing each poor man's cry in the steel; every weary woman moan, flesh on flesh; every ring-hand slap and cuss and quarrel and shiver of flu; of sigh on open sigh; of thigh on crosscut thigh; a jamette's gnashing tongue as she sparks cuss around her saga boys' head – rent to pay and chicken to pluck, yard to sweep and police to beat, and the saga boy only sleeping like cat on the threadbare couch, with one leg up on the back rest, till he up and get dam vex and fed-up of the jamette mouth, and leap from the couch to flex his manhood, to fling on his hot shirt and swagger down to Tanty's Cafe where the Mighty Spoiler holding the corner, drunk like a fish but singing a new calypso, before he head back south.

Nights in the barrack yards of Port of Spain. Stars bright like pin pricks in a cape flung against the darkness. Humble in the corner, the calypsonian lay there, humming bass in his throat.

Kitchener come to Port of Spain because he want to come to Port of Spain. Nobody eh *make* him come. Kitchener was living in La Cour Harpe. La Cour Harpe was prostitution. Was a old hole in the yard, there. But he couldn't afford nothing better. Kitchener come to see if he could make a dollar. The first time I saw a woman underwear was on George Street. I see women sit down with their legs open wide, wide, as a boy in the 50s, so I know what Kitchener had in La Cour Harpe.

—The Mighty Chalkdust

'BOYIE' 1944

KITCH MAKE HE WAY. He didn't look for trouble. He ketch he arse like everybody in the Harpe. But he was ambitious and he had talent. Them times calypsonian didn't have no money. They singing in Carnival season, but when the season done they broken again. People used to call Kitch 'Country Boy' because he come from Arima, and them times, poor fella, he like a jumbie all about Port of Spain, trying to get a break. He hustling, he sleeping in hen house, whorehouse and all kinda kiss-me-arse place. But somehow he always decent; always suit and felt hat and two-tone brogues, paisley tie. And you don't ask a man where he get his money from. But then he start, regular, to sing in the calypso tent and things start to get a bit more rosy for the scamp.

The first tent I know was right in the back of Nelson Street, and I living in George Street, so when they singing over there, I could peep over the wall and see them from where I there in the barrack yard. I would hear all them fellas – men like Kitchener, Spoiler, Attila, even Tiger, Pretender, Lord Melody, I see them sing right there.

At first was just galvanise and palm, sawdust on the ground, but then all them bourgeois people from St James and Maraval start coming to hear calypso. French creole inquisitive. Yankee soldiers coming quite from the base in Chaguaramas just to hear this thing, even Captain Cipriani in the tent, big dignitary and mayor there. So they put bench for people to sit down, and they start charging decent money to get in. Fellas selling nuts, sweet drink. Children couldn't go in there, but being as I was living in the back of the tent, I get to hear them sing. Them days your mother don't even want you to *hear* calypsonian sing. Much less to stand up and watch them in tent. Calypsonian was ostracise, together with the pan men. So if my mother, so-help-me-God, catch me beating iron, or if she find me by the fence watching

27

them calypsonian, she would break a lime branch and bawl, 'Ai boy, bring your arse from there now or I cut your tail!' And I wouldn't let her have to call me again.

Kitch come down from Arima hot! He feel he was the champ; he win all them country show and he like a zwill; he cutting. But it don't work so. Even legend does lie. First time Kitch went to try he hand in the tent, they put him to sit down, they make he wait. His blood was hot, he had good songs, but he have to show respect, he have to pay dues. Eventually they give him a chance and he get by. Yes. Them days somebody had to bring you up, a elder bard, and if you don't know the big boys, somebody have to like you, introduce you, they have to give you a good kaiso name, they have to throw some rum on your skull plate and coronate you.

TANTY TEA SHOP

TANTY TEA SHOP was for the vagabonds. Tanty Tea Shop was Duke and Piccadilly Street corner, right near Silver Dollar whore house. Tanty Tea Shop was famous for never closing. Tanty never wash the pot. The pot on the fire all the time and is corn beef and bread, or saltfish and bread – that's what she selling – and coffee, cocoa, an' she have fried bake and egg, cheese. Tanty like she come from B.G. or Suriname and she have some Indian in she. Dark-skinned, she head tie, she apron clean, she calve fat like pup, busy in the kitchen.

Tanty was the late night place for them jacket man and they woman to come. Even the Yankee soldiers used to leave the base quite in Chaguaramas and come by Tanty. That's where the action was. Jamette skin up on the road with rum in dey hand making one set a noise. Ponce used to hang round that corner. All the boys used to lime there. You sit down there at night and big men talking, plenty hustle in the yard. Who playing card, who have rum, thing to smoke.

But Tanty shop wasn't no real cafe, eh mister – you cyar sit down inside there – was just a wooden counter, the kitchen behind, and Tanty serving you right there. She would put a bench out front on the street so tests could sit and eat their sandwich and drink their coffee. And if you there late at night, after fete or after the tents close, you could see Kitchener and Lord Melody, Spoiler when they come there for their corned beef and bread after the calypso tent close. And if somebody have a guitar, you might get to hear the things they composing.

Tanty place burn down one Friday night and would you believe that by Monday them fellas was in town singing,

No tea by Tanty tonight
No tea by Tanty tonight
Tanty tea shop burn down…

CORONATION CALYPSO
Is Tiger give him his name

THE BARD STANDING THERE between the bamboo posts that holding up the back of the calypso tent. They call him Tiger. Growling Tiger. But what they calling tent is just a shed that thatch. Growling as he sucking orange after navel orange in that narrow yard behind the shallow wooden platform they calling the stage, where old knotty zigar bush that hard to kill does trouble the wire fence that separate the tent yard from the back of the Diamond Penny whore house on St Vincent Street. The Tiger face screw-up: green citrus rind biting the corners of his mouth, his eye squinting, spitting the slippery seeds. His mouth like cardboard box when it wet, and he folding the orange for juice to burst, and it sucking sweet.

Sans humanité.

As the calypsonians arrive, they gather there, behind the stage, by the trench where mosquito biting. Some tests drinking bush wine, some puffing clay pipe, some singing low, say they warming throat till the deep croon come in. The fiddler oiling his elbow with a nip of rum, the sax man sit down on an overturned pigtail bucket, sweetening his old horn, tapping on the pads, twisting the mouthpiece to the exact angle, puffing it, prepping it, sucking the reed. The horn hanging down like child foot between his legs. It get knock much and plenty lacquer crack out, gun brass, but sweet when it blow; is a good horn. The trumpet man stoop, pants' hem reaching up his shin bone, and the seam sharp, and where the socks don't reach, it hairy. He fingering the valves, polishing the bell. Blow.

Sans humanité.

Tiger turn from the darkness and watch young Bean talking with the other singers. He watching how Bean hard-blinking out his words, sputtering like his timing belt break. The young man tall, what they call *lingae*, bent from his waist to trouble the guitar man ear, say he humming song. And Tiger seeing this sideways, leaning forward so the damn orange juice don't run on the good white shirt that his woman starch and press for him that afternoon. And from how the Tiger stand – the bandy knee, the one leg slight in front of the other, resting light on the sharp outside edge of his black derby shoes, you can see evidence of how Tiger used to box before he start to calypso. He ruggedy steep, muscle lean, his fists big like grapefruit and his face know war: scar sided, the grin lopsided, and the eyes – the eyes like flat stone skimming dirty river, only glancing, glancing. Yes, Tiger was worries in the ring. The Siparia Tiger. He would stand brazen against bigger men from Matelot and Cedros. Men with good-good pugilist pedigree, who chasing world title an' thing, and Tiger would tear them and beat them like snake. Men like Kid Ram and Jungle Prince get beat up and down the island, till Tiger win the bantamweight title of 1929, in this colony,

Sans Humanité.

When Sa Gomes send the Tiger to New York in 1935 to record calypso with Attila the Hun and Beginner, and the big men sing their songs and it gone down in the appropriate time, and it come to Tiger time to record 'Money is King', the arranger, Felix Pacheco, get up from his swivel chair and bawl, 'That is not music. Young man, you break all the laws of music, you can't expect these musicians to play this primitive thing you compose. I can't arrange this. I won't.' Tiger watch Pacheco, he watch him frankomen in his face, till all the blood drain out the Cuban eye, and his expression change. Tiger never say nothing, but he watching Pacheco from below, like when pugilist on stool waiting for the bell to ring, ready to stand up and fight, and his voice growl deep and it heartless,

'Boss man, hear my cry. I come from quite Trinidad to record this calypso, and it bound to wax. I bound to sing it.'

And they say he was so sure that quick-quick Pacheco cry, 'Come now, play it again, let me hear it. Maybe I did not hear it right the firs' time... Ooh, it *is* good, yesmanitgoodman,' he say, and he start to score and arrange the damn thing, and it is a classic in calypso. Hear the song the Tiger sing:

If a man have money today,
people do not care if he have cocobay.
He can commit murder and get off free,
and live in the Governor's company.
But if you are poor, people will tell you 'Shoo',
and a dog is better than you.

An audience begin to gather on the wooden benches in front of the Victory tent stage, waiting for the music to start. Tiger watching the young man that Johnny Khan bring to sing in the tent. He hear about him. This country bookie who pants short in the ankle, who wearing a black jacket that look like St Joseph Road prostitute put together and buy for him because he never have no money; and you can't say you singing in tent without jacket. Tiger watch good when the great Attila the Hun himself, walk up and ask the young man to sing, let him hear, and how the young man strain with a stutter to say, 'R-r-right n-n-now?' Attila had say, 'Yes, sing it come. What key your song in?'

And the Arima Champion say, 'R-r-r-r-r...R-r-r-r...'

Attila watch him with compassion and interrupt, 'Ray minor you mean? Is in E?'

'Yes, gi' me in E.'

And Bean sing it. And the fiddle man stoop there in slips to catch the tune, and the bass man wood start to tremble like a woman leg. The country boy grinning, he know he have a good tune. He fling down two verse and Attila say, 'OK, good, good, I want you go on second, before Invader.'

When Tiger suck the navel from the last orange, he throw the pith over the fence in the crapaud land and he call to Bean, 'Young boy... come.' And when Tiger call you, you does come. 'So is you who sing 'Green Fig'? People talking, they really say is a good song. You will sing it tonight?'

Bean smile, 'Yes Mr Tiger, I-I-I–'

'Oh ho, so long I want to hear the damn song and I cyar hear it. I have to wait for you to come to Port of Spain before I hear the kiss-me-arse thing.'

And Tiger bray, but he have he eye on Bean. He must be say something, and Bean bend his neck like drake duck to listen to the swifter blade. Hear Tiger: 'What they call you?' Raising his voice to its elegant tenor and turning from the fence to face Bean straight.

'My-my name? Roberts. Aldwyn Roberts.'

'I mean your calypso name, boy.'

'Well, they call me Bean.'

'Bean? What? You is the Mighty Bean? Lord Bean? Butter Bean? That is no kind of calypso name. Come better than that, man.'

'Well, I win Arima, so they call me Arima champion.'

Tiger laugh, 'Arima champion? What kind of jackass name is that boy? Them name eh good.' He laugh like the laugh been sitting in the back of his throat since morning and only now decide to come out. 'Listen, in kaiso you have to have better name than that. This is big man thing. Tests will merciless you if you sobriquet weak. Look...' and he bring his right hand up to pull his chin and his face get serious, bend his head to think. Then he look at Bean and he say, 'From now, you must call yourself "Lord Kitchener." Anybody ask you, tell them Growling Tiger give you that name. I give you that because I feel you could be a real general in calypso. You have the height... and you have ambition. You know Lord Kitchener?'

'Yes, the Englishman, the general, the field marshall?'

'He used to beat bad, y'know... *Lord Kitchener?* He wasn't easy, poopa.' And with that Tiger ask for a nip of rum and he dash that over the young man head. Then he done talk, he move to stage side to watch the show starting. Bean stop there to think by the wire fence, to let the name roll round his head, for it to mingle and merge with the jungles above the city and the river running beneath, and the sound of the black-back crapaud bleating in the bush. And to repeat the name lightly, like something fragile in his mouth, until it begin to take on its own shape and resonance.

...Lord... Kitchener...

This is the city and this is the hill and these are the ravines where mosquitos are knitting barbed wire in the gullies. This is where the Growling Tiger, shadow boxing at the side of the stage, firing blows to the breeze to compose himself, waits for his turn to step up into the ring.

Sans humanité

When Kitch turn to sing, he sing 'Green Fig', and the crowd applaud, encore, he sing a next verse. The calypso was good in truth, so he ramajay and give them a special verse. Attila was pleased; he pat the young man on his back and give him a bag of navel orange and a bake an' sal'fish sandwich to eat. The young man stutter but he couldn't bring himself to ask for two shilling because he know how things does go. That night he newly coronate, he walk from the tent to La Cour Harpe yard and his foot never touch the ground. The night sweet, ravine stink till sweet, he hearing melodies in the breeze blowing round the bridges. East Dry River. Everybody he pass, he tip his hat. 'Goodnight'. Foreday dawn and the light coming in. Now he in tent in town, so as he walk in the yard, retracing each step he make on that stage. *Lord… Kitchener…* the name keep ringing in his ears.

FEVER
East Dry River Breakdown: V.E. Night, 8 May 1945

First Movement

FROM THOSE JUNK METAL JUNGLES behind the bridge where the
river bank pave, and the water running in the middle crease,
narrow with moss and filtered in the St Ann's Hills, washed down
from the Lady Chancellor ridge, down through Belmont where
the river come soft and trembling, with ripple and silver fish,
under Observatory Street, through barrack yard and shanty town
where flesh upon flesh secretes its own oil and seeps into the
ravine's oil-blackened earth, and the La Basse scent sweeps up
west from the jetty and stinks in the vibration of air and heat and
steel drums that ring like bells from a rugged cathedral tumbling
down from hills above the city, filling the streets with its sparkling
sound, pitch-oil lights lamping the hill tracks coming down from
Laventille, under riverless bridges and through the fog of grey-
green dust settling on the gravel roads and the tin roofs of a
tenement glimpsed in moonlight, way backroads of the mythic,
where people are drawn up close in humble desperation, in this
land, in this land that steep and slippery with stick-fight blood and
rum, hillside small holdings, this world of hard corners and swift
curvatures, of flick razors hid inside jacket pockets for good luck,
of blades between flannel pleats and bright calico cloth, east of
this sprawling sea-swept city, where citrus scent sent from upper
Nelson Street, on the corner by the yaraba butcher shop where ox
blood spill and still sticky on the road since morning, like it don't
want to wash away and fade, fade that now the full weight of night
coming, so people begin to gather in the communal space of La
Cour Harpe yard to gamble and cuss, to lay down the burden of
their day right there on the ground, and who not drown, water-
logged, and who not dead, badly wounded, but most of them was

catching hell, that night that Churchill claim victory over Hitler, and then the whole of town turn upside down.

Second Movement

The iron band gather near the entrance to Harpe yard, where the grass scant and catching hell to grow through the hard dirt and gravel. A barrel-chested young man with a curved stick leans back to beat bass from a big salt-biscuit tin drum. The boom big like a pigtail bucket. He keeps the pulse and swagger, his wrist twisting like a hinge, his bearded face turned up to the moonlight, eyes closed, sweat pouring from his stingy brim. Each blow he pelts sends shivers through his flesh.

The cowbell man has his instrument to his ear. Is really a old church bell he beating with a rail bolt. Each beat tightens his pursed lips, which then slack to a grin. He knocking sweet and, as the metronome of this spasm band, he can't afford to miss a beat, nor the du-dup roll, or the band will slack and surrender. Neither the black Indian on the bent paint-can, nor the sugar-haired man who deals with the ping pong pan proper, leaning, as in gospel, can pause or the band will bust. His neck-veins strain as he plays, crafting a melody from just two and a half notes. The cuff boom grumbles: 'Buglers coming! Regiment, Army band.'

The audience grows. Hilltop women come down to the flat yard in calico skirts that ride up higher at the back than the front, clapping in time, voluptuously wining with the grinning maracas man, flirting scandalously with the iron man. They move to the front where the iron beat is sweetest.

But you still want to know how this music could come from these rancid yards behind God's back, eh? Music from that black triangle of suffering, laughter and sin? How can anything beautiful be born here?

Third Movement

Hear Miss Daphne: 'You eh hear war done, Mr Jaja? What you doing in that room? You say you reading bible, but you know you can't read a damn thing by that pitch-oil lamp. Why you want to strain the lil' piece a eye what God give you? Come outside, man, you eh see people outside? War done, boy, Churchill declare. Let we drink two rum and celebrate!

Eunice Daphne is a tall, hard-boned woman with skin dark as aubergine and a gap between her front teeth; fellas does say she have a bag of sugar down there. She lives in the barrack room next door to Mr Jaja and every morning she walks across the Savannah with a straw basket on her arm. Is going she going to wash wares and cook for some French Creole in St Clair. Now, she stands in the bacchanal yard with her hands akimbo, her wrists folded back on her waist, waiting for Mr Jaja to come down two three step into the yard to fire two shot with she.

'Ignatius Jaja?' she calls.

The old man shuts his bible like a drum. 'Yes... Daphne,' he moans, 'Ah comin'... a comin'.' He turns down the wick in his paraffin lamp, his feet search for his slippers under the table, and finally he steps down into the yard. The iron band are playing under the tamarind tree, a crowd has gathered to hear them. They play rhythm with the mere suggestion of a melody, but melody not so important here. These people need to move – even old bandy-knee, Mr Jaja, leg bend like calliper. Thirty-five years he serve in the Anglican Credit Union in Port of Spain, and he was never late for work once, never take sick leave, never miss a day until his hernia drop and his stones get so big he can't work like used to, and they lay him off, poor fella – but he keep his gravitas and tell people he fire the work.

He lives in one of the good rooms in the yard and keeps it tidy. Jaja have a radio, he have sacred heart picture above the door. He build some shelves, he put down linoleum floor. But he one alone in there, since one morning his common law wife, Mavis, take in with bad feelings and fall out of bed and dead. Now he stands in the yard surveying the bacchanal with his hands clasped behind his back, but his knee can't help but bend.

Hear Daphne: 'Where your glass, Mr Jaja? You know rum sharing and you eh bring no glass?' So Jaja gone back up to his room for a glass, coming back down as Daphne unwinding the cork. 'Is a lil white rum the mister get from the docks – a Bajan something. Must be fall off a ship; it nice too bad. Come, hold your glass, man.'

But Jaja fraid God. He say, 'Not too much. I was just reading my bible; Papa God watching.' But he offering the glass to fill.

'God? A big man like you, Mr Jaja? You believe in them thing? You think God have you to study if you drink a rum? God busy no arse tonight, man. Drink the damn rum or I give somebody else.' Jaja rolls the rum around the sides of the glass, raises it to his nose, then it hit like worries on his tongue, his lip twisting in a scowl. Behind them, lamp light glints on the framed photographs on the wall of Daphne's small room. Fading portraits of hard men born in the late 1800s, with eyes that know life. Harder women standing erect, unsmiling for photographs. The room itself is a chaos of ornaments and doilies. In a shadowy corner, Daphne's big daughter, Bee, is sitting on the floor plaiting her younger sister's hair. Gunshots sound sudden so, and they all look up. Was Adolphus Henry, a cook in the infirmary, who living in a little stilt-house in the yard back, who bust three-four shot from a rickety hunting rifle, cutting the sky in two like is Old Year's night. Henry leaning out his balcony, with a half-smoked ciga-rette perched in the corner of his mouth. He like to wear suit and cummerbund, centre-part in his hair. They uses to call him 'Englishman'. Yes. He was in England once, in 1919.

Daphne and Mr Jaja cross the yard to where the iron band beating. The boom they hear is like bamboo bursting, or boys lighting carbide down on the dry river bank. As Mr Jaja stands there with Daphne, even he, upright Ignatius Jaja, find the little iron band beating sweet. Just so, Daphne pulls away to throw her waist, to dance the juba, the belair, lifting her dress over the mud.

At the arched gateway that separates the barrack yard from Observatory Street, engines buzz, horns blow, bottle and spoon clink, a scratcher man scratches, a bugler blows and a chorus of whistles and voices rises as a victory procession nears the Harpe yard gate.

A young man in a grass-green suit and straw hat enters the yard with his entourage – the chantwelle, a guitar slung round his neck, his hands cutting across the sound hole, fluttering like wings, but the sound hard to hear in all the noise. He walks like scissors cutting, tall in the stride, with his head cocked back, chipping, chipping, strumming, chopping chords, till the b string bust and dangling, but he grinning still and singing, so the people gather round him. He singing folk song because he run out of calypso to sing.

> *Sergeant gimme de day today.*
> *Oh, Monday, Tuesday eh 'nough!*
> *Sergeant gimme de day today.*

And when the gang eat out that one he singing a next one:

> *Me one alone on the ocean,*
> *me one alone.*
> *Murder, fire, blood in the gutter!*
> *Me one alone…*

He bring lavway, he bring chant, he pull kalinda to burn away smoke. He had walked out of the tent just to buy a bag a' salt nuts, when he hear the bugle blow, somebody say, 'War is over'. He gather them calypsonians and they march through town, people leaning out their windows, coming onto the street, jeep horn blowing, a bell ringing somewhere in a distance. They walk until they cross the bridge to enter La Cour Harpe. He leading the way, the chantwelle, he leading the charge.

Now they reach the Harpe, fellas pick up hub cap and rail knuckle, beat any damn thing, to bring drums down from high up some bush-fire hill, from rock-stone quarry, to where they outlaw their faith. The chantwelle, in the centre of this axis, forget himself and come out of his skin. He is a channel; rivers pass through him.

Hear Miss Daphne: 'Kitchener!'

Mr Jaja: 'Kitchener who? Ent that the buck-mouth country boy that uses to sleep on the Madam Holder oven in the yard?'

Miss Daphne: 'Yes, he self. They used to call him Arima Champion –'

Mr Jaja: 'Oh ho, so *he* is the one they calling Lord Kitchener.'

Miss Daphne: 'He real good, you know. You never see him sing in the tent?'

Mr Jaja: 'Me? Tent? You ever know me go Calypso tent?

Calypso tent not for me. But I hear people talking about this Kitchener from Arima, and how he could sing. They say he composing good.'

Then like the rum make Ignatius Jaja merry, he start to fling his tongue. 'Me? I, I is a man not in them thing, not really; tent not for me. I went tent once; once them boys carry me… Calypso, if they have the words… is good, but if not, then no, not so.'

Bobulups there among the men, shaking she roll, her bodice ride up on her belly, her arms swinging above her head. She come with the chantwelles, pick up with them gang from town where she was making her fares. Daphne calls to Bobulups, 'Ai gyal, you passing me straight or what? A-a, and where you pick up them sweet man from?'

Bobulups laughs and shouts above the ruckus, 'But look at my crosses. So much man you have, an' you watching mine, Daphne?'

They laugh proud and reckless; they throw their heads back and dance, their hands on each other's shoulders. Bobulups says, 'Gimme a rum nah, girl, you keeping all the rum for yourself or what?' She takes the glass from Daphne's hand and sucks the rum down whole. She looking for more, but a vibration was passing same time and it carry she gone by the iron band to inveigle the men there with her slack and scandalous mouth.

Mr Jaja goes back to his room. He thinks to pray but rum tell him God not watching. So he falls asleep, face down in his widowers' bed with all his good clothes on. The iron band join the victory procession and start to push out from Harpe Yard and onto Observatory Street, each man beating with the sweet burden of his instrument, feet shuffling. Some man have no shirt and they shining; some don't want to jump but they jumping, and Kitchener right there with them.

Keeeech

Keeeech

Women point at him with their pursed lips.

He turns around and flashes a smile, shakes his head and laughs as if to say, *These women crazy*. But when they call him, he goes to stand at the side of the road with them, stuttering and charming, already knowing his worth as a calypsonian in this colony. They like when he tip his hat, how he stand with one long leg frontwards;

how the seam down his pants could cut. They wonder how he managing, day after day, eating saltfish and nuts, drinking jigger-bush tea, how he always look shave and sweet, soap-and-water fresh, how he able to come out like a jacket man with tie clip and merino vest. But don't ask *him* what happen. You see him alive.

In the yard, Kitch don't look for trouble. Is 'Good morning, Mr Jaja… Yes sir, good morning, Mr Henry, Miss Yvonne good morning… Miss Daphne, good day and how you do?' Is so he pass through, whistling down through the dry river, like he have a grass stalk in his teeth. But when you see him sit down under the big tamarind tree, strumming his guitar and grinding his jaw to make his calypso, don't say a word, or he will suck his teeth and scowl.

The lil' iron band reach as far as Basilon street corner and they stop there and play two-three tune, but is not tune, is pure rhythm beating. The crowd around them like some jou'vert morning bacchanal. Kitchener in the heart of the thing. The band captain, Sheriff, have a scar down the middle of his forehead. He blow a whistle and the band turn back to push for home. Moonlight in your eye and the sirens still a long way down, but the governor ban pan, more so beating in the night. So they have to go back inside the Harpe, victory night or not.

The folk gather there in the yard with the band again, prancing up the dust. Dirt-foot children run between them, playing catch in the pissy recesses between the latrines and the mud, and hide-and-seek behind the yard, with high-pitched glee to be up this late. When the iron band humble and simmer down, here comes The Mighty Spoiler, done spume his guts in the bandon land and feeling refreshed and ready for more rum. He start to sing the lavway with Kitch. They dip and dingolay, they open their throats and sing. And Bobulups, waving the Bar 20 flag like a kerchief, bending forward with her backside cocked out, twist her heels into the dirt and back-back on Kitchener and Spoiler. The lavway is:

> *Oh Lord, glorious morning come,*
> > *Ambakaila!*
> *Oh Lord, the glorious morning come,*
> > *Ambakaila!*

Sing that till morning.

RUSSELL HENDERSON, JUNE 1945

AFTER THE FIRST VICTORY in Europe, I was working in a store in Port of Spain. Midday, the sirens come out and they say, 'Oh, War is over.' Everybody run out in the street. Tests start to turn their jacket upside down – they eh play mas for five years! Dustbin turn over, inside out, anything they could find get pelt an' play. We had two days of that. Well, the Army band was out on the streets too, with the trumpets, the brass and the buglers. And the buglers come in the fête, blowing with the people, they take a lil' touché with the young boys. And is those buglers that fellas start to imitate on biscuit tin and dustbin, lil' pan in hand and kettle drum they beating with stick. And by the end of that day, they was playing – no, not no tunes – see a bugle could play but it can't play flat, is all a diatonic scale, so it playing:

pa pa pa pee pa pa pee…

Them iron man try to play the same thing. But is just rhythm they was beating because the tonal range of their pan was limited, so all them iron band was beating same way. That is why when Kitchener made the first steel band tune in 1944 you hear him sing:

> *Well I heard the beat of the steelband,*
> *friend, I couldn't understand,*
> *it was hard to make a distinction*
> *between Poland, Bar 20 and John John.*

An' even Kitchener was singing the same notes as the bugle, the same diatonic scale. But as he himself get a lil' bit more musical he start to write more interesting music for the pan; for them fellas to try, to extend the range of the instrument. Because, remember, Kitch living right there in the barrack yard with all them Bar 20 iron man – men like Zigalee, Fisheye, Battersby, Ozzie. So if you pick up with Kitchener, you will know exactly where the steel band start.

EUGENE WARREN, 1946

THEM WOMAN IN THE BARRACK YARD used to mamaguy Kitchener. They would cry '*Kiiitch, Kiiitch*', and they could get anything from him. Just give him sweet talk, kiss up the side of his face, rub breast on his back, squeeze his prick – he love them things, an' he love when they call his name, '*Kiiitch, Kiiitch, you so sweet.*' Kitch like to pretend he have money. But Kitchener don't have nothing, otherwise he would be living in St Clair or Woodbrook, he wouldn't be living in La Cour Harpe. Every night he singing calypso, but calypso don't make money, unless you is a big boy in the game.

But he have plenty girls; woman like him, and he could get his lil' mopsy in the yard to iron his shirt for him. He pass by another one up in the quarry – take a lil' stew beef and rice, next one darning his socks. And when these women husband gone up in the hills to hunt, or they gone down on the wharf to work, they giving Kitchener good curry manicou and jungle pig to eat.

He had a Chinee woman, once. Merlin. Somehow she break away from she flock and end up living in the yard. She used to wash Kitchener clothes and feed him and when the night come she give him leg. The woman nice; she clocking forty, but she skin smooth like a cup, and she have she own teeth in she mouth to smile. Things going good, till the mark bust and she find out Kitch was friending with a woman from John-John, a girl they call Sugar Mouth. The Chinee want to kill Kitch now – you know how Chinee does jealous bad. Anyway, one night she get damn vex and pull for a knife, she leggo one cussing on Kitchener, right there, in the yard. If you hear she, 'You sleep in prostitute bed and come by me, you take am for arse! I wash your clothes an' cook an' you do me this – it no good – I show you trouble now. If you want dead, come trouble am!'

People come out to see, but time you look for Kitch, Kitch

gone. So long? How you mean? They not married, so she have no rights on Kitchener. Couple days after she hanging up Kitchener singlet and drawers on the line, she cooking pigeon peas and pigtail for him like nothing happen, and Kitch lie down inside, snoring. Well, don't ask me what happen, you see him alive.

Was so thing was. Melody, Sir Galba, Spoiler, all a we had two-three woman minding we. If woman not minding you, you not a calypsonian. And when a man say he is a calypsonian, it wasn't no skylark; calypso was big man thing. If anybody interfere with you, you have to be ready with a razor in they tail. You didn't 'fraid make jail, you have cutlass under your mattress. Some calypsonian was hustler, some was pimp and unscrupulous, smart-men, some was scamp. Fellas like Spoiler or Melody could sweet con the shoes off your foot while you walking, they would eat out food from your hand like cat, they would thief the cigarette out your mouth and you wouldn't notice.

It was a girl call Fat Cunny Lou that take Kitch from La Cour Harpe and carry him up Basilon Street in the big *cacheau*, where all them prostitute was living. That's why in 'Chinese Memorial' he sing, *Sleeping in me cacheau, in a dream I hearing a echo.*

Kitch used to friend with all them stink-mouth woman. I can't lie. These is women who will go in shilling hotel and bull, or they gone Lucky Jordan or The Wang when Friday night come and they know man just draw their pay. They would wine back on you in the club, kiss you all on your big toe. But cross them and they cuss you upside down and break bottle in your face. Six months in jail.

La Cour Harpe didn't have no hi-class prostitute; is only bat and jagabat you getting there. If you want nice woman, you have to go downtown; you have to go St James or Woodbrook, you have to make a rounds by the Oval and there you could get some sweet red coolie or a Venezuelan rose. I never partake myself. Maybe once, twice at the most. But sometimes I used to hold their money for them, and I know people up on that side, so I could find them a room to do their business in, make sure they safe, that kinda thing.

And we had some good ones. It had Jane Broadbelt and Jean in Town, Black Stallion, Saccharine Irene. The one they calling

Coolie Rosie was a skinny Indian girl with a cry like police horn. She used to bite and scratch like tiger cat when sweetness take she. So town say, not me. Broadbelt was a red woman; always a big belt 'round she waist. She face hard, she cheek sink in, she haggard. But some man did like them thing and would come down in the Harpe just for she. She was from San Fernando and used to take the bus to town every night to sell pussy. Then next morning she hop the train and go back home. She had a man down south and children, but she used to tell him she working nights at Elite Shirt factory. Somehow the poor man get to find out is prick the woman taking and he come down in the Harpe behind she. He jack she up coming round Belmont Circular Road, arm in arm with two jacket man. When he really start to leggo cut-arse in she tail, the jacket man run. Jane bawling: 'Help, help me, please!' Licks. Blows. But nobody go interfere with husband an' wife business.

Somehow Jane get away, and is so she end up staying in town. Kitch used to help she, give she a little change, cause she was living on the street for a while. He would take her for Chinese food, buy she a pow, poor thing, she old, she didn't have nothing. Then she get a cleaning work in the Salvation Army and done making fares. She dead now. She catch a sore foot that never heal and only running pus. Syphilis. She uses to wear long dress to hide it.

The one they call Black Stallion – black girl, very black, black like jet, but she wasn't bad looking. Kitch like she too bad. He was a few years older than her, but he… y'know… he want some too. She was from deep south; she don't know town-man ways. And I observe how Kitch work on she. He sweeten she with gentle-man talk, he buy salt nuts and melon give she, he croon Bing Crosby, he mamaguy she until she give him. When she broken, he would give her a few shillings. One night Stallion stab a man on Duke Street and had to run Grenada by she father. She never come back.

But Bobulups was the queen. Bobulups used to sit down on George and Duke Street corner with a bottle of stout between she leg and a cigarette in she mouth, and when a jacket man pass, she blowing kiss, sailor boy pass, she lift up her dress. Yes. She sit down on the pavement, right there and open up she leg. People passing… she take the bottle and… *lord*. But she could fight; Bobulups used to beat man bad. And if police hold she for whoring or obstructing justice, she tearing off she petticoat, she opening she breast, she stripping naked in the street, and it would take about five police to carry she down, she was strong; a big bone brown-skin woman; she wasn't no pretty girl, and she was heavy, but lord, she could wine like a genie when she hear pan beat and she love nothing more than to make rab with ol' nigger in the street. She go in jail all the time. Six months one time, six months the next. Kitch used to friend with she; they was close; she look after him. Maybe he get a lil' shine one time he was thirsty, I don't know; town say so, not me. But he make up a song about she:

Bobulups, why you beat the officer,
six months hard labour

I cyar remember the rest.

Even when Kitch was making money he wouldn't try to get no classy woman. Is wajang an' jamette, them bony nigger-woman from John-John he like; woman with gap teeth and bandy knee. I used to ask him, 'Kitchie, boy, why you don't get a good woman from Petit Valley or Diego Martin? What you want with these women? A man like you, in your position as a calypsonian now, you could get a nice reds, a decent craft.'

But he would laugh. 'High class woman not cheap, poopa. If you have a woman in the yard, y-y-you just buy she a sack dress or some sweet water when month-end come, or some sweet water and she feel she in class, she happy. But them highfalutin woman from Petit Valley want gold bangle, they want ballroom, they want cherry wine, brandy.'

I say, 'A'right Kitch', and I leave him there with that. Kitch love all them characters. He love stickfighter and knifeman; mobster was his friend, men like Samperlie and Joe Pringay, fellas born bad. He love to be around tight-dress woman in night club, '*Kiiitch, Kiiitch*' they calling him, they arm round his waist, walking in the street after the tent close at night. I would see Kitch on the corner of Observatory and Basilon Street, or stand up drinking a boscoe outside Maxitone parlour with two, three woman around him. An' is from them, from them badjohn and jamette woman in the Harpe, that Kitch get so many song to sing.

Bobulups and Elaine Pow
every night they making row.
When the thing is not the same
they gone in the poker game.

Ruby Rab and Stallion
have a different solution.
When they fail in Charlotte Street
they heading for Cocorite.

Kitch start to make money but he not spending stupid. He from the country so money wrap up tight in his hand. He don't like to talk about his money. You would never know his business. But these woman in the Harpe could get money from him. Sometimes they pass, 'Mr Kitch, gimme a shilling to buy a bread and a tin a sardine, please?'

'Kitchy, gimme a bob to buy a piece of black pudding, please?'

He come like a saga boy, like a sweetman in the yard. When is carnival season, he in the tent. He had songs. He had 'Jump in the line', 'Tie Tongue Mopsy' and 'Chinese never had a VE day' – all these had people talking. But these days he not recording yet, so you have to go to the tent to hear him, or you can catch him on the street with his guitar, under some lamppost, singing. But he making his money, he could afford to buy you a beer, he could afford to buy a bake an' cheese, he could afford to stroll in flannel pants with woman on he arm.

DONAWAH, 1947

DURING THAT TIME when the steel bands was up in the hills, pan men from town used to come up to the Dry River to hide and play. The river bank pave and the river bank high and we hiding them fellas in the canal to practice. This is where I used to see men like Ellie Mannette, Black James and Zigalee. Then it have fellas from Belmont; badjohn pan men from Mon Repos, Never Dirty and Clifton Hill; men like Zanta, Moppers and Didier. Every area had a steelband. Going up by Laventille Hill it have Rising Sun Band, Free French and Tripoli. You come down Quarry Street by Dry River and you bounce up Bar 20 and Alexander Ragtime, Red Army.

Now, La Cour Harpe was a village unto itself. You could be who you want, you don't go there to tell nobody nothing. La Cour Harpe was hard. Hard-hard. Imagine you walking on that side in the early morning and you seeing blood in the gutter. Some man get zwill the night before, some skull get bore, some cocksman burst and leave he thing right there outside the mechanics hall. You have to cross over ravine to go bathe. The latrine almost overflowing, you could fall in. Somebody piss on the wall outside the butcher shop, lord have mercy; when the butcher come in the morning he have to wash that down with disinfectant. Rubbish burning, dog shit piling. When rain fall: mud. When mud fall: you slide. I don't put water in my mouth to talk; it wasn't a nice place to live. But it had a spirit. It had a something in there that was special. Whether is stick fight, cockfight, calypso or moko jumbie, is behind the bridge it come from. And even though the people there was poor-no-arse, they would give you their last piece of pigtail if your belly was empty.

Men from the Harpe was bad like yaz. Bar 20 fellas living there. Men like Sugar Bain, Mokotux Charlie and Ancil Boyce, the captain. Boyce was a saga boy, he wasn't no real badjohn, but if

49

you rough him up he would cut you. He always impeccable: cowboy shirt with pique collar, denim pants, skimmer hat, and when he pass through the yard to go an' beat iron in the riverbed, he always say, 'Good afternoon, good afternoon, Mr Donawah, what mark play today?' And I would tell him whether Centipede, Gouti, Dead Man or Crapaud play, 'cause I was a real-real whe-whe jumbie in them days. Now, Boyce don't work anywhere, but he smoking Chesterfields, and he always have money in his pocket, and he have girls. He and Bobulups was in thing. The story go that one night Boyce was walking along the ledge at the side of the Dry River – remember is concrete there; the riverbed pave – and somehow Boyce fall in and mash up right there. The fellas had to carry him hospital; next day, he dead. That night them Bar 20 boys dye they jacket black and light candle for him. But it had a rumour that the police kill Boyce because he was a big-time iron-band leader and the governor did want steelband to dead bad.

When they bury Boyce, Kitch was there in the cemetery with all them knifeman, pan-man and prostitute. He bathe and brighten up, he smelling sweet. Grey dogteeth suit and the necktie. Because he did know Boyce good. All ah we did know him. Ancil playing pan in the same yard which part Kitch living, and both of them was saga boys. So when I see Kitch in the Lapeyrouse cemetery that day I wasn't surprised. He stand up sombre in the long grass when they lower Boyce down. Boyce family start to wail. Some boys pour white rum in the hole. Two craft put they arm round Kitch waist and ask him to sing, so he sing:

> Ancil Boyce is dead an' gone
> but the iron beatin' still
> Ancil Boyce, he dead an' gone,
> but the iron band beating

People start to clap and breakaway right there in the people cemetery. Now, the police don't like them thing, so it had some officers there and they start to guff-up and bray, they start to tighten up baton in their hand, they start to talk hard. 'Alright. Alright. Allyuh done bury the damn man, leave this blasted burial ground now. Right now!' And they start to break up the funeral.

Things turn tense, like the air ready to burst. Is anytime the police go leggo they hand.

It had a few man with pan beating, even though they know they not supposed to beat no pan in the road. They harden, they beating they lil' tune. They leave from the cemetery and going up Tragarete Road with a dozen police in their tail. I could see Kitch big head up in front with all the Bar 20 bad man. I say, wait. Like Kitch gone mad. But they flag waving and they going through Green Corner, up Park Street, people behind like is a Carnival band they following. They know by law they not suppose to have pan on the road, but they have pan, they have bugle, they have drum. They have Bobulups.

JUMP IN THE LINE
Iron Band Funeral (A chant to kill death)

HOSPEDALES WITH THE BUGLE coming up Park Street, blowing.
> *Roll*

Jack Ben, Swiss and Gri-Gri with the bubblers three.
> *Blow*

Park Street narrow; it bawling. Fathead have the kettle beating, Audrey have the cuff boom. Brake drum iron. Mallet beaten down from the yankee caboose. Whistles, bells, bottle and spoon, bone and teeth. A riot of sound like a storm stirring, surging, seeping through a crack in their agony, with more vamp than harmony. The cortege is no longer mournful on its way back home to the hills. Dust to dust. Dirt to dirt. Unto thy hands we commit our souls: Bar 20 Band from Bath Street.

> *Thousand, ten thousand to bar me one*
> *Ai ai ai is murder!*
> *Thousand, ten thousand to bar me one*

The drums. Drum is breath and drum is life and drum is lung and heart. These men and women play these drums as if their power had too long been hidden in the hot alleys and gutters that perforate these regions east of the Dry River, and having been unable to speak till now, they beat reckless in their supplication. People start follow them across the bridge, moving among the muddy gutters and black-shack alleys with shattered glass and red dirt at their feet. But the police have a jeep.

The police have a jeep and they blowing the horn. They trying to disperse the crowd, but it growing, it growling, it picking up delinquents from all the hard-hell yards going up Observatory Street, Quarry Street – they call them street but that is a misnomer; these are alleyways, passages, colonial roads. Passing Tanty

Tea Shop corner. More tin pan grumbling in the cortege, bottle breaking, a chant, a chant to kill death. Siren send some scampering, but some stay beating iron in the dusk till they pass Oxford Street corner and they going up still. Some warriors stay with zwill and steel knuckle in hand to ramp with the police when the police try to break up the band, and they bound to try, by law.

Is then Bobulups emerge with the Bar 20 flag at the head of the iron band, with the skull and bones flailing in the citrus wind. She waist she rip, she roll, the flag in she hand she fling it, she wave, she wrap it round she, and flash it in them police face. She ask the inspector, 'How a man could fall in a dry river an drown. When the river so silt and shallow that even crapaud ketchin' they arse to bathe?' And when he say was accident, she prong back and arch, hand on her hip, she plait her mouth and cuss him till he somersault in his skin. 'You must be think black people stupid!' And when he go was to grab and desist her, she cuff him in his face and his glasses break in three pieces. People hear it splash on the road. The big man just put a hand on his holster and Bobulups cry, 'Shoot me nah! Shoot me. If you name man, then shoot.' Then a shot ring out in truth, and everything turn ol' mas on Quarry Street.

The police jeep kicking back dirt and sticking, it straining to follow the band through these red dirt and dusty roads. It get turn over on the side of the road and tumble with a crush that sound like carbide burst, with the wheels still spinning. Bobulups and the inspector start to wrestle like dog in the gayelle. She could kick, Bobulups could bite, and he really don't want to hit no woman, but he smelling puncheon rum on she breath, so he start to fling baton blind and a blow catch Bobulups in she chest, in the breast, in her heart so heavy like it could burst.

Bobulups fall on the government road. Gravel eating at her knees, blood and saliva trickling from her mouth. The knuckles of the fist she still gripped the flag with are torn and bloody, pressing into sharp stones on the road. The suffer; the love. All her struggle-life like a vice round her neck now. Time suspend her there on the road with her own heart beating loud in her ears and the salt-bitter taste of blood in her mouth. She feel she could not rise up, she could not reach them, her people. They behind something, a blurred murmur of gossip alone, the incline too steep, the road too narrow. They have nothing else but gesture to fight with. Is now she knew her people, in this moment, she seeing them as they really are, and how they live. Is a wonder, congealed together in their shack-wood rooms, with thin partitions, hid in the rancid gut of this city where decent people fear to reach, overcome by the overwhelming stench of poverty and destiny, but still they clapping blades, mano a mano, they don't fear life nor death.

But Bobulups did tired fight. She tired make fares on George Street corner. Tired of the pimps, of the police, the courthouse, the jail. Fed up of skinning up, sucking and smiling back. Sick of the suffering she saw all around her. The law like it make to downpress them. Bourgeois and politician never pass this way, and see poor people bathing by standpipe. Suffering and smiling like rain fall and sun shine same time. As she staggers to her feet, the sadness of it fills her with wind and lifts her up, upwards and away from the scene, upwards above Quarry Street, till she can see the battle of sticks and stones still raging beneath, the blood-red sun sinking, the ocean dark and deep as death. Erzulie. And bereft at the agonies, the weight she must bear, the muddy inclines and stagnant pools, the hurricane brewing at the interstice of day and night, torrential rain, the lingering scent of a stevedore, the courthouse and jury, colonial awnings, dust upon the roof of time...

Up

Up

She feeling herself – lifted – bliss of this moment – the flag falling from her hands – unfurling to the earth like wings of a stingray – then she is falling through eternity – away from her birth and growth on these dirt-track warrens – the light draining from the sky – red – her head burst like a splash. Then she feel herself fall again, then spinning, spinning, spinning.

And it was then that the young calypsonian held her from falling, catching her round her waist; her weight pulling him sideways. He had seen when Bobulups fell from the blow, had seen when her heel had failed, and she fell, like Spiritual Baptist mothers when the Holy Spirit swept them, the bell still ringing hard in their hands, and he steadies her just by Argyle Street corner.

She fixes her dress, dusting off the dirt with the tips of her fingers, as if she is sending waves back to the ocean. 'You see what they do me, Kitch? Even a woman, even a woman they will beat.' And she sigh like she blowing out the sun.

'Bobulups, you mad, *oui*. How you go see a big police so and want to fight the man, you mad? He coulda kill you? You eh fraid?'

'*Fraid?* Fraid For what? What I must be fraid for? What they could do me that people eh do me a'ready? Beat me? Shoot me? For what? I is just a jamette, boy, a ol' whore. Bobulups eh nobody. Jail cyar kill me. But he prefer hit me a baton. See, is he did 'fraid fockin' me; yes, is he who have to 'fraid, because me eh 'fraid he.'

She cries. But her tears are not tears of sorrow; they are hot with rage. 'Ancil really get a good send off, eh? You eh see how much flowers people bring? I feel is one of them police kill him y'know. Ancil was so nice, Kitch, I must love Ancil. Oh gorm, is one a them police kill him, eh Kitch? They was running behind him and is so he fall to the bottom and dead, not so.'

He takes her by her arm. 'Come,' he says, 'Let us go back in the yard.'

The band and its entourage had dispersed, disappearing into cracks in the gutters and tunnels beneath the street. Boyce was dead, he had been buried in the muddy clay. The war was over. And they walked. Side by side into the big barrack yard on Basilon Street where Bobulups lived. Wood shack and slum. The latrine soon to overflowing.

So swift the night comes down east of the river, lamp light to light the hill tracks coming down. And a muscle in the air ~

THE SPIRIT

AT NOON, when the Laventille breeze billowing warm through the stained-lace curtains of the jamette yards, the sun is blowing down hard from the Belmont hills to the valley of the Harpe and Hell Yard kitchen and the asphalt roads soften, Kitch struggles to steal a few more minutes of sleep under a light cotton coverlet, in the back room of some frolic house. He rests the soft inner part of his right arm across his eyes, seduced to restless sleep by the rustle of leaves above his head, a branch rolling across galvanise. He pulls himself up and walks into the yard, past the croton and the hibiscus tree, to the latrine.

Brother Jimmy, the Baptist Shepherd, is passing in white, uphill to the quarry. Gamblers and wappie card men are slapping cards down and casting dice at the side of one of those wooden houses, where a black dog is tied under, its pink tongue hanging from its mouth. Heat. Same time the ice-man passes. Ice in a humber bicycle basket to chip with his pick, brown crocus sacking over it to keep it cool. 'Ice, ice, ice in your ice! Ieece!'

When Kitch reach Moses's Bar he finds The Mighty Spoiler sitting at the counter finishing his saltfish and bake. Spoiler wipes his lips with the back of his hand and blinks hard. 'Ai Kitch, gimme a cigarette nah; you have cigarette? I want a cigarette, boy.' Spoiler wears last night's brown suit. Stale drunk. Kitch puts his hand on Spoiler's shoulder,

'But you know I don't smoke Spoils. Where I will get cigarette?'

And The Spoiler laughs, rum teeth grinning in his gum. 'Well lend me a shilling then; you see your boy broken here. Moses so kind he trust me a bake.'

Kitchener takes his hat off and places it on the counter. 'I now going by Slate. Moses, g-gimme a cup of cocoa please, and a bake and smoked herring.'

Spoiler sucks his teeth to dislodge threads of salted cod from the insides of his mouth. 'Oh ho, you going by Slate? I will come with you. But your brother don't have dollars, boy, ease me up nah, a lil' nip of brandy, a taste, till Friday?'

Kitch's eyes widen in concern. 'Nah boy, Spoils, all the money I have done a'ready. I still have to go by the Chinese man to print up some song sheet to sell this evening. My money small, boy, I eh holding.'

At the shoemaker's shop, the calypsonians find the cobbler Hargreaves hunched over his work, with the whine of his transistor radio like a bee buzzing in the heat above him, and his bottom lip slung down in concentration. Kitch closes the swinging bottom door behind them. 'Mornin' Mr Hargreaves.'

Hargreaves raises his head, squints, sunlight sparkles on the thickness of his spectacle lens. His face is narrow and dark; the skin shines, his hand still twists an awl to the helm of a boot. Then he peers over the bridge of his spectacles. 'Poke a poke, boy, poke a poke, allyuh just come out for the day?'

'Tent close late last night, so the fellas was down by the bridge liming, was a late one. Snake in the back?'

'He in the shed. All yuh pass through nah.' Then lifting the swinging counter door he says, 'Mind them boots hang up there. Spoils, watch your head.'

They find Slate sitting at his workbench eating butter bread and cheese from a brown paper bag. He wipes his mouth with the back of his hand.

'Ai, The Spoiler and the Lord Kitch, boy. What going on? A lil' hunger take me tail. Come, man, sit down.' And the calypsonians sit beside him on a hand-stitched wooden bench. The one they call Slate is a dark-skinned, slim-boned man with steady eyes.

Slate twists his lunch bag shut, then he rests his elbows on the workbench top. Then he turns to Kitch, 'Tall man, I hearing real good things about you, boy. I hear last week you sing for Harry Truman, is so?'

'Yes, I sing for him. They call for us, so me and Beginner went up Wallerfield and sing. When I done sing, Truman say "Boy, I never heard music so. You're like a negro Bing Crosby." An' he pat me on my back.'

57

Slate swings his head towards Spoiler, but Spoiler just grinning, then he look at Kitchener again: 'He call you "Boy"?' Kitchener begins to respond, but his words descend into a mess of stuttering and the three men laugh together, like washerwomen at the river rocks. 'Joke I making, boy Kitch, joke.' But he watching Kitchener.

Kitchener says, 'Slate, I have a new tune I working out; tell me what you think nah?' Slate rolls the bake bag to a ball and throws it over his back to the bandon land. He drinks water from a pan cup, and picks his teeth with a twig, then he spits and rises from his stool.

'Sing it nah, lemme hear you.'

Kitchener sings. Slate strums his chin, 'Well, it nice. Nobody could tell you what to do now in kaiso, but people have to hear every word you sing. I mean, your diction must be impeccable, and the rhythm of your wording have to be right, grammatically exact, you know what I mean? Sing it again.'

So Kitchener sings and rephrases to fit the gaps between rhythm and melody. Slate, listening with eyes closed, as if he can see the words falling out of Kitchener's mouth, listening for excess syllables and half rhyme. By this time the sun's heat is less fierce and throws long shadows of shade across the yard. Spoiler has fallen asleep, laying back on a bench beside a dasheen stream. The fowl cock crows, the water truck passes. An old woman falls and gets back up.

Sans humanité

Slate say, 'Sing it again, gimme.'

And Kitchener, map out the bass notes, swing the rhythm, the line, the du-dup of a drum, his hands conducting the air, his legs itching to kick.

That night he sings last at the tent and chants the same kaiso eloquently, to applause and ovation. The other calypsonians watching from the eves, and the band, each man in the arena with Kitch, in the alley, and the yard, they with him there. Sing with the necktie twist, the suit-jacket broad, the people eating from his hand. But in all this, still the man is awkward; this must be said. Is like he can't come out of himself, he wrap up in something there and anytime he try to punch out you could see the effort. He

58

shy, embarrass. He have to inhabit his own self. But sometimes he would burst out and rage, the words spitting from his mouth, flinging down spirit and bad mind, making people laugh. Them is the times he forget who he is. Catch him one night when the mayor in the tent, or when it pack-up with white people and you will see Kitchener perform. The night Cipriani in the audience, or the night he sing in competition and win second place – was $15 and a bottle of cacapoule rum – he will walk like a prince, he will buy Chinese food, he will ride in taxi, he will make his way, somehow.

KITCH WAS NEVER NO BADJOHN. Doh mind he big like a robot; when is time to fight he gone; he not in that. He will grand charge: 'Me? I doh want kill nobody, if I get vex and fight with a man, ah go have to kill him, no question! I don't make joke y'know, if any one of them interfere with me, take it easy.' But is just throw he throwing words so people will leave him be, because really, Kitchener couldn't fight.

He was behind a woman in Belmont once, Linda, a lil' French Creole who break away from the flock. This Linda was working as a stores clerk on the docks and through the fault of her own slackness, she end up living behind the bridge with them jamette and vagabond tribes. Linda an' a big-breast woman call J.J. – who I was trying to inveigle myself – was living in a yard on St Francois Valley Road.

But this Linda had a man call Rawlston who was a well-known Corbeau Town stickman who people say kill a man in a bar fight, but police never bother to hold him. Kitch know; the woman tell him about this Rawlston. But Kitch don't care, he still behind the poor woman, he want to get inside. One night me and Kitch meet the two craft in a bar on Charlotte Street. Kitch want to carry Linda home by him, but she say she tired; long shift. Kitch beg, he beg, I watch that man beg until she oblige. He take she up in the lil' bachie he had on Basilon Street, was to badden she head with rum, and make one set of love to Linda.

The next day about 5 o'clock in the afternoon, Kitch coming back from Lum Lee shop with a piece of saltfish in his hand. He whistling like a semp, he pep. When he reach the junction by Bath Street corner he hear, 'Country boy, Mr Calypsonian. I want talk to you, sir.'

Was a fella stand up like a ol' police on the other side of the road, with his hands behind his back. He wearing wasp-waist pants and short-sleeve shirt, stingy-brim straw hat. He build big; muscular; so tall that if he jump he bust he head on street sign. Them arms was thick like hog leg. He call again, 'Country boy, come nah? Yes is you, you is the man I want talk to.'

But Kitchener, like he smell cut-arse, he buck when he see the man. He intend to pass straight. He say, 'Ai, alright.'

When the man start crossing the road to confront him, Kitch stop and start to stutter, 'W-w-what you want to talk to me for?' The fella stand up in front Kitch and swell up like a bull in the road.

'You mean you don't know what I want you for? I feel you know, a smart fella like you. You must know.' Both of them same height, strapping. The man ask Kitch, 'You know who I is?'

Kitch pull back he neck. 'No, me don't know you.' And he backing back, barring the sun from his eye with the saltfish bag, and the saltfish smelling. 'Who you is?'

'Is I who name Rawlston. You ever hear 'bout Rawlston?'

Kitch knee bend and he say, 'But I-I don't know no nobody call so. Is *me* you sure you want to talk to?'

'Ent is you they calling Kitchener?'

'Yes, is me.'

'You know a woman name Linda?'

Kitch face pinch up, he playing like he confused, 'Linda? No, I don't know no, no, me eh know no Linda. Linda? Linda who? From where?'

The more Kitch talk, he stutter, and the more he stutter is the more Rawlston get vex, and the more vex Rawlston get was the more to fight. Kitch start to walk and Rawlston behind. Is so they enter Harpe yard. People come out their house, they smell trouble. Some inside peeping through curtain. Kitchener in front and Rawlston behind. When they reach the centre court, Rawlston pull a razor from his back pocket, flick it and it flash like a mirror in his hand. A simple razor he sharpen like bad mind.

People start to circle round – they smell blood. Kitch backing back 'cause the blade burning his eye, hands up by his chest, showing the palm and the saltfish hand as if to say 'wait'. 'I-I done tell you I don't know no Linda,' he bray. 'I don't want trouble, leave me in peace, man, please me in please, peace, don't want, no trouble me, leave me be.'

When men get damn vex and just before they battle, they does start to talk sideways, so Rawlston, when blood rush, start to stutter and talk shit too, like the words getting heavy in his mouth. 'You, You like nice woman? Eh? Is nice woman you like? Is nice man woman you like nice, eh, woman man nice?' And just so he lunge forward and fling the razor at Kitchener, but the way he throw it was like he was hoping it didn't connect, and in that doubt somehow Kitch manage to hold his hand, and the two of them wrestling there upright, in the middle of the yard, like dog. Kitch holding the blade hand and Rawlston puffing like a cow. He eye open big-big, he cussing, 'Leggo meh hand, leggo meh fockin' hand!' Lord, if he did only manage to wrench way the blade he mighta cut Kitch bad-bad! But Kitchener strong; is cowfoot and butter bean he eating. He hold Rawlston hand tight like a vice and twisting, was to break it.

Rawlston want to bite. He try, and he cussing one set a cuss until vexation like it overcome him. He vex so vex he foaming at the mouth and his neck get stiff with rage. He manage to pull away the hand with the blade, but like he don't know if to cut, or to cry – and Kitch stand up there with the bag of saltfish still in his hand and a lil' blood on his elbow, poor fella, he body trembling.

It was me who pull Rawlston back. I see everything. But it was old Mr Jaja who really hobble in with he bandy knee and part them. 'Look here!' he say, 'All you is big man; it have children around. You cyar do that stupidness here, in broad daylight. Kitchener you self, you should know better. This is the Harpe boy, this is not John-John, we don't behave so here.' He turn to Rawlston now. 'Sonny boy, I never see your face, so you not from here. What you doing in the Harpe? Eh? You want to dead? You don't know the Harpe is a dangerous place?'

But Rawlston have to stand his stand; he pointing at Kitch. 'Old man, you better tell this one, you better tell him don't never interfere with man woman. He know what he do, otherwise I will come an' burn down this whole fucking place. You hear me? I go burn down every blasted thing inside of here!'

Mr Jaja bend his head to the side like he don't hear properly. 'You will what? You will burn down where... the Harpe? Is so? Well, let me ask you something. You know that fella over so?' It was Mr Henry he point to, swinging in a rocking chair in the yard in front his house with his rifle across his knee. And on the other side of the yard, Saga Boy, the stick man lean up on a wall, and the Indian they call Cacique, coming with a three-canal cutlass they say mount with spirit and leaving mark in water. And all around the yard you see men picking up stone, piece of wood, anything. Mr Jaja tell Rawlston, 'You best go from here, boy, now, before these fellas bust 'way your carapace. You take Harpe Yard for some kinda open sepulchre?' Rawlston take in front before front take him, he turn and run through the land behind the latrines, he jump down in the Dry River bank and run – big stone behind him, pelt we pelting, even dog take off in his tail.

Kitch go and sit down under the tamarind tree and he wouldn't talk to nobody. Like he feeling shame. He hand trembling. The saltfish bag greasy how he hold it tight. Them woman come to hug him up, they bring mauby, sugarcake, but he push them away. Mr Jaja went with his old self to talk to the champ, to rub his back, but Kitch swell up like a turkey; he vex to kill priest, but his body don't know fight, and all them tension, so it stiff. He was to stay there until he boil down like bhagee and come back normal-normal. Eventually that whole commess pass, and people could laugh about it, men drink rum on that, people even start to consult Mr Jaja for arbitration in the yard. Kitch sing about it, that same night in the tent.

'YOUNG KITCH', 1947

KITCHENER WAS SMART. He come down from Arima and he hit one time. So they want him in the tents, they want him in the Victory Tent, they want him in Millionaires tent, House of Lords want him. Everybody want to hear what he coming with next. He come with 'Shops close too early', 'Worrier', 'Tie Tongue Mopsy', he come with 'Jump in the line' an' people near tear up the tent. That was 1946. He had another one they calling 'Mount Olga':

> Mount Olga, Mount Olga,
> This is a mountain I climbing,
> I catching hell to climb this hill,
> the more I climb the more I sliding still.
> Me body run down before a week,
> fighting up to reach up this mountain peak.

When them fellers in the yard hear that, they bawl, 'Wee boy! That is kaiso!' Double entendre. Kitch catch them again; it smut but smart. Then you hearing he singing for Truman, he on the American base singing for the soldiers, he down San Fernando, Princess Town. He was doing very well. Eventually he get so damn popular that for the 1947 season he, Spoiler, Melody and Killer decide to start their own tent. They find a lil' yard – 100 Edward Street – they tie bamboo with wire, they throw some bachelor galvanise on top, they put down a few folding chairs and they call it 'The Young Brigade'.

Them old timers like Growler and Roaring Lion was saying, 'Never happen, nobody eh going there. Eh heh?' Pepper on top of pepper – first time it open, the Young Brigade sell out! You couldn't get a seat. People coming from all over Trinidad; tourists, them *petit bourgeois* from St Clair, even Governor Bede and other dignitaries coming in the tent. The Young Brigade become so popular that season that less and less people going to the Victory Tent to hear the old bards, except them high brown and French Creole people who feel they in thing, because they listening to Tchaikovsky an' Benjamin Britten. Even them, after a few weeks, start to go over by The Young Brigade. People love the tent because the music exciting; plenty horn and bass in it, people dancing in the tent like is a fête.

I mean, they had Mighty Killer there and Killer could dance. The Mighty Spoiler there, Pretender, Melody, Wanderer, a fella name Red Soil, and Kitch. Entry not exorbitant either, so poor people could reach inside. $2.00 a head for seat. $1.50 if you stand up at the back. Money coming in, and every night after the show them calypsonians coming down Edward Street singing:

> *Young Brigade again, Young Brigade again*
> *We young and we have the brain.*
> *Tell them we eh 'fraid*
> *We go mash up the Old Brigade*

Kitch big tune that season was 'Chinese Memorial' and when *that* hit the tent, well is now Kitchener walking through the Harpe like a lord. Now he is *Lord* Kitchener; he not Bean no more. You can't call him 'Arima Champion' or 'country boy'; he making style on people. See him with the big trilby and the rayon shirt with the pique collar, the wasp-waist pants, the two-tone brogues. And every week he in the barber shop for a trim, and every other month he get a new suit measure and make.

He had a tailor on Belmont Valley Road that uses to cut and sew suits for him. The fella name was Greene, and every time you pass on the Valley Road you could see Greene – a red-skin Bajan fella – sit down inside his drawing room with a tape measure round his neck sewing, and a wood pipe hang out the side of his mouth, stitching suits, pleated pants. Bespoke waistcoat hang up in the shop. Cloth mark with chalk and ready to cut. Nice cloth. When Kitch go by Greene, he ordering the good wool cloth that come from England, the wool that smooth like baby head. He want the silk paisley lining, he want the jacket cut long and the lapel narrow, he want vent in the jacket back and two-inch fold in the pants. He want two-inch fold. And anything he want, Green could cut. Greene could measure a man from the way he walk. He sewing for Lord Invader, Lion and Growling Tiger too, and these is tests don't imps with clothes, so.

Kitchener was one of the best dressed calypsonians I ever know to pass through Port of Spain. He walking through the Harpe and the fellas saying, 'See, Kitch have on a next suit again, new pants, new shoes.' Only Roaring Lion could dress more better; nobody could touch Lion. Lion would wear pin-stripe tuxedo with African waistcoat, red cummerbund, bow-tie; he bus' cravat, hat-matching shoes, belt-matching hat, watch and chain, monocle, anything, bowler hat, white cane. When Lion walk in a room, big men breath used to pause. Lion like a prince, he always cool, he never fluster, you never see him sweat.

Kitch used to watch Lion good, because Lion have the seppy, he have the style, like he eh even try. Lion? How y'mean? Lion singing in The Village Vanguard, Lion in Harlem, San Francisco. Lion in Hamburg, Lion cutting record and Kitch want to cut one, too. Kitch want to hear his voice on the shellac, leggo throat. He have songs, he want to see the world. And that is normal, no problem. Because when a young man in Trinidad get to be about tenty-three or twenty-four, he does feel like he outgrow the island. Remember, Trinidad nice, but it small, it does get mundane.

So around this time Kitch start talking about going to America. He tell me, he say, 'Len, boy, I want to get out there, I must try my hand.' He see Eduardo Sa Gomes sending Lion, Tiger and Atilla up there to record, and a fella name Houdini was making one set of money singing calypso in New York City, and maybe Kitch feel he could do better. But people have to invite you to go America, you can't just take your boldface self and say you going. You have to have pedigree; you have to get sponsor, your papers must be in order or they would send you back same as you come. Or, you end up like deceased Sharko's brother – living in a cold water warehouse, snow and rain beating you, and you can't get work. It had plenty fellas went through that.

So I tell Kitch, 'Take a chance and go down in the Emporium and talk to Sa Gomes. Ask him to record you.' But like Sa Gomes didn't want him. So Kitch start looking now, for a way out of Trinidad.

'CLEO IN THE YARD', 1947

EVERY DAY KITCHENER PASS by my yard he would say, 'Mornin', Miss Cleo,' and he smile and tip his hat. But in the back there, where we living, it have latrine and standpipe right next to each other, mud, dog shit and galvanise bathroom that smelling of carbolic soap and disinfectant. I was 17. Mammy was a domestic in town. My father dead on the wharf, so we living in a two-room barrack house in the corner of Harpe Yard.

Kitchener used to call me Miss Cleo, as if I was a big woman. And if I sweeping the yard or sit down on the step front he would stop and chat. He had words, he know to make me laugh. His head long like a mango vert but his skin was dark and smooth like cocoa seed. Ma did always warn me to stay away from calypsonian.

Dry River had plenty calypsonian in them days; everybody feel they could sing calypso. But people was saying that Kitchener was special, how he, Spoiler and Melody was the best of the new ones to take over from Atilla and Lion. One Friday night, me and Ma was coming down Edward Street after church. It was the night they put Sister Ruby down on the mourning ground. In those days Baptists had to hide to worship. Mammy stop to talk to Miss Patsy in her yard and I could see straight over Miss Patsy back fence into the other yard, where they had the calypso tent. I leave them talking and go by the fence and I see Kitchener and the rest of the calypsonians standing by the side of the tent, all in suit and tie. Kitch was singing, he was playing a guitar, and I wave and he wave back, he smile. And he start to come and talk by the fence, but same time Mammy bawl, 'Cleo, what you doing there? Who you talking to?' I had was to run back.

But the next day, the Saturday, I was sitting on the step, minding my business, shelling pigeon peas. Mr Kitchener pass, whistling, feather in his hat. 'Hello, Miss Cleo, hello, good day, you is just the one I want to see. I have something for you, y'know, yes.'

I giggle, I shy. 'Me? What you could have for me?' And I fixing my clothes to talk to him. He put one foot up on the step next to me, his shoe was shining like a trumpet, and he tell me close my eyes, and when I close eyes he put a mango in my hand, a ripe starch mango that warm and smooth. The sap run and stain from the stem, it firm and nice, but my mother – lord 'av mercy – my mother see me from the kitchen and bawl, 'Cleotilda, Cleo, bring your tail in here.' Kitch run.

And when I go inside Mammy beat the back of my leg with a swizzle stick till it welt. 'I tired tell you don't talk to them fellas! Them calypso man is no good. They want one thing, one thing they want. A young girl like you. You is my one piece of daughter, Cleo. O gorm, you go carry on until they gi'you big belly. Is that you want? Eh? I carry you church, I try my best with you, I even get Leader Jimmy to burn garlic and pray for you. I smoke asafoetida in the damn house and you still in calypsonian tail? After I bust my liver string for you? Please Cleo, don't let me see you talking to any of them calypso man again, or I will send you to live by your Uncle Billy in Talparo, and you could mind pig and milk cattle up there.'

I take a chance one evening, just before dark when the sky turning red; Ma was in church. Kitchener was sitting under the sandbox tree that hanging over the ravine. He was playing his guitar. When he see me watching, he call me. I sit down there with him and he telling me to sing. I laugh, 'I can't sing, what you want me to sing? You is the singer, sing.'

'But a pretty girl like you, you must have a voice to match, and I can tell it is the voice of an angel.' And he went to kiss me, but I turn my head so he meet me on my cheek. Is not that I didn't want him to kiss me, is 'fraid I did 'fraid if anybody in the yard see and tell my mother. So after a lil' while pass I tell him, 'I have to go home, Mammy coming home just now.'

'Pretty girl, don't mind your mother. How old you is?'

'Twenty-one.'

He smile with a full set of teeth, 'Well, you is a big woman now, y'know, you could do as you want. A nice butterfly like you, you must be free to fly. Why you don't come back tomorrow, when your mother gone to work, and we will go for a walk round the savannah. You like boil corn?'

And is so things start. I would lie and say I going to take shorthand lessons in Belmont, and me and Kitch would hop the bus and go Carenage to bathe. I had to hide. Once he take me matinee to see *Black Beauty* – first time I see inside a picture house. Once I ask him, 'But Kitch, a fella like you, you must have so much woman, what you want with me?'

And he hold my hand and rub the inside of my wrist. 'That is just calypso life, for show. Those women mean nothing to me. All I want is to get in with a girl like you, *doux-doux*. Anywhere I go, I taking you.'

'I want to go America,' I say. 'You will take me America?'

And he laugh. But when people poor, sometime even secret they can't keep, and the talk went round that me and Kitch was in thing. It come back to my mother and when I reach home one night I meet she sitting on the step, waiting on me with a bible in she hand.

'Where you was, Cleotilda? Lessons finish late?' And she calm.

'Yes, lessons now finish, Mr Richards keep us late, and –'

'Keep you late? Then tell me how the arse I see Richards going up the hill since five o'clock this evening, and he tell me no classes today? Eh Cleo? You gone back in that country nigger tail?'

She give me a bad cut-arse that night with an old police belt. Mammy used to beat bad, y'know. And the next day she put me on the bus with three dollars in copper money and send me by Uncle Billy in Talparo. A whole month I stay on the farm. When I come back to La Cour Harpe, I hear Kitchener gone. Gone where? He gone Grenada to sing. He gone Curaçao, St Maarten.

But my mind on him. I can't lie. Every time the dog bark I looking out in the yard. And when I lie down to sleep I could still feel his arm round me, like when we was in the cinema, like when he did take me to the hotel in George Street, first time I knew these things. I was still smelling the sweet soap on his skin. I hearing his voice. I wait till Christmas for him, then I pick up with a ping pong man from St James. Mammy didn't approve of him either.

SHERIFF, THE BARBER, 1947

I REMEMBER WHEN he was going because he come through the Harpe and tell everybody. Christmas was coming, people was buying their pig leg and sweet biscuit, and you could smell the oil paint in the air all down the avenue. From where I cutting hair in the barbing shop on Bath Street corner, I see Kitch coming down the road. I see him go by Miss Dolly parlour to buy a sweet drink, he gone across by Caesar shop, he buy a *Gazette*, he stop to ol' talk with the fellas outside the poor house and then he come by me, where I put linoleum on the bare dirt and hang up two mirror and Paul Robeson picture, in my lil' place where I doing my work to feed my children and charging five cents a cut, eight cents with shave, where I sharpening my razor on the leather strap I nail to the centre post.

When you is barber you does know everything that go on in the area. You know how fast man hair growing, you know when you see a man come for a trim when you could expect him again, in four weeks or five, depending on if he have dada head or Indian in he blood. You know who with who woman, who getting horn and who horning, who lose thing and who thief, who going bald and who have moss on their neck. And when men sit down in barbing shop, they does gossip like crapaud in moonlight. Is there men does look for work, plot, scheme and organise to make their manima.

Three old man was there liming that Monday morning, sit down against the wall as regular, chewing roast peanuts with they back teeth and talking about things and times. I now lathering Bill Frank beard with the shaving-foam brush. Bill big throat prise up. Just so the strip curtain shift and Kitchener hop in, light on his foot like a mantis, brown linen pants, white shoes, white shirt open down and a black hat swank down on one side like star boy; peacock feather in the band. He grinning like a stepchild. 'Mornin'

Mr Billy, morning, Mr Frank, Mr Murchison, Sir.' He turn to
me: 'Mr Sheriff, the boss, I need a lil' trim, I travelling tomorrow.'

I stop with the razor in my hand. 'You travelling? OK. Where
you going?' Because even though Kitch and them calypsonian
always on some hustle, I say I will give the man a chance to talk.
'America,' he crow. 'I going Aruba and Curaçao first, but I trying
for America really, is there I want to go.'

Bill Frank raise up his head from the chair, all the cream foam
thick on the man face.

'America? How the hell you going America? I eh know calypso
making big money so. America don't want no ruffian y'know, they
have plenty there.' Bill Frank breath bad, like the last thing he eat
was rotten ham, about a week ago, and he laugh with the big throat
and lean back in the chair. The other men laugh like they coughing.
I start to shave Bill now and Kitch stand up in the centre of the shop
like he can't find a pose. He lean up by the sink, he looking out the
window, he reading magazine. Then he ask me, 'You see Melody
for the day yet? Melo owe me $10 an' he dodging to pay me. He like
a rumour I hearing, but I can't see him nowhere.' And he chuck and
chuckle, but nobody laugh with him.

I wipe the scissors on my apron. 'Not today. I eh see Melody
since yesterday.'

Jus's so Murchison close the newspaper he was reading. 'Every
ass and he uncle want to go America. What America have that
Trinidad don't have, besides snow and skyscraper, and one set a
ketch arse?' Then he gone back in the paper, like he make more
of a statement than a question, like he say more than he wanted
to say. Murchison old and cantankerous, he nearing ninety – even
he don't know how old he is.

Sun coming up strong now and Bath Street wash white with
the light. Oban Billy push back his cap. I watching him, because
Oban Billy is a cocoa hound, he not from town, he from Matelot,
and he don't put water in his mouth to talk. He used to blow bugle
in the army band till one eye blow out like a bulb and the other
one get dim with cataract, and I never expect him to say anything
good, but he lean in the scene with gravel in his throat and
surprise everybody. 'Well, that is good news, boy. I glad for you.
Go, go and make your name, this kiss-me-arse place eh have

nothing for you. You have ambition. I like that. And you can sing too. Yes, man, is good to leave this blasted place.' And he suck his teeth.

I have the shell-handle razor shaving round Bill Frank ears and I turning his head to suit the blade. Bill gone back in Kitch tail, as if Oban never talk. 'New York not easy, poopa. My brother in New York since last year Christmas, he ketchin' his black arse in Harlem, say he working doorman – when the mark bust is ponce the man pimping. New York? Police ketch him; eight weeks in jail. So who is you? Eh? You come from country with two-three good song and just so you say you going America? Look, don't make me fall off this chair this early morning.' And that make the rest of the tests bray on the bench like old mule. But Bill Frank didn't done with the *mauvais langue*. 'Calypso have no future, boy. Long time, when it had men like Lord Columbus, King Lancelot, *them* was kaiso singer, not this stupidness you young fellas coming with now. Attila is a master calypsonian. Executor still singing good. Lion could sing, Tiger, even Killer have something. But you, you just start, boy, you eh even make one damn record yet and you talking 'bout America? You best take your country bookie arse and go and plant peas in Arima. Yes, or stay in the damn Harpe and mind the child I hear that jamette have for you. America don't want you, boy; forget that. If you was good, Sa Gomes woulda send you.' And the men laugh again, hard. Bill Frank reach out his hand, to slap Kitch on his arm, as if joke he making.

'But Mr Frank, you feel, you feel, you feel I want to stay in Trinidad? Tiger, Attila, Lion, Invader, all of them fellas travelling. They does go all New York, Chicago, they does go Boston, they recording for Decca, for RCA. Houdini making one set of money in New York and he not even a real calypsonian. So I say, well, is my time, I must take my chance. Attila give me the contact up there. Invader know people, calypso making money in America… I know people in Brooklyn… I have good contact in Boston…'

But the boys forget Kitchener. They gone back in their own business. Kitch lean up by the window like a imps. Bill Frank handle him rough; he get weak. I feel sorry for him. As I washing the razor in the sink I turn and tell him, 'You go get through, man;

forget them fellas, they only making joke. Come back about three for your trim. I have plenty head to cut today.'

When Kitch gone, Bill Frank steups and shake his head, and as I soft-brushing his neck with talcum powder and taking off the sheet, he grumble, 'Every kiss-me-arse calypso boy want to go New York. But you think is just so you does go America? If was easy so, all a we would go.' But the laughing simmer down in the men on the bench; they maybe get the sense that Bill Frank eat tiger cat that morning.

I look out the lil' window above the sink and see Kitchener walking down Observatory Street; he head up in the air and he waving to people as he going down; he tall, he outgrow the Harpe. And as I leave that vision to wash out the lather brush, I watch Bill and the other men sitting on their old decrepit arse in the barber shop, making joke on the man ambition, and I watching Kitchener again. He quite down the road. He stop by the Indian people shop, he crossing the bridge by the poor house, he disappearing into the sun, and just so something touch me inside, out from nothing. I even surprise myself. I wipe my hands in my apron and stand up in the middle of the floor.

'Is so black people bite-up, eh? We don't like to see our people prosper. The boy trying he talent, he trying to catch a chance and instead a' wishing the boy luck, Bill Frank, a big man like you, instead of encouraging the man, you make him feel like a fool. But what you do with your life? You work on the rail for twenty-five years and never make engine-man. What you have to show? You still living in a one room in Gonzales, you have so much children you does forget their name.'

Bill laugh; his skin can't get pierce with that, I know. He stand up there fixing his clothes. 'Look,' he say, 'I is a big old man now, Sheriff, my skylark days done. I never travel, is true, I go give you that, and I poor no arse you see me here. But them young boy make a lil' money and they feel they in action. Oh, this one going New York, this one going Panama; they running here, they running every kiss-me-arse place. What Kitchener could do in New York? I bet you when he reach he don't have his papers correct and they send him back. Kitch not so good... you find Kitch good?'

I didn't answer the arse. I watching the street. I know once a man catch the vision of the outside, inside not good enough no more. So as I stand up there with the apron slack round my waist. I was wishing I could go with Kitchener, too, away from this place, just to see what outside there.

Then Oban Billy take the chair.

I wish you knew Kitchener. He is nearly seven foot tall, and is blacker than a whole deck of aces of spades. He has rhythm in his ears. In his knees. In his fingers. In his elbows. And in his soul. He is one of Port of Spain's outstanding calypso singers […]

Lord Kitchener sang to us in a taxicab. Harvey McMillan, who is travelling with me, and I picked him up shortly after midnight on our way from Port of Spain to the Pan American guest house, where we were staying while waiting for the plane to Belem, Brazil. He rode with us for about an hour, and I wish I could put on paper his accent, his words, the mad time he beat out with his hands on the door of the cab.

I wish, too, that I could give you an adequate picture of the jungle which holds Trinidad in its arms, and the size and color of the moon that rode above the jungle. The jungle, the moon, the strange calls of the birds, and Lord Kitchener's songs formed an unforgettable picture…

All the music he had was the hum of the motor, and the time he beat out on the doors and cushions of the car. 'Mr Henry,' Lord Kitchener said, 'What do you want me to sing about? And Mr Harvey, what is your pleasure?'

— Henry McLemore
Schenectady Gazette Aug 7 1947

LORD JOOKING BOARD, 1948

CARNIVAL COME and Carnival gone and calypsonian broken again. Some of us take the boat, as regular, gone up the islands to catch them small island Carnival and to make a few bob in them tourist nightclub in Curaçao or St Croix. This trip it was Kitchener, Melody, Beginner and me, the Lord Jooking Board. We on this boat call the *Northern Eclipse*. Bobby Khan organise. Curaçao and Aruba have hotel, they have nightclub, they have casino for people to sing in, they have tourist coming there from America and Holland, so it have money to make. You sing your lil' 'Mary Ann' or a nice 'Rum and Coca Cola' and you could make ten dollars a night easy, plus tips.

And is not just tourists; the locals want to prance, plus, it have Trinidadians living in these islands too; men who come to work on the oil refineries. These fellas away from home, so when they hear a Lord Jooking Board coming from Trinidad – bring rum, come out – they want you sing whole damn night. My song for '47 did call 'Fishing Pole':

> *Well the girls in town want to know*
> *how Jooks catching big fish so*
> *River cold or river deep*
> *a catchin' from grouper to carite*
> *and when I hook them they bound to roll*
> *when they see the length a my fishing pole*

You hear kaiso? That is kaiso. That tune cause plenty ruction in town. Sa Gomes wanted to wax it, but they rob me in the calypso competition. They put me 7th, behind Lord Woodslave. But you ask me about Kitchener. Well, Kitchener never really go out of Trinidad to sing, properly I mean, as a bonafide calypsonian, before the trip he make with we. I hear he went Grenada once with Galba, Pretender and Small Island Pride, but that was banana boat thing. Where they sing? This time we going quite Curaçao and Aruba, so is a big boy engagement Kitch find himself in, and he whistling like a picoplat when you see him on the boat.

Now, Kitch was good, but I did find he too hurry. He wanted to do everything one time. He hear the big timers going America to perform, so he want to go. He see Lion in the Wang in a polywool suit and he jealous; he must get one too. He see Invader driving Austin Cambridge; he eye get long, he want vehicle too. Melody pick up a white woman; he want one too. The boy was ambitious. But calypso is big man thing; you can't rush it. They tell me he good, I tell them, 'Wait, let we see how he peruse, when it come to proper composition. He still can't beat Attila or Invader when it come to lyrical proficiency, and in picong duel, I didn't think he able, not for instance, with a man like me.'

So *krik krak*, the story go: we on the boat and I smoking my cigarette cool there on the deck. We now pass Bonaire Island and we heading to Curaçao. The ship engine humming and the night blowing a lil' cold on my skin, so I fold up in my jacket. Mr Kitchener come up from below deck; he wearing check triple-pleat pants with suspenders, white shirt, the trilby; he like a star boy in a Western – he eh dress for boat, he dress for dancehall.

He come and lean with his back on the deck rail. 'Ai Jooks,' he say, like if me and he is friend from long time, 'you ever went Curaçao before?' I watch him, but he don't look like he even expect a answer. He looking out to sea – star-boy pose – one foot up on the rail and the other one bend like a cutlass.

I say, 'Yes man, I was there last year with Galba and Lord Brett. It don't have many a these islands I ain't sing in yet.'

He want to know everything bout Curaçao. What the people look like, if the woman nice? What music they does have there? They have jazz there? They like calypso? The food nice?

Now, I did like the fella, eh. I had nothing against the boy, but eventually I had to ask him, 'Look man, what do you at all? You's a police? Why you have so much question? When we reach Curaçao, you will see everything for yourself.' I flick my cigarette in the sea and I suck my teeth. But Kitch in my tail. He want to know about making record now. He know I make a record in

Barbados, so he asking me, 'The studio big? What it have in the recording room? The machine have plenty button? How much button? What kinda microphone? How much they paying?' And the poor boy stuttering like his engine spoil, spitting in my face.

Soon as we reach Curaçao that night – I mean the men just tie the anchor – Kitchener want to go nightclub. We passing through Willemstad and he eye get big-big when he see how pretty the little city was. They have nightlife, they have restaurant, bright light, glass-front bar, and them brown-skin, thick-bottom woman. Yes, Curaçao nice. He want to roam. Beginner say he tired, Melody drunk, but Kitchener want to spread joy. I don't want him to get in trouble; he don't know the place and since my head was a lil' tipsy from the two white rum I had on the boat, I say a night breeze go straighten my head, so I say, 'Leh we go.'

In Willemstad it have a bar they call The Bira Ront and a local calypso band does play there some nights to entertain the tourists. When we reach there it pack with people and a quintet playing on a lil' stage: guitar, wood bass, trap set, clarinet and piano. The piano man was Boyie, a big-belly Indian I know from St James who living Curaçao for years. They playing their rumba while white people eating lobster and flying fish. The tables they eating on have candle vase and flowers; it have real palm tree in every corner. The roof is wood slats like a shed, thatch on that, chandelier in the centre. In there all you smelling is tobacco smoke and rum. The waitresses dress in tight skirt and yellow blouse, yellow allamanda flower in their hair and they twisting through the crowd with trays of rum punch, cheese and pineapple sticks. It noisy. Is a good place. The people not really listening to the band; the band just there for background and vibrancy. The locals sit down by the bar at the back, watching the show and drinking their hard liquor; the men there seeing who eye they could catch. Me and Kitch go and lean up by the bar; we order a couple stout.

The lil' band playing sweet. They play 'Mary Ann', they play 'Linstead Market', they play 'Shame and Scandal' and then they call intermission. Boyie come straight to where Kitch and I lean up. He hear about Kitchener. 'So you is the "Green Fig" man?' He say, 'Sing something with we, nah? And Jooks, you too, boy, both a you have to sing. We can't have two great calypsonian in the Bira and eh taste allyuh hand.'

Kitch jump up. 'Why not? Well, yes, that is no problem at all at all at all.'

I say to meh self, 'Lord, this country bookie go embarrass me here tonight. We not getting pay to sing here, we have we engagements, plus, you don't come in people place and just get up and sing so. It not professional. This ain't no rum shop. But Boyie want we up there, so he go and he buy two shot a rum, cigars, cutters. I say, 'OK, alright, we go try a lil' something.' Because in truth, one set a white woman in the place drinking white rum and lime, and I have my eye open. It have hotel upstairs; I not stupid.

A-a! Bram. Music start again. Boyie introduce Kitch and Kitch jump up on the people stage. He call for 'ray minor' and start to sing some song he calling 'Jump in the line'. The audience applaud him decent. Is a good song, yes, it nice.

Boyie introduce me, 'The great Lord Jooking Board from Trinidad,' and I start to leggo kaiso in they waist! I give them a piece a 'Fishing Pole'; they bawl like ten Tarzan. I give them 'The Donkey Can't Bray', and they laugh they belly full. But as I ready to come off, Boyie come and pull down my shoulder and say, 'Gi'we a lil picong duel nah? You and Kitch, a lil' extempore?' I laugh, 'cause I don't really want that. I tell the Indian, 'Boyie boy, people have to prepare, the band have to know how to play it, men have to be sharp. And you can't put a veteran calypsonian like me against a youngster; picong duel is a serious thing, I don't want to embarrass Kitchener in front all these white people; it wouldn't look good.'

Kitchener come, 'Who-who-who say picong? I hear picong? Me and Jooks could do something. Why not?'

Music leggo – bram! It not the real extempore music they does play in Trinidad, but the boys trying their best. I turn to Kitchener, 'Listen boy, let we just give them a couple verse eh? Light thing, slight. You take front.' But I could see he eager to go up. He start his verse,

> *Many nights I been wondering,*
> *who teach Jooking Board to sing*

79

Yes, many nights I been wondering
who teach Jooking Board to sing
He face hard like rock stone
he so ugly no woman don't want him
he better go back Grenada
and leave Lord Kitchener alone

I say, 'Wait, what jail is this? Like Kitchener really feel he could tumble with an experienced test like me.' The people clap him hard, they raise glass and they watching me. Things get hot. The band start the melody again and I step forward:

Ladies and gentlemen
thank you for your hospitality.
Now watch this young man carefully,
I'm going to send him to casualty.
I know him since he was a little boy
Yes, since he was small…
And if I tell you a next thing… a next thing I say
If I tell you…

And I don't know what happen, but I bust. I bust right there. I couldn't bring nothing else. You could believe that? Right there in front the whole damn Bira Ront, the Lord Jooking Board bust. But is ok. I did never want to embarrass the boy, and I really wasn't ready for picong duel anyhow, my mind wasn't on that. And the stiff rum I drink on the boat must be tamper with my head, because I never bust before. He catch me weak. But he good, I go give him that.

So after the Bira, when we walking back to the hotel, the big street empty; it late. Is only a few drunk fellas outside, and them Curaçao police in shorts pants and sandals. Just so Kitchener ask, 'Jooks, you vex with me?'

I watch him and laugh, 'Me? Nah man, vex for what?

'The lil picong I give you, I notice after that you turn a lil' funny with me.'

I ask him, 'Who teach you to extempore so? Executioner?'

'Is Pre-Pretender teach me,' he say, 'and Tiger show me a lil' thing too,' but he watching me to see if I grinding malice. Few day later we gone Jamaica to play, and when time to go back Trinidad, he get a work in a club in Kingston and decide to stay there.

BILL BUCKLE, 1948

THE DANCERS USED to come on first, they used to open the show, and they dance the juba and the limbo in their 3/4 pants, and the women in raffia skirts and the flower bra, they will dance under fire in that limbo there. Elena, then Litico and Sandra. Then Madame Jeffrey the acrobat would contort, spin plate on her head and bend back in crab back. We had a comedian, a Black Chinese fellow from Trelawny name Long Ting. Some nights we get Dora Misingham, she was a classical singer, and she would play piano and sing before the intermission. And then the master of ceremonies would introduce Lord Kitchener, and he would come out with his top hat and tuxedo, sit on the stool there and oh he would sing calypso with the Sugar Hill Band behind him. I remember him doing 'Mary Ann', 'Sly Mongoose', and people used to love that. Then I would come out, Bill Buckle; I uses to croon.

Saturday night, the Sugar Hill Club was the place fi' go. It was in St Andrew, down Red Gal Ring. Is all dark wood in there. It have plants and palms and the bartender pouring good rum an' lime, tonic and Scotch, liquor galore. The bar maids used to make plenty tips. English people, French people, Canadian, all of them sit down there to eat their pepper shrimp and rice while they watching the show. Sometimes men like Lord Fly and King Cinch, even Lord Creator, would come backstage and beg Kitch teach them a few calypso.

We did a show once, just me and Kitch, was on a Monday night in a little place called the Big Penny Club in May Pen and something happen with the promoter and him never get enough people in there. It was embarrassing; about twelve or fifteen people in the club, lord. So before the show, me and Kitchener go see the big man in his office behind the club. I remember him well; was a half-white man call Mr. Carmichael, a fat man. I say,

'Mr Carmichael, bare fifteen people here, what to do? Sing? Or we cancel? Either way you have to pay we, you know.'

He say, 'Yes man, no man, sing, you must sing. People will come; it early.' So we sing. Kitch do his thing, I do mine. 'Hi de ho, they call me Bill Buckle,' I uses to croon. The room catch about twenty people, and 'bout half a them was the band, waiter, barman and chef. When we go in the office after the show, Mr Carmichael crying, 'Oh, lord, fellas, so much money I lose tonight. Ease me up, man. Pressure… Ah beg you take half the money now and the rest next week.'

I get vex. 'But Mr Carmichael? A so you a go on? You insist we do the show, now you must pay we.'

But Carmichael in a daze. Debt sharpening he big toe. Band to pay, bar man, bar maid, rent to pay, police to feed. Then Kitchener start to swell up. 'I-I-I for one need *all* my money tonight, tonight, tonight – I going England in a few days, I can't wait for you. Monday night never good for these cabaret, but I is not the promoter. I come to sing and I sing, so I wants my money, tonight, tonight, tonight.' And his hands trembling.

Mr Carmichael stay giving prayers – how we should see the situation and have a heart, how he don't have the money. I watching Carmichael because I hear he carries gun, but I size him up, an' he don't look like no gunman to me. He pat Kitchener on his arm. 'Take the half and share it, Ah beg you, come back next week for the rest. Bill, you will get your money, a beg you, believe me.' But like something fly up in Kitchener head and he pull for a drape and he rip that down from the window, he lick off a glass from the desk, he kick a cupboard and it spring open, then he collar Carmichael in his throat and Carmichael cry out: 'Lawd! Have mercy, no bother beat me, no beat me. Look, look, take this.' Y'know, that scamp had the qualie roll up inside his jacket all that time?

The next I hear about Kitchener is that he gone England. A ship did pass through Kingston harbour charging £28 pound a head to England. Kitchener gamble to hop 'pon that and gone; he take a chance, but he spend his money wise.

PART TWO: LORD KITCHENER

Build me a road let me walk on the sea,
to see the mother country
                    — The Mighty Viking

'CENTIPEDE', JUNE 1948

ALLYUH SEE HIM THERE? The one they calling Lord Kitchener? See how he sit down there on that bench facing the sea? He singing his calypso, humble and sweet, he not troubling nobody. You see how the boys gather round to hear him sing? Is because he does remind them of who they is, he does sing them full of hope, sing them out from fear. Because I will tell you something for free; even the most cantankerous man on this ship does frighten when night come and all you seeing is bare black ocean, and the big ship start to rock up on the waters of Babylon. And you in the middle of nowhere and nowhere. You in between your own self.

I know Kitchener from Arima. But he won't remember me. His father deceased, Pamp, used to shoe my Uncle Ben mule. And many time I go by Pamp with Uncle on the mule cart, I would see Kitchener as a little boy, running about the yard in he tear-up pants. 'String Bean' they used to call him. But I sure he forget me. I hear him tell people he going to sing in nightclub in London, how is record he want to make. They telling him sing, and he singing, and he could make up things on the spot. But England is a funny place. Back home you could see straight inside your neighbour house, you know what he doing, you know what he eating, how much money he making. But in England everybody does think you doing well, because you can keep your business private. You might be smiling, yes, but deep down, is suffer you suffering.

As I stand up here and the boat rolling, I could look around and tell you all who never travel before, all who know sea and all who never even put one foot on boat. I know from how they walking, from how they fix themselves in relation to the ocean. Some sit down quiet-quiet inside their cabin, but they watching how the sea-line rise and breathing, and they holding on deck when they walking, because it have no branch in the sea, if the wind blow.

Fellas does feel sweet when Kitchener open he throat to sing. Long as he singing, we feel safe; we eh go dead. You leave maybe your mother, your wife or your children behind in the islands; what you will do in England, eh cowboy? Where you go sleep? What food you go eat? Who go give you a overcoat if it snowing? Coverlet if it cold? Where your clothes washing in the white man country? What work you could get? You ever hear about cooking rice under your bed? You say you coming back but you can't say when.

Some does want to play card till three in the morning, 'cause they can't sleep. Some get seasick and hide to vomit like when woman making baby. Well, yes. Some does cry, oh! How they want to go back home, oh! How they make mistake, oh! How England don't want we. Is 'fraid they kiss-me-arse 'fraid; they 'fraid the lash, 'fraid the uncertainty. All some of them know about England is what they get teach – about the King in Buckingham Palace, how London Bridge falling down, and 'the sweet green fields of England with the sunshine overhead' – they know the language. But those like me who been there before, who serve in the war for his majesty, anyone of us can tell you: England is a dread, dread place, it prim on top, but it sour at the bottom. Is nothing there, really, for we. England like a big hole we does fall in. Is true. I know they don't want we there, but we coming. Is them English have to be accountable for all that happen and keep happening.

Sometimes Kitch and Lord Beginner would go down in the galley and they play music down there; jazz, calypso and what not. A young boy, Dizzy, had a trumpet and he does blow good. Another test from Dominica have a mouth organ, one had a tambourine, one man make a pair a shac-shac from dry peas and two bean can. Kitchener, well he could play guitar, he could sing, and then somebody make a box bass with a crate, and Kitch will to play that like a bitch. I goes down there some nights and gamble, and the cook might throw mercy on us and fry up some liver and onions for the boys. Who have grog bring it out, who have weed, smoking. Is all these things does make the crossing bearable till we land at Tilbury.

And when you land in the mother country, who you is to the

English? You don't know if you coming or going; you papers say England but you born in Trinidad, and you not of the place you reaching yet – and when you reach you is a immigrant. But let me refrain. The ship is a pendulum, it like a bell clapper that swing, you on a journey, see; you not of the place you leave behind – that gone, is a memory, home gone, at least for now. The blue hills done fade, the bay, the mountain, the forest, all that gone, water pass, business fix, we go settle for cold for now, metropolis.

LONDON IS THE PLACE FOR ME

FOREDAY DAWN, THE SKY is ashen grey. The sea washes from the waters and the river begins to lash at the ship's bow. Estuary. The water here is dank and slow and dour, like the scent of snakes in damp country bush. Along the Tilbury coastline there are dark and sleeping hills, a few factory chimneys that pout fog, blink lights. Saplings and crab-apple trees. Marshland and the fisheries, port side warehouses and shippers offices. The morning opening sickly, diseased and dull. Silt. The white foam forms a trail, the engines churn, through sediment of oil and blackness.

Dark figures crowd the prow of the ship: black faces peering from the top deck. Some have footholds in the riggings, others hold their hats and jackets shut against the wind. Silhouettes of their dark mass, and then the buzzing hum of their voices, travelling across the water. The ship begins to turn slowly into dock, it asserts its draughts and trim, it rests on its keel, and then the engines die with a groan. Those on the shore cannot fathom the depth of field, likewise as islands are often underestimated on maps by cartographers, so too the ship's true scope overwhelms the eye.

The men on the boat can see the crowd gathered on the docks to meet them, and they wave. They put fingers beneath their tongues and whistle. They have seen shipyards and ships arriving before. They know what to do. Their faces are taut and starched by six week's sea blast. When they come down the gangways with their sea grips and baggage, their shoes are the only things shining in the dull light.

A young man steps onto land, he feels the air with his face, tastes it with his open mouth, the sea smell, the moisture on the tongue. One suitcase or box case or bundle tie-up with twine, the soft suit, the pastel-coloured seersucker shirt, the trilby, the brogues burnished from kneeling between the varnished pews on some evangelical Sunday morning in the tropics, with the bread-fruit branch knocking on the roof of the sermon. But he stands here now, on the wooden jetty, upright in England, the land he had imagined for so long. A photographer fixes his image; flash bites his eye.

A reporter in a black wool coat, black hat, his red face round and impartial, Pathé microphone in hand. He pulls his bulk up the gangplank to the deck. There are a group of men there, leaning starboard on the top deck, smoking slow cigarettes, waiting for the jetty to clear so they can come down to England in style. The one who sings is the centre of their circle, and the reporter wants to see who stands among them with the song. The calypsonian emerges to face the mic and camera eye. He wears a wide brimmed trilby, fawn brown, pinched at the crown. A polywool suit in indigo blue with wide lapels and padded shoulders. Black tie, criss-cross patterned with white near the knot. The trousers are high-waisted and hold two-inch folds. They fit so loose in the thigh that the sea breeze flaps the pleats.

The camera operator sets his tripod on the roof of a car on the jetty below, and zooms the image of the calypsonian down to earth from the deck. What appears to be close in his lens is actually distant and this is why the film stock cannot capture the fine details of the calypsonian's face: the rigid bone, the cat-eyed blink. Instead, the image he records is dark and simple.

'Now, may I ask you your name?'

'Lord Kitchener.'

'Lord Kitchener. Now I'm told that you are really the king of calypso singers, is that right?'

'Yes, that's true.'

'Well, now can you sing for us?'

'Right now?'

'Yes.'

London is the place for me
(mimics the upright, wood bass)
London this lovely city
    (the right shoulder rises, the beat runs down)
You can go to France or America
India Asia or Australia

91

but you must come back to London city
(wood bass in the throat, the rolling, country Baptist diction)
Well believe me I am speaking broadmindedly
I am glad to know my mother country
I've been travelling the countries years ago
but this the place I wanted to know, darling

     (tap-tap of the beat against the railings, and his shoulders ducking and clenching, releasing the rhythm, the lavway, the drum)

London, this the place for me
(he can hardly contain the motion of his body)
(mimics the wood bass, the rattle of the cornbird's throat)
Two verses is all he sings.

The wind on the river blows up ghosts behind these men. Look how cold tightens their smiles, and in the sombre, dim dawn, when the calypsonian finally climbs down the gangway with his beige canvas suitcase, he looks to the sky, always the sky, but cannot find the sun.

More smoke. Smoke upon smoke.

COLD IN THE WINTER

KITCHENER, KITCHENER! Yes boy, come, don't stand there, move. Yes, you're in the way, man, and these people don't care; they will knock you down. How was your journey? It's long, hey? I did it in '44. Terrible seas, cold. I was sick, night an day for the first three weeks. You was sick? Lord, when you catch that seasickness, you feel as if your whole belly rolling. Here, give me the grip. It heavy, boy; what you bring? You bring a sack of coconut? You bring a bag of yam in England, boy? I hope you bring a heavy coat; that saga-boy jacket you have there nice, but it won't help you; it thin. This country cold, boy. Nobody ain't tell you England cold? But if you feel it cold now? Wait, you wait till December or even January, and you will see how quick you find a winter coat. See all those chaps? They been here before – might be soldiers – see how they have their duffle coat hang on their arms like gentleman? I tell you. Come, we will catch the trolley bus. Where Pearl and I live is Bayswater, not too far from here. In fact, you're lucky I'm even here. We're getting married on Saturday. Of course, you have to be there, man; I might even make you sing a song or two. But of course. Look, there's our bus. Let's cross. Mind the road. How things back home, boy? Heh? I hear those Americans still in town; they feel Port of Spain is theirs now. I know the Governor, Shaw, I know he don't like them there, but England only manage to come through the war because of the Yanks. You know Bain? You know Fisheye? Jumbie from Belmont? How those fellas? How those boys from Woodbrook with the steelband? Sweetest iron band in the land come from there. How you mean? La Cour Harpe? Nah, La Cour Harpe don't have iron like Woodbrook. Joke I making, man; take it easy. Bar 20 was good. Well, give me the new calypsos nah? The ol'bards singing good? Atilla still singing that same song? He's good of course, but no variation in melody. Ah, and what about Tiger? Red Soil? Well, I know Lion's doing well; Lion all about. What about that short fellow, from the country – panyol… ah, yes, Lord Pretender? But we have time to talk. I want to know what all those boys are doing. Not much calypso here, my boy. Not really. English people very set in their ways – music hall, vaudeville, jazz, classical. There are a few bands here, and those fellas that come up with Al Jennings. Rupert Nurse, Fitzroy Coleman, they play at a place called The Antilles. But is not like home. I miss Trinidad bad, boy, bad. Especially the food. Oh boy. Can't get wild meat and bush rum here, you can't even bring them back from dream. Oh, don't mind him, he doesn't want to sit next to a darkie; let him be, that's how these people are. You will learn how to deal with them. I don't mean you will learn to accept it, no, because you shouldn't accept it, but this England is a curious idea. Imagine you're on the bus, on the street, minding your own business and a child will rub your skin to see if the colour would rub off, an old woman will touch your hair to see if it real. Once, I was in a pub in Birmingham and a man was talking to me good-good, a white man, pleasant chap. All of a sudden, the man bite me on my hand like he want to eat me. I get so confused, I couldn't move. You laugh? The chap bite me, I telling you. I had to run from that place. I was vex till I frighten. They will make you feel uncomfortable, but most of them, they hardly say anything, they just watch you, cut-eye. Or, they smile that snide smile they have. And then, of course, there are some hooligans who like nothing more than to interfere with you. They like to stab the boys. I mean, they would be stupid to tackle a fella your size, but you have to be aware, you have to keep alert if you walking alone at night, because they may come from behind. Simple fact is English people don't want us here; they don't like us eating out the same plate. And that will never change. That's how it is, and… and… Alright, this is our stop. Hand me the grip; careful how you step down. Come. Mind the road. Wait! This is not Trinidad, pardner; I tell you, they will bounce you down.

MY LANDLADY

THE CALYPSONIAN TURNS in a cool cotton sheet on a narrow bed in the guest room of a high-ceilinged apartment. His ankles are tangled in water; he reaches for a vine above a green river with overhanging mango branches and the ripple of swift fishes escaping to the mossy gutters of the river. River dove and iguana. The stunning buzz of ciçadas. Down in the valley in the shack-wood smithy, his father knocks a horseshoe into shape and dips it in the cooling pan. Even from the river bank, as he aims a slingshot into the tall bamboo, he is sure to hear the horseshoe's hiss.

He wakes to the sound of Miss Pearl moving out in the hall, fussing over her hair, scraping gum from the bottom of her shoe, filling a kettle and cussing, and then singing folk songs in the same high breath:

> *Do you know Mr John Boulay – tim-bam*
> *That man from Charlotteville? – tim-bam*
> *he owe me one dollar bill – tim-bam*
> *He owe me for something – tim bam*

He rises. Still feeling the undulation of water rolling under his feet, a week after he stepped off the *Windrush*. The room feels dry, the air artificially hot and brittle. Dust in his throat. But he waits. He is reluctant to step outside while Miss Pearl is getting dressed for work, for to appear in the hall or the kitchen this early in the morning would be to remind her of his imposition on her and Edric, for this temporary room and board. When finally he steps into the small hallway that runs between the rooms he finds Miss Connor fixing her hair in the drawing-room mirror and speaks with delicate politeness. 'M-m-morning, Miss Pearl, morning. Like you going out early today?

'Yes, I have a meeting at the BBC. I just made some coffee. Go on, it's on the stove.' And she rushes past him into the bathroom to brush her teeth and gargle. She is a tall woman, broad-shouldered, fair brown and Creole with oval eyes and windball calves in her heels. When she walks with purpose, the floorboards creak. Kitchener waits until he hears the faucet open, and close.

'London busy, eh? Everybody have somewhere they rushing to go,' he says.

'Of course, there're no hammocks here.' She answers from the bedroom. 'This is not Arima where you could ride donkey cart and suck orange all day. People have things to do.' She laughs, moves, pulling a breeze into the kitchen to drink the last cool dregs of her coffee. 'Was it Brixton you went last night? How was the Tropico? You sang?'

Kitch prepares his mouth but it will not sound. He folds his eyes to suppress the glitch of his tongue, moans, time is running out for a response, but then at the sharp top of the breath the stutter releases. 'Yes, I sing. I went to sing. Plenty people there. I even see a few fellas who stowaway on the boat. If you see them, like them is more English than the Englishman.'

Pearl touches the sides of her neck, her wrists with perfume. In the kitchen, Kitchener turns the third spoon of sugar into his coffee. 'Edric say he know a man who want to record calypso, a West Indian fella. A Mr Simmons, you heard of him?'

Pearl appears at the doorway fiddling with an earring and an ear. 'No, I have not, but Edric knows a lot of people. You really think you could make a living from singing calypso, though? Maybe you should think of another job of some sort. Something to fall back on.'

'Well, yes, but if a man don't dedicate he life to what he love, I feel he wasting he time. I want to record, maybe play a few shows, then we will see. I come here for that. A man have to try.'

'Edric tells me you left school at twelve or something. And do you have a trade? I don't know, but me, I couldn't just turn up in England with nothing and with two hands swinging. I would be so afraid. You're not worried?'

'But what it have to 'fraid?' Kitch says. 'If I bust I go back to Trinidad and plant peas. The only thing I know is calypso, so I have to get through. I bound to.'

He listens to the door's creak and close, to Pearl's quick footsteps down the stairs, to the front door opening, then firmly closing. He looks out the kitchen window and watches Pearl walk, then run, between traffic, across Bayswater Road, disappearing into the light of morning, a bright gauze falling over the street as the sun begins its arc.

A man have to try.

KITCH IN THE JUNGLE

FOR THE FIRST TWO WEEKS after the Windrush docked, the arrivants would walk from the deep shelter at Clapham South to the New Pacific Bar in Brixton. The men dressed high and broke-dick slick, the heat of their islands remained in their bones, and their brown skins were still dark and shining, not yet dulled by the cold. They came to drink and to see which spare craft they could pick for prick. It was there that Lord Kitchener decide to get up one night and sing with the house band. Not on a Sunday night when Cyril Blake or Rupert Nurse was in the band, and the place was jam, but on one dry Tuesday night when a long-stones piano player called Conrad Prieto was in session with his trio.

Kitchener recognises several men from the *Windrush*; men who were dry and dour on the crossing, who would offer only simple sentences, who could be seen shivering in the sea breeze. Now these same men were posing in their high-waist trousers, leaning on the bar, drinking gin and warming women's ears with sweet talk.

The house band have no collective name, besides, and are setting-up to play on the narrow stage, against the wall, right where people passing for the toilet. In fact, sometimes, in lulls between songs you could hear men pissing in the urinal behind. The stage is garlanded with green, white and orange bunting; old and curling, left over from St Patrick's Day, and there is a long bar at stage right, where drinkers are leaning to talk.

Brady, leaning there too. The old cuss Brady from Kilkenny, salty in his tweed. Silver haired, his eyes are glazed with Scotch. His back is noticeably arched, so he appears pious and considered with his drink in his hand. Conrad Prieto is still feeling round the piano keys for a tune when Brady catches a vaps and shuffles across the floor to the stage.

'What band is this? What you play, jazz?'

Conrad raises his weary head from the piano. In his eyes there is the slack gaze of a too-queried man, 'Yes, a little jazz, but we more play calypso music.'

'Cal-yp-so? What's that? Come now, lad, I hope y'don't mean that jungle music. That's not what we want 'ere.'

The pianist coughs a laugh to appease and diffuse the old man, make him go sit in a corner and beh-beh on himself. The band begins to play, straight away with pepper and step: 'Stone cold dead in the market', 'Wash Pan Wash' by King Radio, 'Jou'vert Barrio'. Three songs deep and Mr Prieto rises from his piano stool and speaks into a microphone. 'Ladies and gentlemen, please welcome now the man... look, he just come from Trinidad, Lord Kitchener. Give him a big welcome, he now reach in England. Kitchener... Lord Kitchener.' And Kitchener, who has been pacing a dim spot at the side, enters centre stage. The quartet play a legato, minors in the chords, swinging thirds, 2/2 in the beat. Kitchener begins:

Imelda bawl 'Murder' when Kitchener was leaving Demerara
Imelda bawl, when Kitchener leaving Demerara
I jump on the stage with the Lord Pretender
Imagine how I sing with tie-tongue Mopsy in British Guiana
Imelda say –

A hand reaches up into the song, to pull the microphone from the singer. Brady. He holds the chrome stand at an angle, like a neck bent in supplication and the lone loudspeaker squeals with feedback. Brady stands there for a moment, suspended, with his scowl and his stagger, as if he is waiting for the band, the singer, the bar man, anybody, to say something, to explain, to save themselves. But the tune is broken, the wood bass gone fickle, the drummer hand stick, the piano weeping in a ditch of knives and the singer does not sing.

The audience start to rumble and guff, but no one steps to Brady in that gap in time.

'You call this music?' Brady asks, in seriousness. 'I've not under-stood a single thing, not a single word. It's nonsense what you're singing there. What is it? It's complete nonsense, that's what it is.'

Kitchener's mouth opens, but makes no sound. His eyes bulge and stare. One cool bead of sweat rolls down the side of his face, with his arms slung down. *Act or be impacted upon. Do or be done to. Take front before front take you.*

Conrad stands beside Kitchener at the front of the stage. 'Come on, man,' he calls to Brady, 'give him back the microphone. No one trouble you. What you want in this?' But his pleading eyes do not assuage Brady who holds fast to the mic stand.

'I said play the jazz, lad, that's what you boys should play. And you, mate, you can't sing. Get yourself off. Off!'

A string of bunting tangles to Kitchener's shoe as he jumps down from the stage. It rips, pulling a string of small Irish flags, pinched from their thumb tacks. A heat begins to build in him, a rage so nervously hesitant, vexation collapsing upon itself. He pulls at the microphone stand, still gripped in Brady's hand. His voice is awkward and tremulous, pushing against the plot. 'G-Give it, give me that, man! You mad or what? Give me the damn thing!' Brady's grip is feeble; the pull shocks him to stumbling. Then he bucks back and raises his hands, palms up, as if in a question. There is a pained and bitter grin in the corner of his mouth, but his moment is past. He drifts to the far end of the bar, knocks his shin bone on a bar stool, and calls for a double Scotch and fades.

The band kick back. Plot is how you tell it. The trumpeter pierces the air with the cry of his horn, the rhythm jumps, and Kitchener sings. Sing it now, sing it away like everything else. Let it go. Humble down deep in the song.

Throw.

Oh lord, Kitchener I want to go
let me go, take me to Trinidad.

WINSTON 'CORBEAU' FRANCIS, 1948

WHAT HE WANTED MOST was to hear his voice on the shellac, to see
the stylus wind across the wax. So when he record one take he
would beg Mr Jones, the engineer, to play it straight away,
because he want to hear how it sound. And he would stay smiling
there, in front the machine, with his hands behind his back,
bending forward with his ear press to the speaker. 'Play it, play it
again gimme, lemme hear.'

They call the place The Manor. Was in Morden. Renico
Simmons put up the session, Hummingbird Records. Was the
first time Kitchener get record, properly, and we there behind
him in the band, playing music like beast. Rupert Nurse there,
Fitzroy Coleman. Lord, we shaking up like jumbie in that basement. And I look up through the one window it have in there and
see the leaves leaving the big crab-apple tree, outside in the Manor
grounds. It was autumn. I hearing motor car passing in the
distance, train, people going about their business, and I say to
myself, 'But wait, like England don't know we here at all.'

Look how I beating them bongo drum till I coughing up blood.
We put all we spirit in that music. Is eight song we record that day.
Eight. Straight. Kitch call for 'Chinese Memorial', run the tape,
we run that down. 'Steel Band', 'Jump in the line', all get wax in
one take. And no matter how Mr Jones tell Kitchener that is best
to record everything first, and then to listen, Kitchener have no
patience. He want to hear every note, he want to hear every word,
as it going down in history.

CALYPSO CLAMBAKE

An unusual commotion was caused in Parlophone's Abbey Road Studios last Monday afternoon (30th). The occasion was the first recording session in this country of genuine Calypso music played and sung by Trinidadians. And to mark the date, Parlophone threw a cocktail party and arranged for the press and calypso lovers to witness the recording.

An interesting point about Calypsos (which were described in these columns last week) is that they are always sung by men. There are no women Calypsonians. On this date were two well-known singers, Lords Kitchener and Beginner, accompanied by Cyril Blake's Calypso Serenaders. They each sang two of their own songs: 'Underground Train', 'Nora' (Kitchener), and 'Dollar and Pound', 'Matrimony' (Beginner). Among the audience were chanteuse Mona Baptise, Mrs Rex Harris, Mrs. Steve Race, Lord and Lady Donnegall, Iain Lang, Humphrey Lyttleton, 'Frisco' Robin Scutt, Edgar Jackson, Max Jones, Sinclair Tralli, Bert Wilcox and Tom Cundall.

The band comprised Freddy Grant (clt), Cyril Blake (gtr), Fitzroy Coleman (gtr), Brylo Ford (quatro), Neville Boucarut (bass) and 'Dreamer' (conga drum). This session was the brainchild of St. Denis Preston, who organised the group and supervised the recording.

— *The Melody Maker,* February 4 1950

CRICKET CHAMPIONS
Llewelyn Barrow interviewed in Harlesden, London
by Michael Myatt

MICHAEL MYATT: Were you living in London at the time of the 1950 Cricket tests?

Llewelyn Barrow: Yes, I was living in Kilburn. Dyne Road, Kilburn, near the railway, in a one-room there, in a house with some Irish people. I was working in a biscuit factory in Harlesden at the time.

Myatt: What made you leave Trinidad in 1949?

Barrow: Well I was only twenty-four. So you have to remember that we was young men, and as young men we want adventure, we want action, we want to see England, see what it like, see the sights; we want to see the mother-country. Now, don't think we had no understanding of the thing. We know England not easy, we know they don't really want us here. But we coming as man, we name 'British West Indian', and England is the mother country. Don't let people tell you West Indian was stupid, that we come England cap-in-hand, expecting the King to meet we off the boat, singing how 'London is the place' and all that. White people was spitting on we in the streets.

Myatt: But tell me about the cricket – West Indies versus England at Lord's in 1950, the second Test. How significant was that match for West Indians in England at the time?

Barrow: Well, boy, that day, I think since I leave Trinidad, that day in Lord's, when the West Indies win that cricket match, was the best I ever feel, up to that time, as a black man in England. West Indies beating England at Lord's? When we lose the first test, everybody head bow. The boys didn't play well, the wicket didn't favour we. They beat us by 202 runs. But then, at Lord's, at Lord's we start to throw fire on them. We beat them bad-bad, at the cradle of cricket.

Myatt: So you felt proud?

Barrow: It was more than proud, yes. We was proud of the cricket team, of course, but we was proud of weself too. West Indies team did represent we, and we was fighting up like man in the empire to show England that we could stand equal, that we could beat them. Because, if you really want to know, those days we talking about, lord, a man couldn't get a room! Chinee man can get a room, Jew man can get room, even the coolie man getting – if he have money, but nigger man walking 'round all day and door slamming in he face. It was hard. Room you get dilapidated and smelling of cat piss. Shoe have hole and you looking for work. It take me three months before I get my lil' work at McVities, and when I get that, I hold on, I hold on.

Myatt: So did you suffer any direct hostility?

Barrow: Direct? Listen. I used to try to always dress smart, y'know. You never see me without jacket and good pants, shoes polish. I used to think if I look sharp, the English people would see me as a respectable chap, but that didn't work. I remember coming home from work one night and I buck up on some Teddy Boys. I walking, whistling my lil' tune, and I hear, 'Oi! Sambo, go back to the jungle!' It was four of them, walking behind me. Well, I carry on. But one come and spit on my jacket an' blood rush in my head one time. I turn and hold the first one I ketch and I bring out me ratchet blade. I did fed up, I did want to kill 'im, to chook him, but something tell me, *No Llewlyn, let him go, leave him.* And I let him go, and the whole a them run.

Myatt: So, going back to that day at Lord's, in a way you felt, it seems, like West Indians were settling scores. Would that be fair to say?

Barrow: Well yes, but you know, even with all the pressure England put in we backside when we come here, how they treat we like animal, we did still love England.

Myatt: Can you tell me about the game itself, the last day of the second test?

Barrow: I was with the fellas in the G stand, right there on the ground, right behind the boundary line and, from early, we could see England was in trouble. They was chasing runs they couldn't make. When Ramadhin clean bowl Washbrook for 114, and then Yardley, Evans and Jenkins fall quick-quick, the West Indians that was there – and we couldn't have been more than 150 or 200 strong – we start to make one set a'noise. Man beating iron, man beating bottle, one man had a bugle, and every time he blow, we bawl.

All now the English people face red. They know a sweet cut-arse book for them. Johnny Wardle come, he make 21 and get out lbw, stupid-stupid, and then Alec Bedser, but Bedser was a imps, he couldn't bat. Ramadhin bowl him for a duck, and that was that; the Indies win by 326. The umpire just grab up the stumps and run. West Indians invade the grounds. Plenty confusion boy. We even try to go in the pavilion, but police stop we. If you see bacchanal.

Lord Kitchener there with his guitar singing and prancing all round the wicket, an' we following him; a fus he singing sweet. Rum come out, the bugle blow, who have shac-shac shaking, whistle, you blowing. Them days we never had flag to wave.

Myatt: So Lord Kitchener, he was leading the crowd?

Barrow: Well yes, he was popular. I see a officer – imagine this – a police hold Kitchener by he arm, hold him to arrest, say, 'Young man, you can't do this here; this is Lord's.' A white man tell the officer, 'Let him go, man, you can't see is happy the people happy?' And the constable let Kitchener go.

Eventually we leave the grounds and we go down Park Street singing and beating anything we could find, dustbin, old wood, anything. I even see a couple man with Congo drum, I don't know where them come from, might've been Africans; some of them love their cricket y'know. People come out their house, looking out their window to see us pass.

By that time my head bad with red rum and stout, I eh know my arse from my uncle. I following. We move down Baker Street and then we cut down Oxford, Regent. I hear people say we going Piccadilly, we going in the heart a town. Kitchener was in front with the guitar still, and he singing all the way (sings): *Those little pals of mine, Ramadhin and Valentine.*

We dance round Eros twice like cannibal, singing that. Police shaking they head, but they not bothering with we. We not hurting nobody. Then we cut up by Glass House Street and we hit Soho, and the group start to scatter out.

Myatt: And what was there in Soho? A club?

Barrow: There was a club there, yes, the Paramount, a West Indian club. We get there now and start to drink, we drink till we weak. If you see people. All kind a people was there, not only West Indian, English people, Indian, African. Music playing and people celebrating. It was wonderful, man, wonderful. I hear Kitchener and Beginner and a couple other calypsonians was going to come back and sing there later that night, I wanted to stay in town, but I was drunk bad, boy. I don't even know how I reach home. I fall asleep face down in my bed; in boots, singlet, pants, hat, every damn thing.

CALYPSOS, BANDS AND WAR DANCES
IN LORD'S VICTORY RIOT

LORD'S, June 30 – Across this sacred sward of cricket, when the last English wicket had fallen to the West Indies, swept wild rejoicing crowds. Leading them was the gleaming blackfaced Calypso singer, 'Lord Kitchener'.

Right around the ground he went in an African war dance, all in slow time.

'Kitch', with a khaki sash over a bright blue shirt, carried an outsize guitar which he strummed wildly.

'Do you see that patch of ground moving over there?' said a cricket wit. 'That is W.G. Grace turning in his grave.'

Wild-looking West Indians in dungarees, scarlet jockey caps, or zoot suits, after this victory over England yelled: 'We want to go to Australia.'

A sober-minded M.C.C. Official said: "It is unlikely – in fact it isn't possible. But I wouldn't like to be on the other side if they did."

— Trinidad Guardian, June 30 1950

LAURETTA, 1951

HALFWAY DOWN WARDOUR STREET there was a club called Jigs, in the basement of a shop and Cyril Blake worked there. Cyril played the guitar and the trumpet and he would sing 'Frankie & Johnny' and 'St James Infirmary' just like Louis Armstrong. Sometimes Kitchener worked in that club too, and that is where I first met him. One night I went there, and Cyril told me that there was a tour coming up, playing a few American army bases in Germany and did I want to go. I said 'Yes, of course.'

There were six of us in the troupe. Two dancers – Dot and Dash – a pianist, myself; Cyril and Kitchener were the singers. We were in Germany for about six weeks, in spring of 1951. We started off in Stuttgart, then we went to Heidelberg, Frankfurt and then Wiesbaden. I remember the night we got to Wiesbaden. As soon as we got there, Kitchener disappeared. I don't know where he went. There was a rehearsal the next morning with a new pianist and Kitchener arrived late, after the rehearsal had started, looking like he had slept in his suit. He came to me and said, 'Gimme your comb.' Not, 'May I borrow a comb please?', No, just 'Gimme your comb.'

My hair was quite greasy at that time; I had pomade in it to keep it neat and set, and there was grease and hair all at the top of the teeth, so I said, 'No, I'd rather not lend you my comb.'

He said, 'What? Just give me the comb.'

'No,' I said, 'I won't; it's not clean.'

And he went really horrible, using all sorts of bad language and nasty expressions, like, 'You think you're this and that. You feel you're too special to lend me your comb? You feel because you're half white your comb is too good for me and my knotty hair? You think you're too white to lend me your comb.'

I thought, oh well, that's not nice. But it didn't bother me because we only performed together, I did not have to talk to him otherwise. After the show we hardly saw him anyway, because he would be off doing whatever he was doing. I think he had a ball in Germany; every night after the show he would leave whichever army base we were playing at and go out on the town. Sometimes with Cyril, sometimes with the American soldiers, sometimes by himself. But somehow, when it was show time, he would be ready, oh yes, immaculately dressed in his navy-blue suit, his white shirt and red bow-tie; his shoes would be shining.

It was all cabaret really. We would all sing something together at the beginning, to open the show. Then each of us would do our act. Dot and Dash would do their dances, then I would come on and sing a few songs with the pianist, and then Cyril would do his numbers, and he would introduce Kitchener, and Kitchener would do his songs, singing and playing the guitar. He would sing, 'Ugly Woman'. He would bring the house down. He was a very good artist. He could pick someone out of the audience and sing about them straight away, and I suppose he was charming when he wanted to be. People liked him. But I didn't have much in common with him as a person. I found him a little bit rough.

CYRIL BLAKE, 1951

Talk about a land which enchanted me.
Is when I spend my vacation in Germany.
I walked around in the bright sunshine
romancing my beautiful fräulein.
But when I told her I was going away,
in the German language the lady say,
'Oo la la liebling Kitch – Oh,
wiedersehen meine Apollo.'

— Lord Kitchener, 'Liebling Kitch'

IMAGINE WE GO in a bar in Wiesbaden. Had to go down, down below a restaurant and it dark and it smell kinda funny down there, and dampness not good for my chest, it not good for blowing trumpet. But the dancers gone back to the hotel, the piano man and singer gone, and Mr Schreiber say how we can't come Wiesbaden and not try some of the local bock beer.

The bar room grand, with dark-wood floor and chandelier. German people down there smoking pipe and drinking their liquor. It have big leather armchair, some old painting of men hunting with horse and wood gun on the wall. All the drinks bottles hang up and shining behind the bar, barrel o'beer and crystal glass and some accordion music playing easy over the loudspeaker, a woman singing in German, what sound like duck bone stick in her throat. A few hard-face German man watching we; they suppin' their brew from big tankard and watching we. But that is normal thing. I used to that. It don't worry me. They could watch how much they want; to look is free.

We sit down at a table, a waitress come, and Mr Schreiber order a round of the bock. Then Schreiber son come and join us with his young girlfriend. The boy must be about 20, 21, he don't look

110

like he even start to burst yet, but he have a slim, blonde craft on his arm and like butter can't melt in her mouth; she softly spoken.

But it have a next room. It have a next room in the back, through a doorway and it dim in there, like they have candle light there, flickering. I want to see what in there, so I go to the W.C. and when I come out I go and stand up by the door to peep in now, and see two giant sit down there with elbow on table eating meat straight off the bone, like dog, some big-big junk of meat they holding, blood dripping, and they have no rice, nothing, no knife, no spoon, just meat in their hand, chopping. So I watching. One of them turn and catch my eye and he watching me watching he as he eating the meat, but he wouldn't turn away. He wearing glasses and the candlelight blinking from the lens. I watching him back; I not afraid.

Even from where I standing the meat have a fresh smell, like flesh beef and vinegar. Is the kind of smell that does go up inside you and make you feel sad. So I go back to the table and I ask the promoter, 'Mr Schreiber, what they eating in there?' And he look around twice, left and right, and he lower his voice, like he don't want nobody hear,

'Bear, that is bear they are eating there.'

I lean back, 'Lord, bear?'

Schreiber say, 'Yes, they are eating bear. But please, please, don't look at them.'

All this time Kitchener sit down there like a schoolboy; he talking to Schreiber boy, but he watching the fräulein. He don't care the girl fiancé there, he winking at the girl. But when he hear 'bear' he look round. 'Is B-B-B-ear allyuh say they eating in there?'

I tell him, 'Yes man, blood running down their hand, the meat look raw.'

Kitch buck. He turn to Schreiber, 'Wha-what kind of p-p-place is this you bring we? This place not for us. What place is this?'

But he want to see the men eating the bear for himself, so he straining his neck to see. Mr Schreiber say, 'Please, let us drink. Don't look at them anymore. Mr Kitchener, you want another beer? Cyril, you?' And he looking for waiter.

Now, we sitting on a table in the middle of the room, so one of the bear men just lean forward and he could see we, and I could see he, the same one with the glasses. The man shoulder wide like motorcar bonnet hulk over the table with big meat in his hand. Just so, his chair push back and scrape on the ground. He stand up. He about 6 foot 8, and from there, he taper down. The hair slick back, jet black; it shining. The head too small for the body. He wearing a long black fur coat; the wool thick and it hanging off him like it just cut from the bear. I know was trouble when he come and stand up at the table between Kitchener and Mr Schreiber and he watching me frankomen in my face. Is then I realise that one lens missing from the glasses and the other one crack. He say, 'Who are you? Don't you know Germany is for Germans only? And you are as black as night. How do you feel?' And he grin like a goat. I didn't answer the fool. He watching Kitchener, he watching Schreiber, he watching the fräulein, he watching Schreiber son, he watching me. Kitch straighten up. 'Mister, we not look-looking for n-no trouble here. Just a drink we having, as friends.'

The fella just watch Kitchener cold. Mr Schreiber jump in and try speak to the big man in German. But it sound like the man leggo one cussin' in Schreiber arse and Schreiber sit back down. The man stand up there with his hand on his hip, like he waiting to see if somebody, if anybody was man enough to step up and say something. So I stand up, like man. The beer glass tight in my hand, I ready to break it on the table edge if it come to brawl. I hear Schreiber son say, 'Mr Cyril, no, no. Do not upset.'

The big man bend his head to peep over the glasses frame. 'Aren't you afraid of me?'

And I say, 'Well no, we are all God's children here, so I feel safe.'

When I tell him that he blink hard, like a twitch, not a blink, and his breathing get heavy like his engine stall with the bonnet open. He put his hands in his coat pockets and he prong back on his heels. He look in everybody face. He survey Kitchener up and down, from the trilby to the brogues and then he ask him, 'Who are you? What are you doing here?' But Kitch watching Schreiber, like he want him to answer, but Schreiber reluctant to get cuss again. The man ask again, 'I asked you a question. What are you doing here?'

Kitch shrug his shoulder. 'What you mean what we doing here? We having a drink; you can't see that?'

The man turn back in my arse. 'Don't you know where you are? Where are you from?'

I laugh, I trying to play it cool. But I don't like people ask me that question at all, at all. I put my hands on my waist and I push out my chest, 'Why you want to know? You is a police?'

'You are musician? American? My name is Eberhard,' he say, 'I have no problem with you, but my friend wants to fight you.'

The friend, coming to come behind him playing shy, he wouldn't look nobody in the eye. Big like a ox, both hands tattoo, tattoo on his neck, tattoo on his face. His overcoat burst down and dirty and the buttons hanging off because his belly big like a flour bag and he have 'bout six or seven chin and smelling of blood and cigarette. Is cokey he cokey-eye, he can't see straight, but he spraying hate and spit like he want us to dead. He voice like pig drag to slaughter. 'You are not for here. Go out. Now!'

But I decide I not going one mothercunt. I not moving. Why I have to 'fraid? Because we in Germany? Just so Kitch get up and he move from the table. What will happen? I just laugh. Things tense. People in the bar watching. I put my glass up to my mouth and I drink the last of the bock beer down – was really a good brew, thick, like syrup. All the time I watching the brute fix in his face, the glass warm in my hand.

The bad-eye one squeeze he fists an' squeal: 'You are not welcome here. You must leave!'

Kitch say, 'Who say so? Who say we have to go? You?'

I know Kitch. Kitch revving up his motor and if he get a flying start he will forget he don't like to fight. But I don't want fracas in the people bar. The promoter, like he screw to his seat; he son sit down there like a mook, with his hands on his knees and he fräulein like a swan, she neck bend down. I leave them sit down right there, and I pick up my trumpet case, easy-easy, and me and Kitchener walk out from that place.

All the walk back to the hotel we never say one thing to each other. It shake Kitch up; he was trembling. Big as he was, he fear altercation. But he have to maintain. He have reputation. And all I was thinking as we going through the town was thanks, Papa God, that I didn't have to bat them man, and damage my good trumpet hand.

OH HE WAS THERE, of course; we went together. Men like Roderick Haynes, Black James and Spree Simon in London and Kitch not there? Never happen. Dudley Smith? Tony Williams? Them was pan self. Ellie Mannette, Betancourt, Pan DeLabastide, Boots. All these was boys from Port of Spain and Kitch know them good. Remember, he used to live in La Cour Harpe, right where those fellas used to beat their iron. So when we hear that TASPO coming to England for the Festival of Britain, we make a lime and went down to the South Bank to hear them play.

That day, good sun, heat like back home. We reach early and walk round, watching all the exhibition, the Skylon, the this one and that. A few of the boys was there already; Trinidadians from Notting Grove, a few Jamaican tests from Kensal Rise. Everyone in a good spirit. White people strolling with their parasol. The Thames flowing cool, she rippling in the sun.

Me and Kitchener stand up by the Festival pier, right by the river, waiting for the band to come out. They have chair arrange there, microphone set up, television people with their camera, crowd start to gather. Two young boy come and wipe the chairs. Kitch just watching with hands behind his back, and every now and again he would hum something. He restless, he can't mellow, is not his way.

Then one by one the players start to come out from inside the Festival Hall with their pans around their neck. Lieutenant Griffith coming behind with the baton in hand. Everybody in the band wearing Hawaiian shirt and pleat-waist khaki pants, trilby hat. They take a bow, sit down on their chair. Then Lieutenant Griffith face the band. He raise the baton and he watching every pan-man straight in their face.

Pa dong pa dong! Is start they start. The crowd give a cheer and they gone with a mambo. One time Edric Connor and McDonald

Bailey start to dance and break away in the crowd. Boots Davidson have the cuff boom pumping like is wood bass he strumming. Lord, the tenors bright. Kitchener watching the band, he concentration deep. Kitch is a man did go down inside music. He watching round at the crowd, he watching to see how the white people watching, how they listening to the pan, how their foot take it. They don't know nothing about pan, so they watching to see how the sound producing.

The rhythm take a white woman and she start to shake she waist. She come in the little circle where Griffith conducting and she making bacchanal. I don't know where she learn to dance steel pan but she wining good. A police come and ask her to move, but she oscillating on the sergeant and all the man decal an' braiding get press up and ramfle. But Kitch not taking she on. He turn to me, 'Them pan look rusty, boy, like they eh prime. Must be seablast. Black James tell me the seamen didn't handle the pans pr-properly at all; they eh care for them. Is just oil drum nah, so they throw the pan like is ol'iron. But they sounding good, an' it have pan inside there that I never hear, new pan them boys make.'

Bam! The boys leggo 'Johnny', the Houdini song. Griffith singing:

> Ah look a misery, wherever I see Johnny.
> All you people will be sorry to see
> the grave for Johnny and the gallows for me

Tony Williams start to go down in the rhythm and lick the tenor boom till Kitch catch a vaps and start to tremble. I shame for him because you know how English people does watch we. But he take a small dance, on the side, he couldn't help it, and them fellas in the band start to grin when they recognise was Kitch. Last time they see Kitch was Port of Spain, and that is a good four years. Kitch tip he hat, and I nod my head, 'cause some of them recognise me from when I uses to wrestle in the quarry.

When they done their repertoire, Griffith conduct them to simmer the last note, to trill it and it fade. Griffith pull down the hat from his head, he bow, the fellas stand, they bow and the crowd applaud, and is gone they gone. But hear the black magic:

116

walk as we walk and is like the pan still sounding, ringing on the river, going down beside us. Kitch want to walk now, he don't want catch no underground. As we going along the Embankment he say, 'I find they didn't play enough calypso. And how, how they… I did expect them to play a lil' longer, so much good calypso it have, they didn't even play one of Lion songs, or even, or even a…' And that man talk about pan till we reach back in Bayswater, pan like a jumbie in his ears. We was to catch up with the boys at the Paramount, later that night.

CAMERA ON YOU
The BBC, London, August 1951

THE LIGHTS OF THE STUDIO surprise him. Tungsten heat. A chaos of spotlights illuminating plywood palm trees with mint-green fronds. The pastel-washed veranda and the swinging kitchen doors, the sky-blue backdrop. And then the male dancers come, dressed in turquoise silk with billowing sleeves, three-quarter pants with ragged hems cut at exact angles for pulling seine nets or stepping through Hollywood jungle undergrowth in muddy bare feet.

The women follow behind, lifting their floral skirts and dancing delicately. They have sharpened their toes with red nail polish. To twirl. Rouge on their cheeks, their black hair tied back and decorated with a pink dupoini rose, broached to the left side, like lilies of the plantation. Olive oil caresses the knots of their limbs and the lower branches of their bodies. They tie their white blouses in a knot at the waist and their smiles brighten the room more than the bulbs in the rigging above.

Then the steel pan-men come with sticks in their hands and their instruments hung by straps around their necks. They wear short-sleeved shirts of floral seersucker and pleated beige flannel trousers. Same old shanty-town armpit that under these lights start spewing their rancid scent.

They begin to play. But these verandas overlook no ocean. These ochre shores look up no hill, no Dry River. The corbeau, who avenges corpses in the *labasse* and flies over the land, hissing through its beak, is missing. The Shango bells that ring at eight each night, sending jumbies tumbling down from chapels hidden in the quarry, are missing. The crapaud poison and fetish mirrors, the thunderstones and dried navel strings are missing. The badjohns with razors for teeth, who lime outside the Greedy Jordan on a Friday night, likewise the women waiting to cordon and kiss them on their necks are gone, like incense burning in the Mechanics Union, like Hell Yard and George Street fight. Halogen won't make sunbeam. White paint don't make salt spray. This scene is in black and white.

Boscoe hefts the horizontal limbo stick. He runs his fingers along its length, ceremoniously, waves it above his head, replaces it between the two upright staffs which stand in the middle of the studio floor. Then he stands back to assess the limbo rig. Its smooth staffs, black with white rings, the horizontal held up with a sly hook of nails so it stays. Then he dances, with his arms akimbo, wrists bent inwards at the waist, shaking his elbows back and forth; his legs press, instep and back, twisting, his bare feet scraping the floor. The women dance around him, circling with excitable steps. They hook elbows with the men, gesturing, as if to speak plantation talk in some abstract bongo yard.

When Kitchener sings, the cardboard palms sway, the sea spray splashes against the studio doors, the lizard and agouti hide in the gully grass, among the gaffer wires, where a green river runs to the sea, between the stout cocoa and the guava fields. Poised there, with the song in his throat, with the talking-drum's rhythm fluttering in his double-breasted suit:

> *Ah ha, never me again,*
> *to go back on that Underground train*
> *I took the train from Lancaster Gate,*
> *and the trouble that I'm going to relate*

Fitzroy Coleman's guitar inveigles the space, shuffles in duple time. Then the wings of the cornbird have flown and the sea recedes to night and sleep again.

To black. In a minor key.

BUT IT IS AMAZING to see when he come in the studio and he set up a tune, and he have pieces of paper, microphone there, he loosen the tie, he push back the hat and he going to sing. He will take a run through first and when he feel it ready he say, 'Right, let's do it.' And we leggo music, *bram!* An' he would kick out his foot and dance like he on stage, like he forget we was in the studio.

What a lot of people don't realise, though, is that the producers and the recording company had a lot to say in what get record. Sometimes they would even get so fast with themselves they will go inside your song and tell you how to sing it; might be a word wouldn't work in the song; they ask you to change it.

For example, 'Tie Tongue Mopsy' was a tune Kitchener sing in Trinidad, one of his most popular songs; it was a Road March before Road March, and that year, 1946, he come second in a big calypso competition in Port of Spain. But when he come to record it in London, the producer, Denis Preston, say, 'Kitchener boy, people don't know it here as 'tie tongue'; make it 'tongue tied'. And poor Kitchener ketch he arse to turn that one around. All how he try he couldn't get the words to fit in his mouth, he struggle till he sweat. Musicians laughing in their horn. He try another take, he buck, the damn tape rolling and Preston shout, 'Oi! Hold it, hold it, Kitchener, break, break.' They call him in the back, in the production room, and Preston talk to him. When he go back to sing he singing:

> *Last night I had a romance with a tongue tie mopsy*
> *who then convince me that she so love me*

See that? He wouldn't sing tongue *tied* at all! He tongue tie he self. 'Tongue tie' is the best he could do, poor fella. But I think even when Belafonte sing 'Mama look a boo boo dey', he change the thing around and pronounce it different. He couldn't sing it exactly how Lord Melody sang it, no; Yankee people can't understand a damn thing what Melo singing, they can't catch the lingo. So Belafonte soften the edges lil' bit, make it accessible; he make it so anybody could understand what he singing, without changing the meaning of the song. That is the art. And I would go as far as to say that if you can't do that, you're not a true-true entertainer.

PICCADILLY FOLK
12 April 1952, Manchester

Football and footballers, at Manchester
you find the headquarters.
City and United, a wonderful performance is expected
from Manchester City and United.
Three cheers for the city of Manchester

Lord Kitchener, "The Manchester Football Double"

ONE BRIGHT SPRING NOON in April, a train pulls in to London Road Station and Liverpool supporters begin to chant and claim the station concourse. All is motion in red, black and white as they push out onto the street singing fighting songs. Kitchener steps from the train like a dandy amongst the undertow. The one they call Spider beside him, walking with his cynical gait, assessing the scene. But it is not Kitchener's grey serge suit, rather, the honey-coloured trilby with the peacock feather in the band; the audacity of this hat is what Ras Makonnen see first as he waits beside the ticket office. He is a dark, barrel-chested man of thirty-nine, this Makonnen, and his three-button blazer drapes abundantly about him.

When Kitchener has managed to pass through the crowd, Makonnen smiles and approaches. 'The Lord himself. Mister Kitchener, how are you, sir?' Makonnen does not rush his words. Each is humble and considered. He extends a thick fingered hand with three gold rings. Kitchener shakes the hand firmly.

Then Spider greets the big man, a floppy newsboy's cap leaning jaunty on the side of his head, his jaw slim-boned and rigid, skin stretched tight so that each ridge remains prominent.

They walk. Kitchener is looking sideways into Makonnen's face, the rivulets and contours, the craters and the ancient scar above the left eye. Makonnen turns, 'So this is how it is when

United are playing at home – it's a mess. Police have a hard time with the supporters. I'm more of a cricket man myself, but since you say you like football, I say OK, I'll come along, but really, it's not for me. And mind yourself as we passing through the crowd, some of these scousers, they pick your pocket, they could thief your watch straight off your damn wrist.' He laughs, impressed at his own patois.

Spider sucks his teeth. 'Thief *who* watch? My watch? Who will thief my watch here? Nobody not touchin' this, you mad? Fish will clap first.' And he coughs, like dull blades clapping.

'Well I love my cricket too,' Kitchener says, 'but-but-but I like the football, because it have the excitement. Is a long time I want to see United play at Old Trafford.'

'Yes,' says Makonnen, 'but you see the kind of people that follow football?'

Spider flicks his cigarette butt in a culvert; then he spits with a hiss. 'Football have its people, cricket have its people. Just because you don't like football, don't mean is not a nice game.'

'I never said I didn't like it you know, Spider. I just favour cricket, and as a West Indian…'

Spider has stopped, so Kitchener and Makonnen must stop and look back at him. 'What you saying? You saying me and Kitch is not West Indian?'

'No man. Look, don't vex with me, both of them game is Englishman invention anyways, so it don't matter. Is just that the West Indies team does a lot for us, y'know; it's a lot of pride there. You don't agree?'

Spider sucks his teeth. 'Pride?' Makonnen never respond, he know better. They walk among the crowds through the city centre, down Whitworth to the corner of Chorlton Street, where Makonnen's white Morris Oxford is parked. The skies are clear. Sunlight glints on the roofs and awnings, wrought-iron balconies, tramways and viaducts, the fountain and the library yard, imperial architecture, grey-stone turrets and the spire of a cathedral.

They put their luggage in the car boot and Kitchener sits in the front passenger seat, Spider in the back. The interior smells of leatherette and cigarette smoke. Makonnen tumbles the engine and turns to Kitchener. 'The game finishes round five, so after we could go to the club, have a meal, and you could see how we set things up there for you tonight.'

Kitchener winds the window down. 'So how big is the club? How much people it holding?'

'Well, we get around eighty, a hundred if we lucky. Saturdays are usually the busiest, so don't worry about that.'

'You done say you have a wood bass in there, so I, I satisfy with that already. Gimme a bass and a sweet craft and I happy.' The men throw their heads back and laugh.

In Moss Side, supporters on their way to the stadium crowd the streets. When Makonnen, Kitchener and Spider have passed through the turnstiles, they walk up the several wide concrete stairs that lead out to the deafening rage of the stands, where the sky opens up and the majesty of the field overwhelms them. It is like entering a high-ceilinged cathedral. The green field is trimmed tight and marked by bright and gleaming white lines. All around them are packed terraces, a riot of noise and colour. Then the players enter the arena. Manchester in their red and white trim, Liverpool in black and white with red-striped socks. Busby on the touchline. Byrne, Downie, Rowley –

Manchester United 4 - Liverpool F.C. - 0

By dusk the chants have faded, and the Liverpool supporters have made their journey back west, lest dark catch them in Manchester. United fans gather in the streets. They spill out from pubs, milk bars and chip shops, they play jukeboxes, they lash the beer of victory on the streets, they confuffle the road.

The Cosmopolitan club is a converted dwelling house, four stories high, with dark wooden door frames and heavy pine doors. Up one flight inside, they come to a small bar. The room itself is empty, except for a few stools along the bar, and a few chairs and tables laid out on the floor. Makonnen goes behind the bar. 'Scotch, Spider? Kitch what you fancy, a good rum?'

Spider does not answer. He surveys the room, peers around corners with his hands closed behind him.

It is Kitchener who runs his hand along the smooth, dark bar-top. 'I doh drink heavy y'know, just give me a stout or something light.'

'Stout? A big man like you afraid of hard liquor?' Makonnen laughs, a big throaty laugh that weakens his bulk. He puts a hand on Spider's shoulder for support. But Spider does not laugh with him, and the hand soon slips away.

Spider leans his elbows on the counter top. 'What Scotch you have there; you have Johnny?'

I have Johnny, but I have some Bells too, I have –'

'Gimme a shot a' the Johnny.'

Makonnen has to crack the seal of a new bottle for Spider to drink Johnnie Walker. He tips a drip or two to the floor, a toast for those too dead to drink. He gives Spider a highball glass with a generous layer of whisky at the bottom. When Spider takes the first sip, he scowls from the sting of it.

Later, from an upstairs window at the Cosmopolitan, Kitchener watches people arriving. West African students, white boys in denim and patent leather, young women with chiffon scarfs and beehives and bandy-legged West Indian jazz men in zoot jacket suits. The scent of stewed chicken and beans weaves its way up from the kitchen downstairs. Kitchener can hear Makonnen's voice as well, rising and falling between the plays of the jukebox. The room he stands in is bare except for a few folding chairs stacked against a wall, cardboard boxes with worn edges, a long mirror, a pine coat hook and Spider, drunk in a corner, strung out across an armchair.

Kitchener fixes his tie. It is almost showtime. He buttons his jacket, and then he takes careful steps down the stairs into the crowd. Although there are less than fifty people there, he swings his step, he cocks his head to the side, and he walks among them, as if is he and he alone they have come to see.

MARJORIE, 1953

To speak of the red hair lady
a woman of natural beauty,
she keeps to that natural fashion
no changes to cause attraction.
She appeals to me – through simplicity,
if is the last thing I have to say
hand me the redhead girl everyday.
So it is the redhead, redhead,
oh that is what I said,
I must catch a redhead before I dead.

— Lord Kitchener, 'Redhead'

I WERE ENGAGED to a Yankee soldier. I were going to New York; it were all arranged. Then one Saturday morning my friend Martha came round to the house and said there were going to be a West Indian dance at The Cosmopolitan and did I want to go. I said, 'Yes, why not?' Martha loved music, but she loved the black American soldiers even more. Sometimes we'd go to The Blue Bungalow in Moss Side, or The Red Spot, where the black GIs would be drinking and listening to their be-bop music. We'd dance and drink beer. Sometimes they even took us to the Army base in Warrington with them.

We wore pencil skirts and sleeveless bodices, high heels. I were very slim and had bright red hair in those days. Martha were an Irish blonde with a full bosom; oh she were gorgeous, our kid. It's at The Blue Bungalow one night that I got together with one of the soldiers and we got engaged and I'd promised to go to America when he were discharged.

When Martha and I got to the Cosmopolitan that night it were already busy. At that time The Cosmopolitan was one of the few places in Manchester where everyone – black or white – could dance and get along. In those days, there weren't many places where you could go and jive or jitterbug; most places had signs saying, 'No Dancing'.

I didn't know anything about calypso, nothing at all. I had heard about it, yes, but I didn't know what it were, not really, or where it came from. They didn't play it on the radio in Manchester, so I were curious. Then I saw this tall black man with a lovely yellow hat walk across the floor and stand by the side of the stage. I could tell he were a performer because he had a guitar, and people were shaking his hand and patting him on the back. Then the master of ceremonies got up on the stage and said, 'Ladies and gentlemen, welcome please the calypso king from Trinidad, Lord Kitchener!' And the man started to sing and, well, he were very good, charming, very tall and handsome.

I didn't understand a lot of what he were saying; one song were about a comb or something, another about a woman called Norma, but they were so catchy, and he were so funny how he sang them. Martha and I were near the front, so he would smile and wink at me while he were singing, but I weren't thinking it were anything; all singers did that. But during the intermission he came over to our table and asked for a dance, and while we were dancing he were asking me my name, telling me how he loved redheads and asking me, 'Where do you live?' 'What do you do?' 'Are you married?' all sorts of questions. I told him I were going to America with a soldier that November and he said, 'No, you don't want to go to America; it's a bad place.'

I said, 'How'd you mean?'

'They're very rough in America. They don't know how to treat their women, especially those soldiers, and a delicate thing like you. No, don't go there.'

He said he were supposed to go back to London the next day to play another show, but if I'd go out with him he would cancel it. I said, 'You'd do that just to go out with me?'

He said, 'Yes, why not?' And he stayed in Manchester till Monday.

★

We'd only known each other about six weeks when he said, 'Let's get married.'

I said, 'You're sure? That's so quick.'

He said, 'Yes, let's get married at Christmas.'

I said, 'But you're crazy, you hardly know me. Are you sure you can live with me?'

He said, 'Yes, I'm sure.'

But my father wouldn't allow it. He said it were too soon and we should wait a bit.

So we waited a few weeks and we got married on the 12th of May 1953 in the registry office in Albert Square. I wore a beautiful white wedding dress my father bought me from Lewis's on Market Street, with a silver tiara, pearl necklace, veil, white gloves, white shoes. Kitch wore a blue serge suit with a white shirt, black bow-tie. Afterwards, we went to The Cosmopolitan where Mr Makonnen had laid out a spread for us. There were a long buffet table with all sorts of food – cheeses, hams, little sandwiches, roast chicken, lamb, Chinese food. Upstairs they had cleared the chairs so people could dance and Kitch played there that night with a local band.

Mr Makonnen said, 'Marge, Kitch, don't you worry, I will take care of everything.' And he never charged us a penny because when we got married we didn't have much at all, no furniture and only a little money. Kitch were popular in London with the West Indians, and in the clubs, but when he moved to Manchester, it took a while for him to start getting regular work.

There was a fair-sized coloured community in Manchester at that time, with the port at Liverpool nearby, and the Americans who came during the war. There were a lot of African students too, and black families, mostly in Moss Side, where we lived, and Kitch got to know them all. There were a lot of clubs in the area, and once Kitch got in, he were never short of places to play. He were playing bass in those days, jazz, not much calypso, but he would sing a few of his own songs when he got the chance.

When he weren't at The Cosmopolitan he were at The Belle Etoile or the Forum, or playing with Granville Edwards in Salford or Stockport, or he'd be in London recording or playing at some club in Soho or Notting Grove. He played all kinds of music but he loved Nat King Cole, Louis Jordan, he loved Edmundo Ros and we had a lot of jazz records at the house – Charlie Parker and Dizzy Gillespie, Miles Davis. He was always busy but he weren't making enough money, so I still had to work. He said, 'Oh Marge, I don't want you to work, can't you stay home and look after the flat?'

I said, 'You can't even make the rent most months and you want me to stay home? Stay home and do what?' He didn't like it, but what could he do?

MARTHA, 1953

Marjorie I am tired of you
For you are not really true.
For every time I walk down the strand
I can hear you were loving up some Yankee man.
Ah going to beat you – he was a big Yankee man.
Ah going to beat you – he was a rough Yankee man.

— Lord Kitchener, 'Marjorie's Flirtation'

WE USED TO GO to the clubs and get the darkies to buy us drinks. Mr Smith's Cabaret on Whitworth Street, Maples, The Brunswick Tavern. We'd sit on their knees and smoke their cigarettes, we'd dance with 'em. Those days were all stiletto heels and pencil skirts, big hair. Marge were a beauty, she were, with that red hair and her figure – all the boys liked her. And Marge, she never had children, so once the fellas got to know that, they were after her like flies.

And the black GI's loved the English girls, so we'd take them down to Alexandra Park. I used to say, 'Marge, it's not good to go with them, you're a married woman now.'

It could be midnight and a GI might say, 'Hey, let's go for a ride in the jeep, let's drive to Stockport, let's drive to the Pavilion and back, let's go down to St Helens.' And driving at that time of night, when it were quiet, with just the radio on in the jeep, and the forces station playing that jazz, them were good times. We'd get to a club in Stockport – I think it were called Imperial – where the drink were cheap, there was jazz and where we could dance. Somehow we always made it back to Moss Side before morning. I don't know what Marge told her husband.

We looked out for each other in those days. When I were working and didn't have a babysitter, Marge would look after my little boys. If she made a few bob and I didn't, she'd give me a few pounds. And I've never seen a woman love a man as much as she loved Kitch, she did. And once he started to make good money he would buy her expensive clothes, ermine, silks. He'd take her to London with him, to the Mayfair Hotel, the Dorchester. She met Nat King Cole in London, she met Paul Robeson. Shirley Bassey came to the house once. And when she knew that he were coming back from London – he might have been recording or had a show – she would always be dressed her best, waiting for him at Piccadilly Station.

MARGE, 1953

WE WERE LIVING TOGETHER in a two-room in Chorlton, near Old Trafford. It were hard to get flats in those days, as a mixed couple. I used to have to go and see flats by myself and tell the landlords that me husband worked in London, and only came home on weekends. Otherwise, when they saw Kitch, they would say we were too late, the flat were taken.

That first place were terrible. Just two rooms we had; bedroom and kitchen, toilet outside. We had a little two-burner oil stove and we used to cook everything on that; rice, meat an' porridge. Paint were peeling from the bedroom ceiling, the wallpaper were fusty and mouldy and the whole place smelled pissy and old. I think someone must've died in there. When his friend Spider came and saw the place he said, 'But Kitch, what's wrong with you? You're mad? You can't have a nice woman like Marge living in a place like this.' It really were a grotty little flat. Damp, cold. But we spent our first Christmas together there.

Then I remember there was a Mr Shallit who came to see Kitch one evening. He owned a record company in London and he came all the way up from London to beg Kitch to leave the record company he were with to go with his one. They were sitting in the little kitchen and dining area we had, and Kitch told him he would sign with him, but before he could sign anything he needed a new place to live, and he asked Mr Shallit to drive us across to Heywood Street in Moss Side, and he showed him a house and said, 'That is the one I want.' And Mr Shallit wrote him a cheque for £500 right there, to put a big deposit on the house. That's how we managed to move out of Chorlton and buy the house in Moss Side.

But we had to get a guarantor when we applied for the mortgage, because banks in them days wouldn't give a black man a mortgage, much less a musician, and a woman couldn't sign on her own. Halifax gave us a mortgage and that's how we managed to move out of Chorlton and buy the house on Heywood Street in Moss Side, and that's when things started going a bit better for us.

In fact, most of the calypso boys are ordinary chaps, ruffians, nondescript fellows in the community with no status. In this sense I'm talking about a mass-culture in the West Indies, because the masses were setting the pace. Not a particularly big pace either, for if you really knew your high-life songs and transcribed the patois into English, you would find it frustrating; they all boil down to sex and woman talk. Now, there may be higher forms in some of the islands but generally when you take these famous calypsonians like Lord Kitchener, and strip down their material, there's nothing else.

— Ras Makonnen *Pan Africanism From Within* (1973)

ARCHIE 'SWEET MAN' VILLAFANA, 1953

KITCH WENT THROUGH a lil' phase when he was living in Manchester, when he was very influenced by Ras Makonnen and the whole Pan African thing. He start to go to meetings at The Forum, he start to wear pillbox hat and sing about Africa. At that time, it had a lot of black communists also living in Manchester, and Kitch start to seek them out.

Many nights we sit down in Ras Makonnen office, upstairs The Forum, talking about African independence and West Indian self-government. This was the African Service Bureau; men like Padmore and Dubois; Nkrumah pass through there. But Kitch was a country bookie, boss, he wasn't no scholarly fella, he don't have time to read book. So when them big boys start to talk heavy politics and throw highfalutin word, Kitch used to just nod, 'Umm hmm, yes, yes, that is true.' But he bluffing, he don't know one arse. All Kitch know is how to squeeze white woman breast and sing calypso. He singing cabaret for all them white people in fancy hotel, but he want to talk about if you black and if you brown. I used to be shame sometime to hear him talking to men like George Padmore, men who really know what the hell they talking 'bout.

Just so in a meeting Kitch would make a brash statement, like: 'Fellas too lazy in-in-in Trinidad, boy, them scamp only want to drink rum and eat roti. They not ready for self-government.' Once, he even tell Makonnen, 'If God make we black, it must mean something.' And Makonnen leggo one laugh, but he watching Kitch.

Once, Kitch tell us how a mad woman knock off his hat when he was walking through Chinatown in Manchester, and how he get so vex that he accost and cuss up the poor woman. He convince that the woman don't like him because he black. I say, 'Kitch boy, don't say that. She apologise to you?'

He said, 'Well yes, she apologise, but these people, they deceitful you know.'

Makonnen and I watch each other and smile. Kitch wanted the woman charged. He wanted to go to court. He liked them kind of thing, to dress up in a new suit and go to court, and he want to defend himself, he want to talk. He had another thing he used to do. Kitchener would see a policeman and then start running, and when they run him down and hold him, he would say, 'What, a man can't run or what?' Or if the police stopped him he would say is because he black. Or they jealous because he married to a white woman. Then you hear him sing:

> We give our love to Africa – me and Roy Ankrah
> That's why I want to come back home – Africa
> That's why I want to come back home – Africa
> Lord, I tired roam – Africa
> I want to come back home – Africa

It's a very good calypso but how much of that you think Kitchener really believe? You feel he really see Africa as his home? Never happen. Trinidad is all Kitchener see as home. Sometime Melodisc will tell him, 'Kitch boy, so and so happen, sing about that.' And he will compose a kaiso; for him is easy. Sometime he hear something on the radio, BBC World Service, something happen in Africa, Nkrumah say something, Eric Williams say something in Woodford Square, and he catch inspiration, he put his mind in that place and he write a song.

Now, it not hard, as a black man, no matter who you is, to find your place in the struggle, but Kitch only going there for three or four minutes, then he coming back out. Don't get me wrong, he make some great tunes, but Kitchener was a performer, he in that barrel there, he not *really* active politically. Not like Makonnen, or even someone like Edric Connor or C.L.R. James. Kitch was a man around; he know plenty thing, but he wasn't no deep political thinker.

1953, SONNY GREENE

HOW YOU MEAN *if* he was doing it? Kitch was a hustler, he was poncing. But them days those things was prevalent plenty. You broken, you not working nowhere, but you have to look good when you going out with the boys, so you pick up some spare English mopsy in the Safari, or some bar in the Grove and firstly, they don't mind black man, and second, you moving round, you know. You don't have two six pence to rub, but you giving she what white man cyar give she, so she say she love you, she even defy she father for you, and next thing she have to leave home and come in your bachie, your one lil' bedsit room where you cooking rice under your bed, and washing your clothes in the sink, and she saying how she will do anything for you. Where she will go now? The family disown she. What you go do? You have to ponce she.

People hawking up sandy and spitting on she when she pass because she with you, but she love you. Lord, next thing you know, she on the game and you collecting, you making sure she safe, nothing special. The Jamaicans was the worst, but the Nigerians wasn't too far behind in that.

It easy to scorn, but a man can't get work, can't get a decent room. Some days you lucky for piece a'chicken, even, to put in your belly. You in the people country; it not yours. Then winter hold you in London with just the gabardine coat you get from the Salvation Army, and it have no lining. But you have a big prick and when you shave and brush back your hair and you splash some Aqua Velva on your neck, and you put on the dog-teeth pants with the penny loafers and step out in Soho. So when you finally catch a craft, you say, 'Well, is fire for you.'

Now, a fella, if he have the experience, as soon as he walk in the club he could spot the one that love black man, just from the way she look at him, something in she eye, from the way she put she mouth. She may have a lil' kink in she manner. She may give you a smile. So you go over and ask her for a dance, and she will talk and skin and grin an' thing, and she buying drinks. These is woman who love nothing more than to lie down under nigger man. I see some tests getaway bad when it come to these women; man will break bottle and shank one another, they will fight in the road. Another thing you find is that some white man will bring their wife to a club just to leggo black man on them, like beast, they like to watch their wife get bull and break, to see she leg shake up.

It have two kind of fellas: those who into the white scene, and those who in the black scene. Kitch? He was in the white scene; I never know a man who could eat white meat so. Even when we was in Trinidad, he love nothing more than them big-bottom redskin woman. By the time he hit England, he love the blonde, the redhead; he leggo a lion in their tail.

That house on Brook Street. Two up two down and is ketch arse season. The woman up there doing all sorts of things. Kitch know she trade and he let that carry on because it bringing in a lil' change and he not making long money yet from calypso. Plus, Kitch is a man like nice thing, he like to flam, he have gambage to maintain as a calypsonian, so, what he could do? He let it run.

Neighbours start to notice and talk, they peeping through their curtain. A black musician and a white woman? Music playing all hours of the night and all kinds of people coming and going? The Old Bill pay a visit one day and put a stop to that. It was in the papers. Remember, Kitchener eh no imps, he used to live right inside the red light district in Port of Spain, then he pass through Jamaica, so he know about them thing.

Eventually everything was alright; he pay the fine; he even sing about the whole incident.

> *Your wife is my wife and my wife is your wife*
> *The more we are together the merrier we shall be*

Then the recording people give him some good money and he buy a next house in Moss Side. Maybe he pay about two thousand thousand for it. It was a good house, and he was doing all right.

Kitch had his ways. But he was very private. He talking to you in private, but he not talking too much. 'Cause he have he lil' secret side too; he have his girls, and he playing horses. He's a popular man, and good looking, so women want to climb all over him. Poor fella. What he could do? He might have a beer, or a wine, but he wasn't no drinker. He might have a pull if it pass, but he wasn't no smoker. Pussy, that was his vice – and horses.

EUGENE WARREN, 1955

I USED TO BEAT PAN for a side on Henry Street, a steelband call 'Dem Boys', and I remember Kitchener used to send down songs every year from England. 'Mango Tree' – we beat that. 'Old Lady' get beat. 'Nora' – we beat that. But that man sing a calypso in England, in 1955, and he send the calypso down and it reach Port of Spain on Carnival Sunday. Imagine that. So when we in the barrack yard on Henry Street, one of the boys come and he say, 'Ai, Kitchener new 45 just reach.' And he bring it out with a lil' record player for we to hear it.

It was a big thing in the yard to hear this tune that Kitchener send and we make a lime out of it; fellas come with rum, some bring their pan, woman come and sit down. And on that record, one side had a tune call 'Constable Joe', about a Grenadian who paint a mule in Cumuto so he could thief it and all this kind of stupidness. But on the other side was a tune call 'Trouble in Arima', and when we hear *that* tune we bawl! We couldn't even catch we self, a fus it sweet. Big men was jumping, 'Play it again, play it again, gi'we!' And as pan men we want to play it in the band.

But was Carnival Sunday, eh. Fellas painting costume, some painting pan, getting ready for jou'vert in the morning, and my band captain was there in the yard, and he stand up and say, 'Who could play it? Allyuh feel allyuh could play it? You could play it, Scholar?'

'Yeah man, I could play it, but what about the tune we done prepare to play?'

He say, 'Forget that.'

So we arrange the whole tune one time, right there in the yard, and jou'vert morning, as foreday dawning, we band we head red, and the band hit the road. We beating the tune and singing:

I go fight them – is trouble
in Arima – is trouble
if they beat me – is trouble
well is murder – is trouble
Tell me mooma – is trouble
and me sister – is trouble
and me brother – is trouble
no surrender – is trouble

When we coming down George Street now, heading into town, Casablanca steelband block we. They coming up and we going down and they stop right in the middle of the road so we cyar pass. We have followers, mostly women, and Casablanca have plenty followers too, an' them from Belmont, they irascible. One badjohn walk up and he say, 'Allyuh cyar go in town with that tune. Best turn and go back up the road, go back Henry Street.' Behind him Casablanca waiting like an engine to start sharing cut-arse, and we was only a small band compared to them. So my captain say turn back. And as we going back up in the barrack yard on Henry Street, everybody still singing:

Is trouble – in Arima
Is trouble – is manslaughter
Is trouble – tell me mooma
And me papa – trouble

And would you believe? The people with Casablanca start following us, they leave their band and come, and we had a big jam session on that one Kitchener tune, right there, outside the barrack yard on Henry Street.

LORD, THE TROUBLES WE HAD in Manchester. Not from my family; they were Irish and they 'ad no problem with Kitch at all. My mother liked him, even my father thought he were a decent man. Kitch weren't a bum, he were always working, he were always well-dressed, presentable, a gentleman. But it were the people in the area, in the town, that gave us the most trouble.

Kitch used to buy me beautiful frocks and I used to dress quite pretty. But people used to spit at us. What could you do? You could say something but then they would call you a 'nigger lover', or 'a whore', it were hard times we went through. One time, just before we got married, we were walking down Deansgate going to the pictures and a man passed us in the street and he spat at me. I were so upset, and angry. But Kitch said, 'Leave it.'

I said, 'What do you mean "Leave it"? The man just spat at me. Aren't you going to do anything?' But he didn't, he never did.

Once Kitch were performing at a hotel in London with Edmundo Ros and it were my birthday. So as a treat Kitch brought me down to London with him and we were staying at the same hotel. It were quite a fancy hotel and, oh, Kitch used to love it when everybody looked at me in this bloody hotel, when we came down for breakfast in the morning.

One morning, I came down wearing this red suit he'd bought me in Swan & Edgar in Piccadilly. Kitch were in a suit and tie, as usual, with the hat. I said, 'We're only going down for breakfast, Kitch, why are you bothering to dress up?'

He said, 'You have to dress good around these people.'

That's how he were. Always concerned about how people saw him, how he presented himself. He used to tell me his father, Mr Pamp, were the same; he always had to be the best-dressed man in the village, and it used to drive his mother potty.

We were having breakfast in the hotel dining room and this

man were sat facing me on another table, behind Kitch, with his wife. He looked like about fifty, short, a fat man. He looked at me and Kitch and then I heard him whisper to his wife, 'Disgusting, isn't it?'

She didn't answer. She just gave a little glance back. But then the man turned up his nose and went like to spit at me. I thought, *Lord, what have I done?* I didn't say anything. I just sat down with me breakfast. Kitch didn't know what were going on, he hadn't seen. But the man were staring at us, with his knife and fork in his hands. He mumbled something. So Kitch looked at me and then he turned round and looked at the man and said, 'Sorry, I didn't hear.'

The man put his knife and fork down: 'You hard of hearing, darkie? I said its disgusting isn't it, the two of you together. This is a five star hotel.' And then he just continued eating, he didn't even acknowledge Kitch. He said something to his wife and she looked back and smiled at me. Kitch was still looking at the man. He was sitting on the edge of his seat as if he were going to get up and do something, so I put my hand on his and said, 'Leave it Kitch, leave it.' But I wanted him to do something. I wanted him to get up, to hit the man, to let him have it!

He said, 'This is my wife, you know, so mind your mouth.'

'Your bloody wife? Come off it, mate, she is not your wife.'

That's when Kitch stood up. He said, 'W-What you saying? You mad?' He was stuttering like a baboon, I'd never seen him so angry. But the man's wife wouldn't let him get up. That bitch. And I s'pose when the man saw how tall Kitch were, he didn't want to anyway. So he and his wife left.

When we were going back upstairs, Kitch went to the concierge and told him that the gentleman had been rude to me. The concierge said he would speak to the manager about it, but nothing ever came of it. Nothing ever did.

KITCH BLINKS AGAINST sleep in the light of spring flashing through the train windows; the swish of green, the crooked and unbroken slur of wooden fences lining undulating fields. He is alone in the compartment, with his suitcase on the cold steel rack rocking above his head like a crooked metronome. The sound of the engine hissing steam and the wheels tumbling along the tracks are like the sounds of the forge where an anvil is being beaten. His father, Pamp, with his hard back bent over the bench, with a mallet swung in the smoke billowing up from his tempering basin, *kikuyu, kikuyu* he tempers the steel, *ki-kuyu* the iron singing when he brings the mallet down,

BUP dee dip BUP dee dip BUP dee dip – BAP

This music fills the smithy with a swirl. Sparks of sound perforate the night as young Bean stands behind his father, watching the flex of muscle in his father's back, the blacksmith's shirt tight with sweat. He watches the elegant strength of Pamp's straight-legged stance before the crucible. Outside in the yard, chickens make their beds in the guava tree, frogs croak in the dasheen streams and a lone corn bird sits on a barbadine vine and waits for an opening in the music so she too can sing. But the sound that blows is the whistle of the train rolling across Hertfordshire. The landscape moving, from fields to warehouses, to the backs of suburban houses, neat gardens, chimneys and shops, cars waiting at railway crossings. Kitchener wipes the sleep from his eyes with the back of his thumb.

At St Pancras he alights under the dull lights of the station. There is no colour here, just the brusque bustle of bodies and the smell of burnt oil and smoke. A man approaches, his head bent slightly to the side. 'Singer for the Chesterfield? How you do? You just got in? Good trip? Everything all right then? Let me give you a hand with that.'

144

The driver's eyes are drawn close together, a bushy black brow spans them. Furrows run deep in his forehead and then the black hair greased tight to his skull with cream, dull not sheen, a bald spot peeping from the top. He wears a stiff grey blazer with a metal badge on the left breast pocket, black pleated trousers, low crotched and tapered at the heel.

As they are driving along the Euston Road, the driver asks, 'Where you from then?'

Kitchener, in the back seat, turns from the window to answer. 'Trinidad,' he says. 'You know where that is?'

'Where?'

'Trinidad.'

'No mate, sorry, never 'eard of it. Where is that, Africa?'

'You know where Venezuela is?'

'Heard of it, yeah. South America?'

'Trinidad right there at the top, top of Venezuela.'

'Don't know those parts at all, me. Never left England – well, except once I went to Dublin on the ferry. Don't count though, does it? Not really.'

Marylebone Road. Passing Madame Tussauds, Baker Street Station, red brick townhouses with white-rimmed verandas. 'There's a lot of you lot coming over, aren't you. These days. Don't get me wrong, I think people deserve a chance, and if you can bring something to the table, then all right then, no problem. I have nothing against anybody really, just the lazy ones.' He laughs. A crucifix swings on a bead chain from the rearview mirror.

Once, in the butchers' shop on Withington Road, not far from his home in Moss Side, Kitchener was talking with the butcher who was cutting fat from a lamb joint. Then, swinging his cleaver down, and drawing all stray expression from his face to show his sincerity, the butcher spoke, 'Nig-nogs are people too, pardon my language like, but some of yous' are good, hard workers. I mean, I wouldn't want me daughter bringing home a darkie, but I wouldn't say they're bad. The other day an old darkie come in here, I said, "What can I do for you ma'am?" She said, "Three pound a shank." I tell her, "Them is expensive shanks." She say, "A'right, I want them." So I cuts them and then she starts to moan about the price. I said nine bob. She says "Gimme for seven shillings." I said, "Look love, this ain't the jungle, if you want prime shanks you have to pay. We don't barter with bloody shells here!"'

When the butcher brayed, from the back of his throat, Kitchener heard himself laugh too, but not as loudly. The butcher wiped his bloody hands on his apron. 'And what can I do for you today, young man? The tripe is fresh, fresh oxtail, lovely pigs' trotters they are, lovely.'

'So you're performing tonight, at the Chesterfield? Fancy spot that is, the Chesterfield. I never been in myself, but I've worked the route, you know, picked up people, dropped them off there. They got doormen and ushers there, plush carpets, you know, that sort of thing. Champagne. That's a good gig you got there, I'll give you that. People like Doris Day and Louis Armstrong goes there. You like Louis Armstrong?'

Kitchener leans forward, he can smell the beeswax on the driver's scalp. 'I hear Princess Margaret is coming to the Chesterfield tonight for the show. You-you know about that?'

'Princes Margaret? Coming to the Chesterfield to see *you*, mate? Never.'

'Well, is so I hear.'

'Can't see it. Who are you, Nat King bloody Cole? You never know though, she loves the nightclubs, always in the papers at some speakeasy, cigarette in her hand, so maybe you're right, maybe she is going to the Chesterfield. But it won't be to see you, mate.'

West. The midday sun makes harsh shadows on the streets. The sky opens up and trees canopy the road. Kitchener remembers Hyde Park in that first green summer of 1948. He sees himself in the landscape of his remembering. How, in his melancholy for an imagined past, English streets became streets in Trinidad. How Bayswater reminded him of the rum shop roads through St James. From his room on the fifth floor of the Chesterfield Hotel, he gazes emptily into the haze of the early afternoon. The busy road, the trees glittering in the sunlit park, like the sun when it lay gauze-bright along the northern range, above Arima, wild island countryside, and beyond the hills, the blue Caribbean.

FOOTBALL CALYPSO

Princess Margaret – a calypso fan – has bought one hundred copies of the latest disc by Trinidad's 'Lord Kitchener'. Thirty-four-year-old 'Lord Kitchener' – real name Aldwyn Roberts – sat down at his Manchester home immediately after Manchester City's 3-1 win over Birmingham in the F.A. Cup Final, and composed the calypso.

Until recently the two Manchester teams, City and United, were deadly rivals. Then City won the Cup and United became Division 1 League Champions, and along came Lord Kitchener to compose a musical tribute to both teams. Result: "The Manchester Double" is expected to sell 150,000 copies in the next three months and will be used as a signature tune at their football grounds next season by both teams.

"Lord Kitchener", who has been in England since 1948, has recorded about 100 calypsos, including the highly successful calypso in honour of Princess Margaret's Caribbean tour.

— *The Daily Gleaner,* June 15, 1956

SWEET HOME

WOOD BASS. It's lower bout has the low-slung gait
of a black market woman. Its curling scroll, the head
bent from an ebony neck. The bassist leans
against its curved shoulder – *Volute. Busetto –*
leans against the parabolic curvature of the bass back,
the balance-beam leaning to the end pin.
The bassist gives a grin to the devil, stiffens,
is devious in the face as he plays pizzicato
with a Baptist swing, humming its hymn.
Something in the way he hums distils
the pious centre of diasporic sound – the marrow
between the beats. His whole body moves
back and forth, and sideways fastest,
syncopates the roll, till the groove bursts and notes hover
from wood breast to his and then through the room.
Wild island jazz. Power in each brush, each stroke
of wrist. Fingers, bent like the brown twigs of a guava tree.
The big string swinging its pendulum settles, still,
is pulled once more, rattling the drummers snare.
Its skin recoils – *tsst t/t/t/t/ tsst* – sound moving
                    deeper into the ear.
The audience, at first so casual against the rim of the dance floor,
begin to shift at their tables. Men in blazers
and low-crotched khakis, red-headed women
making small steps in heels and a-line skirts,
black communists in brogues.
The saxophonist puts the mouthpiece to his mouth and blows,
hard and high, and the heart is trembled, the cry is sounded,
the wound is pleasured. The sound is a green river running
through an orange field, with cornbirds weeping above.
            Sly Mongoose.

The saxophonist tilts his bell
to drain the lung water from his horn.
                    Jump in the Line.
Sweat buds on the bassist's forehead; he wipes his face
with the sleeve of his shoulder. Braces pull
taut against his chest, his shirt sticks to his wet back.
He loosens his tie. He tips his hat brim back
so he can wipe the sweat, and then he opens his eye
to the faces in the audience. Tonight,
in the musk scent of the bass wood,
he tastes the pull of home. He hears
the ocean calling him, the trees rustling
in the red rayo valleys of Laventille, nights
in the jungles of Port of Spain.
Is so sometimes in the cigar smell
of the bar's leatherette corners, or
in a woman's dank liquor breath,
he meets his memory leaving and arriving,
between past and present, in the perpetual now.

The drummer plays a paradiddle, rolls from hi hat to floor tom,
cracking the snare with a sharp lick.
The bassist pulls his hand across the strings,
makes them fumble, then he fondles their slack and sway,
until the instrument gives up its mystery notes.
                    Jou'vert Barrio.
Outside on Oxford Road, rain washes the street,
headlights burn holes through the spray.
Later that morning in Moss Side,
he will sit in his linoleum kitchen,
with black coffee and a guitar, composing calypsos
until dawn begins to whisper through the trees, until dew
settles on the hillsides of Arima and pastures east of Wallerfield.
The damp land in the country morning, the semp bird
sucking on the soursop fruit, the cow dung and frangipani scent
of the countryside call him away from another winter.
A river, green with moss and young parakeets.
Oh Trinidad.
          Wind through the trees.

150

Melodisc used to sell his records in Africa, so Ghana-ians, grow up on Kitchener, Nigerians too, and just like Trinidad, they look to England, and anything that come from England is good. So when you listen to highlife music, you can hear a connection to calypso. Is Lord Kitchener responsible for the birth of calypso and high-life music in Ghana. Kitchener had good musi-cians, he had good songs, good chorus. The Mighty Terror used to organise the chorus, and the sound of the music awaken the Ghanaians. Kitch singing about Africa, but he eh going there. He singing 'London is the place for me', but he don't know London. That is the creative mind, and that is something you find with many calypsonians who sing for tourists. You like it? They sing it.

— The Mighty Chalkdust

THAT RECORD, 'Birth of Ghana', he could've made a lot of money with that record. I remember when he wrote it. It were winter, 1956, and we were living in Moss Side. He and Mr Makonnen were always talking about Africa, and he called me in the kitchen one day and said, 'Margie, hear this one, I write a tune for Ghana.' And he sang it for me, tapping a box of matches on the table to keep time.

> *Ghana – Ghana is the name*
> *Ghana – we wish to proclaim*
> *We will be jolly, merry and gay*
> *the 6th of March, Independence day*

He went down to London to record it and then, when it were pressed, we both went down to London so he could present it to the Ghanaian people.

We went to Mr Shallit's office on Shaftesbury Avenue, and there were an African man there, in robes and glasses, and so well spoken, quiet, well educated. He were there with a bodyguard and they both took photographs with Kitch. The African man were telling Kitch how he would arrange everything for him to go to Ghana for the independence celebrations. He said, 'Bring your wife, its not a problem at all, you will stay in the President's house; we will take care of everything; you will fly first-class to Ghana.'

But Kitch just smiled and shook his head. He didn't want to go. Mr Shallit were shocked, he were saying, 'But Kitchener, you're making a big mistake. You should go, you will sell millions of records, you will make so much money!'

'I'm not going. Send The Mighty Terror instead, or send for Sparrow, he will go, Sparrow will go anywhere.'

I said, 'But Kitch, think about it, you're always singing about

Africa and about Black people, why wouldn't you want to go to Africa?'

He said, 'Africa? Me? Go Africa? Go in that place, with all that bush? Not me.'

The Ghanaian fellow heard him, he were so embarrassed, he smiled. 'No, don't say that, man. How can you say this?'

But no matter how they asked Kitch to reconsider, how they begged him to go, Kitch wouldn't go. 'Send over the record,' he said, 'I don't have to go quite Africa. I really 'fraid them wild animal they have there, them Lion and Tiger cat.' They wanted him to go. But he never went.

KITCHENER DUE FOR U.S. TOUR

PHILADELPHIA – Lord Kitchener, England's top calypso singing star linked with the Melodisc recording label across the pond, will be brought to this country early next month by Jolly Joyce. Joyce took Lord Kitchener under his managerial wing last month while in England looking after his prize rock and roll property in Bill Haley and the Comets.

Joyce is building an all-star calypso revue around Lord Kitchener for a nationwide tour of theatres, clubs and concert halls, kicking off April 19 at the Metropolitan Theatre in Brooklyn, N.Y., for a 10-day stand. Lord Kitchener's touring will point toward Hollywood where he's set for Sam Katzman's forthcoming 'Calypso' feature at the Columbia lots.

— *Billboard Magazine,* April 6 1957

'BLUES' 1957

Nobody could tell me
about New York City.
The place is a paradise
but the women an' them wouldn't treat you nice.
The women – in New York City
The women – they have no sympathy.
Uptown, downtown, the village too,
boys, they have no uses for you.

— Lord Kitchener , "The Women in New York"

LOEW'S THEATRE WAS only half full. Geoffrey and Boscoe Holder there, Tito Puente, Maya Angelou and Lord Flea. The limbo dancers slipping and bending low under the limbo brim, and the bongo drummers beating up a boom. Maya come out and she sing she calypso. Is Yankee calypso, but she perform it good, sing in bare feet.

Lord Flea come strumming guitar like is drum he beating and shaking his head like a madman. He gone down on one knee, he caray like a crab, he shake up. He and his trio make one set of mess with straw on the people stage. They call it Mento. All man in three-quarter pants. The audience give him a roaring applause and he leave the stage hot for Kitchener. Kitchener come out in his suit and he sing his sing, but like he can't get over. West Indians there, but is few, and Yankee people don't know what the hell Kitch singing 'bout. They may listen and laugh, *'kee kee kee'*, but they can't understand the *double entendre*, the leggo, the lavway, they can't count music in a 2-2 beat.

Poor Kitch. He stand up there by the side of the stage waiting call for encore. I playing trumpet in the quartet. We playing hard. We trying to excite the people to call him back, but they clapping

155

slack. *Bon'jé!* Geoffrey Holder come out clapping like a seal. 'Ladies and gentlemen, come on, the King of calypso, from the isle of Trinidad, give a hand for Lord Kitchener! Do you want to hear some more? Let me hear you! Encore, encore!' And out of politeness a little bubble of clap rise up and someone whistle and with that Kitchener run back on as planned. But the audience, it dead. Dear me. Interval.

When Tito Puente get on, he leggo one set of Latin bacchanal on the timbales. His band was hot. Licks like fire. People in front get up from their seat and dancing, till the ushers had to come round and beg them sit, 'cause they blocking the people behind. Kitchener watching Tito from the dark at the side of the stage. He looking despondent so I tell him, 'Brother, don't worry with these people y'know, they don't know better; your calypso too pure for them. They want Lord Horse and Lord Platypus. They want Belafonte.'

Kitch watch me and then he turn away. He say, 'I-I-I not taking that on. I come here to work, so is OK with me.' But he bite up, I know it, and both of us could hear how Tito have the audience like fowl for crack corn, eating out of his palm.

Geoffrey Holder run come hug-up Kitch. He still in make up. In fact I feel Geoffrey put on this whole thing so he could prance round in cosquelle and costume. He telling Kitch how wonderful he was, how he love his music, and how much of an honour it is to host him – a master calypsonian – in New York City. Is so Geoffrey is, he heart big, he gregarious, plus he cunning smart with mamaguy to make a dollar. When he un-brace Kitch, he leave one set of glitter on the man tuxedo, glitter on Kitch face. But Kitch grinning like a snake, right through.

THEO 'PICO' BRITO, 1957

THE MINI BUS OLD, it smell like sixteen man piss in it. That is how we travelling. When we cross the turnpike and we reach New Jersey, we go in a restaurant to eat and wait for Jolly Joyce. Joyce have the money. We go straight inside and sit down round a big table. Is seven musician; a mixed band, black and white. Menu on the table; the boys hungry.

But it have an old white man outside on the street. He put his palms together at the side of his eyes and he staring at us through the window. Kitchener ask me, 'Pico, why that man watching we?' I tell him the truth.

'Maybe they not used to seeing black people eating in here. Is a Italian place and Italian people funny.'

The waitress come across. She have buck teeth and heavy set, one set of spot on her neck; moles. She mouth slack from chewing too much gum and she underarm odorous. 'Can I take your order, please?' The fellas order. Kitch say he never had pizza so is pizza he want. He want ham and minced beef, onions, mushroom, plenty pepper. The woman look up from she note pad, 'Pepper? Like black pepper?'

'No, pepper sauce, hot pepper.'

'You mean hot sauce?'

'Yes, the hot pepper sauce.'

And we waiting for Jolly Joyce. Joyce say meet him at two, and it's minutes to three now, and it have people in the restaurant playing they eating, but they watching us hard. Is like they watching us like we thief something and they know police get the tip-off and coming, so they just giving us the side-eye and waiting; they not approaching or saying anything, they waiting to watch us get bull. But I know them well, I know all their tricks.

I remember once I was playing with Lord Macbeth in Florida and some white boys give us words outside a cinema. They spitting on the road and hissing, 'Nigger – Nigger.' They threaten to hang us from sycamore. Macbeth don't want trouble, but I have my dagger in my waist so I not afraid. If you show them you frighten these people will rough you up, but if you brave, they gets confuse. And if you corner one alone, they like sloth – they can't walk on flat ground. So I tell Macbeth, 'Mac, walk tall, man, walk on.' And as we walking past, I watch them reprobate straight and hard in they face, with just the handle of the blade showing. Not a man move.

It have a next old man behind the restaurant counter with a box jaw and a dirty apron, shirt sleeves roll up – must be the manager. He's a likeable cuss, but he look like a' old police or navy man, 'cause he glancing at us like hawk watching meat. But when the pizza come it come good, and people hungry, so we eat. It eating nice. We tender though, because the old man watching every bite.

Kitchener bend his whole pizza and put it in his mouth. I say, 'Kitchener, gosh boy, they don't eat pizza so,' and the juice from the pizza dripping – *plap plap* on the table. The rest of the fellas eating and talking like nothing happening. Anyone that watching would think these boys simple, that they not aware of the danger. But these is musician that travel through America; they know these situations and they aware of everything around them, so they ready to take in front before front take them.

The manager start to sing some jackass thing. He have a deep croon, but he's no Pat Boone. Every second note cut rough and out of tune. He watching us, he wiping the knives and he watching us. Then he walk over to our table, wringing his hands in his apron, like if he just castrate a pig. 'Boys, if you don't want anything else, I'd prefer you to pay up and leave.'

The old man still muscular. The shirt pull tight, the muscle print, the forearms hairy. I sure he have a rifle behind the bar. The waitress staying behind there now; she see big men talking. Then Kitchener put in and surprise everybody. 'But why we have to leave? We, we not causing problems. We waiting for somebody.'

But the old man disregard Kitchener, he look around the table and start to grind his jaw, 'Boys…'

No problem. When we get back on the bus, Kitchener say, 'One move and I woulda cap-capsize table, chair, juke box everything in there!'

I just laugh. I know if the Italian did only squeeze Kitch throat, Kitch woulda start to cry: 'Please, please mister, mister, please.'

We drive up quiet through New England; the old man sour the spirit. We heading north to Boston. Massachusetts white fence and lawn, dark coming down.

Jolly reach Boston with Bill Haley, just before showtime. He had all kind of excuse why he never make New Jersey. 'Bill here had a problem with his airplane,' Jolly say. 'Flight was cancelled; had to drive him up from New York myself. I'm sorry about that boys, but come on now, calypso time!' And he raise both hands in the air and start to shake his waist – one hand had a bill roll – good Yankee currency. He feel the boys laughing, but all skin teeth not grin; they not laughing with he.

AT FIRST HE WOULDN'T TALK about America. I'd ask him, 'Kitch, how was it?' And he'd just say, 'Oh, it was all right. It was OK.'

Eventually, after a few days, we were having breakfast and suddenly he said, 'America not for me. All they want is the Belafonte calypso. And so much racialism there, they beating people and hanging them; it worse than England.'

He had made some good money in America, but I don't think he were in a hurry to go back. No, something happened to him in America and I think it had something to do with how he were treated. He weren't treated like he were in England. In London, and in Manchester, everybody knew Kitchener. All the musicians knew him and he could move around, in all the right circles. So he felt special here, he was the king of calypso, and I think he loved that. But in America, who is Lord Kitchener? Nobody knows. So when he performed I don't think he got a good response. I don't think people understood what he were singing about.

I asked, 'So how were New York, the show you had there?' Because I heard so much about New York.

He said, 'New York? Imagine they bring this-this-this Yankee woman who say she is a calypso singer, she come out and sing in long dress, barefoot, she sing one set of cabaret. But she get encore, people want she come back. They bring the one they call Lord Bee, a Jamaican – what Jamaican know about calypso? Again, nonsense. But they love him. He could perform, I give him that, he even singing one of my songs! It have plenty fellas in America singing my calypsos and they not even putting my name on the record. Lord Macbeth for one. But this Lord Flea or Bush Bug, or what he name, they want him for movie, they want him for television. He travelling all over the country and calling calypso 'mento'. But what is mento? Is just calypso turn upside down. They turn the rhythm upside down and call it mento. You think this Lord Flea could go Port of Spain and sing that? Never happen. Even Sparrow better than him.' And he went on and on.

'So what kind of show were it? I asked him. 'A cabaret?'

'Well, yes, they had all kinda masks and costume,' he said. 'Big performance, artistic. Is not to my liking, this "Bal Masque" thing.'

I said, 'But Kitch, it's a cabaret show they were putting on, so you have to expect that.'

'Expect what? What Bal Masque have to do with calypso?' He were fuming. 'When you call for calypso, put it high first, then after you could dance your dance and call it anything.'

He wrote a few songs about America, one of them were 'The Women in New York'. I hated it. Kitch – everywhere he goes, he's looking at women. But in that song I think you can hear that America were disappointing to him. So he were glad to come back to Manchester and he called Rupert Nurse straight away, so he could start recording again, as soon as he could get down to London. It were about this time that he started talking about going back to Trinidad.

DRINK A RUM
Christmas 1957

BOSCOE CALLS INTO THE kitchen from the living room. 'Sing for us Shirley, sing. But Shirley, you should know that song is not authentic calypso. You sing it well and Belafonte too, but you can't fool Trinidadians with folk song and ballad.

> *Day-o, me say Day-o*
> *Daylight come and me want go home*

'That is when they cutting down wood tree in Jamaica and want to go home. Duke Ellington say 'Come Sunday' – same thing, Sunday come and they don't want to work.

> *Come Mr Tally man, come tally me banana*
> *Daylight come and me want go home*

'That is when they pick banana branch and the boss man will count it to pay them, but that's not calypso, Miss Shirley. You should know, you're from Tiger Bay. Why they make you sing that song? Kitch, Kitchener, where you? Look how your guitar lean up there like it lonesome, man. You call this a Christmas party? Pick up the damn thing, man, and show Shirley what real calypso is.' But Kitchener is upstairs, looking for the bottle of rum he hid under his bed.

Shirley makes a slim curve as she leans on the kitchen doorframe with a jewelled hand on her hip. She tilts her head to a smile as she lights a thin menthol cigarette. When she pulls it from her mouth and exhales, she says, 'Boscoe darling, I love that song. So what if it's not a *real* calypso? It's a lovely song.'

Walk into the kitchen where four women are seated at a table with wine and conversation. Their feet are crossed at the ankles and their dresses are blossoms and choruses. The sweet cinnamon scent of perfume hovers over them, among the haze of cigarette smoke. They hear when Boscoe stands in the middle of the living room and sings:

> *Is trouble – In Arima*
> *Trouble – If they beat me*
> *is trouble*
> *In Arima!*

His knees bend, his hip dips, he holds his glass high, with the small finger splayed.

> *Oh, tell me mooma*
> *and me poopa*
> *is trouble*
> *in Arima*

'Now *that* is the real calypso.'

The women laugh. Marge is at the kitchen sink twisting ice cubes from their trays. She has sprat fish frying on the cooker; the pan hisses pearls of flame when she cracks the ice and takes it into the living room. Tom Phillip there, from Jamaica, Kitch there, Boscoe dancing. When Marge returns to the kitchen with the empty serving tray, the drawer of gossip is shut. 'Oh ladies, the men are lonely out there, we should go in,' Marge says. 'Kitch is putting some records on; only Shirley's dancing. Come on.'

Snow falls and settles on Moss Side. Christmas trees blink from terraced windows. Car hiss on the wet road. Shirley is standing over the gramophone with a glass of whisky in her hand, watching Kitchener stack six 45s on the changer. Kitch straightens his back and a record drops from the spindle, the stylus arm, rising from it's resting position, moves to bear down on the wax: Fats Domino: 'Blueberry Hill'. Shirley sways her sequined hips, sashays to the middle of the room to dance. Boscoe leans back in an armchair, sips his watery grog. Another 45 drops from the spindle. Boscoe rises from his seat to dance to 'Mr Lee' with Shirley, lightly holding her at waist and hand.

With nimble feet he twirls her, his ankles bending out of his brogues, rocking on the balls of his feet. Kitchener has a bottle of rum in his hand, cradled like a trophy. Starched white shirt and pleated navy pants, red bracers. He cracks the rum seal and lifts a window to splash the first taste to the earth. They toast to health and strength and raise their glasses, knock them there, under the tungsten chandelier.

Tom Phillip gasps dramatically from the sudden sharpness in his throat. 'What kind of rum is this, pardner? Is dead you want kill me?'

Boscoe scowls, coughs, 'Wow, now this, this is the raw puncheon, the kinda rum the Indians drink when they're cutting sugarcane. Where you get puncheon rum from, Kitchie?'

'I know somebody did coming up,' Kitch say, 'so I put in my order.' Kitch circles with the bottle to refill their glasses. 'Drink, Tom, man. A big man like you, you fraid hard rum?' But one sip is all Kitchener is taking himself. His glass can sit on the window sill till morning, till it evaporates. He won't drink it, lest his gullet blaze. Give him Peardrax, Whiteways. He walks across to the sofa where Ruth and Beatrice are sitting. 'Miss Ruth, you don't want some rum?'

Ruth waves her hand, 'No thank you.'

'Beatrice, you? This is good rum you know, from Trinidad. Try a bit?'

Beatrice smiles and lowers her head, 'No thank you. Rum affects me badly. If I drink that I'll get crazy.'

'Nothing wrong with that, you can get crazy if you want, all of us is friends here.'

Beatrice folds her legs and cups her knee with clasped hands. 'No, I better not.'

Kitchener notices how her high heels hold her to a point, her calves in a gossamer nylon, like the swirl of a violin, perfect and holy, the curve of her thighs in her skirt. Then he goes to the gramophone to replenish the spindle with 45s. When Dizzy Gillespie's 'Tin Tin Deo' begins, Shirley, still in the middle of the living room, throws a hand into the air, twirling her wrist, her head leant back. And when Nat King Cole's 'Calypso Blues' follows, she pulls Kitchener like a drunk aunt at a wedding, and the sudden tug splashes his Whiteways of Whimple. 'Oh I love Nat King Cole! Dance with me!'

Kitchener is grinning so deep that the black gaps above the jaw teeth are showing. 'Miss Shirley I can't dance like you; take Bill. Look-look, Boscoe want to dance you.' He is blushing like a buck-toothed boy, dancing with her at arms length; the polite dance of a married man. But he cannot deny the musculature of her hip, the power in her proximity.

...to take me back to Trinidad

Marge comes from the kitchen with a tray of fried whitebait piled high and hot on a plate, and a bowl of mixed nuts. Then she pours herself a drink: small rum, lemonade, ice. She lights a cigarette and dances the slow dance of shaking hip and elbows raised.

...is black the root is blonde the hair...

They are all dancing now, except Boscoe, dyspeptic and sprawled on his soft chair, and Tom Phillip, sitting next to him, rolling ice round his glass, sipping his sip. When Kitch and Marge dance, fingers entwined, they move close and far, back and forth. The overhead light shines through the thinning hair at the top of Kitchener's head like a torch in a forest. He turns from his wife to dance with Beatrice, palm to palm, her waist all shimmy and shake, twisting her shoulders. He giggles at her prowess in the dance and leans forward to grin in her ear.

Boscoe rolls his head against his chairs' headrest to face Tom. 'Where Beatrice learn to dance so, boy? She can dance. Tell her if she's ever in London to look me up, I'm always looking for dancers. I'll tell you one thing, though, cause you're my friend and I like you and I'm drunk.' He lowers his voice to a throaty whisper. 'But mind your woman with that fox-mouth Kitchener. You see how she smiling, dancing with him? Watch him. He can hardly talk, but when it comes to woman he can talk sweet, plus his business long. If a man like Kitchener hold on to she, boy, tell you, you never get she back.' His laugh leaves his mouth open beyond the laugh's last sigh, rolling his head back around, just as the next record drops from spindle to turning table. Marge has gone to the kitchen to finish her cigarette.

Tom cracks an ice cube with his wisdom teeth. He notices,

now, the gentleman's poise with which Kitchener pours his woman a drink of rum, like a camp butler, with his head cocked to one side, in supplication, how she takes it to her lips and then pulls it away from her face, as if its very scent were repulsive, but how she drinks it, straight. He wants her to look his way so he can indicate his displeasure, but her head won't turn left enough to view him.

Outside on Brooke Street, stars shine down into puddles of rain. A train grumbles in the distance. Marge comes back from the kitchen, wiping her hands in her dress. Glitter in the corner of her eyes.

Blink and the scene will change.

I grew up listening to Kitchener; he was a hero to me; I always admired him. Growing up in Port of Spain, my father was one of his biggest fans, and so I get to know about him, hear all his songs. I even learn a few of them when I was coming up.

When I win the calypso crown in '56, was $40 and a crown from Angostura – but the result was, people start asking me to go here and go there. They ask me to go to England in 1958, and when I get to England now, I asking all about for Kitchener. They tell me Kitchener living in Manchester; he was a top musician there, not just calypso; he was playing bass in a nightclub. So I went to Manchester to meet him because I never meet him before and I want to know the man. When I went to the club and finally meet him, I shook his hand and said, 'Mr Kitchener, I'm very pleased to meet you etcetera, etcetera.' And he look me up and down and he say, 'So-So you-you-you, you is the young fella they talking 'bout? Sparrow? But you-you don't look like much to me.' So I just make a joke and say, 'Well, Mr Kitchener, looks can be deceiving.' And he watch me.

— The Mighty Sparrow

RUDY ALLEYNE, 1958

SPARROW REALLY DIDN'T know Kitch, because when he start to make he name in 1955, Kitch was in England almost eight years already. But he had heard about Kitchener because Kitchener was a genius; he knew the history. Plus, Melodisc used to send Kitch records down to Trinidad as soon as they press. Bam! Radio Guardian get it, bam, Tripoli Steelband playing it, and everybody in Port of Spain talking about the new Kitchener record. Fellas used to wait on that, and when it drop, was like a bomb.

Kitch knew about Sparrow too, of course. He hear about this new singer, he hear Sparrow music, he know Sparrow getting popular in Trinidad and calling himself the 'Calypso King of the world'. But good as Sparrow was, the old man know he could always outshine him with his compositions. One night we upstairs in The Belle Etoile playing All Fours and somebody put on a Sparrow record. Kitchener say, 'What this Grenadian know about calypso?' The boys laugh, but men like Makonnen, who from British Guiana, don't find it funny.

Makonnen leaning back in his chair and give that half grin he gives when he vex. 'Kitchener man, you have to move away from that way of thinking. We is all one people. That kind of talk is what keeping us back from progress. This big island, small island stupidness, you realise how bad that is?' Kitch eh say nothing.

Kitchener have the brain and he know how to record, he could write good songs. But Sparrow had a sweet, sweet voice. It sweet but it strong. And he was a handsome fella, too; woman love him. Another thing, Sparrow had a full head of hair, but poor Kitch was going bald, he always in hat. He would wear trilby and stingy brim, fedora, bowler hat, beret, all kinda thing. He wouldn't let people see he head so, especially women; by the time they see that, it too late. In England with how it cold and the rain and dew, it make sense to wear hat, no problem. But all that was ruse, because when men losing their hair they does develop a liking for all kind of exotic hats, fur hat, top hat and baker boy. If you have hair on your head you never wear so much hat. Some man have it in the centre and they good on the side, some taking it from the front, but the back good; some have it in the crown, lord, but once it start to go, no matter how you beg, it eh giving you nothing back. Kitch had it both ways – front and crown – so I know he used to watch Sparrow head; he envy Sparrow muff.

I feel in fact they envy each other. Sparrow envy Kitch because Kitch is the master calypsonian. Kitch could write calypso about a mango tree, a big stone, about a woman who tongue-tie – anything. He have melody like rain. Sparrow can't do that, not like Kitch, never happen. Kitch, now, envy poor Sparrow because Sparrow have the golden voice and the charisma, he have the seppy.

While Kitch was in England, he keep hearing how Sparrow doing things back in Trinidad. Sparrow come and win the Calypso King in 1956 – he had 'Jean an' Dinah' – don't mind they say that was Lord Blakie song he thief when he an Blakie was in the house of correction, and he come out first and say is his. People does say all kinda thing.

1957, he come with 'Carnival Boycott' and 'No, Doctor No' – good compositions. He start his own record label and putting out music. He have top musicians working with him, men like Roderick Borde and Cyril Diaz. He come and he win the Road March in '58 with 'Pay As You Earn'. Kitch can't deny the song good. Sparrow is King in Trinidad, and Kitch? Kitch up in Manchester in the kiss-me-arse cold. The old man know the young boy could croon, but he want me to say it. He ask me, 'Rudy boy, you find he good?'

And I have to mamaguy Kitchener, to lie. 'He green in calypso, man; he don't know nothing; pop song he singing there.' But I used to buy all Sparrow record as soon as they come out. I can't tell Kitch that. Then Sparrow sing, 'Teresa', an' even Kitch had to bawl, 'Oh lord, that is kaiso.'

LINFORD BRAMBLE, 1958

WHEN WE REACH THE STUDIO and come to record, Rupert Nurse will just hand you the chart, and if you mouth slack or your knowledge fail, when the chart say blow G and you blow B, he will just watch you cut-eye and smile to make you know he hearing. If you a semitone out, he know; that mean don't do that again. He's a old army-band man, he don't mess around. Al Jennings bring him from Trinidad with the All Star Band in 1945. 1-2-3 and he watching you frankomen in you face. Play B again, see what will happen.

'Sorry Mr Nurse, I just learning the tune.'

'But this is not a school, and I am not your teacher. You don't come here to learn, you come to play, and you getting pay. OK, 1-2-3, let's go!'

Men like Willie Roach and Joe Harriott, who like to play free, had to straighten up and fly right, because when it come to recording, Kitchener don't like to waste time or money. He will hum the bass how he want it or he will play it himself if he have to. Sometime them English musician, their rhythm twist, they can't play calypso. It have a way Kitch does want the bass to rally with his voice. He play bass on 'My Wife Nightie' same way; the bass man couldn't swing the rhythm right, so Kitch say, 'Gimme the bass, lemme try.' And the try was the take.

He will lean on the piano and skin teeth with Russ Henderson. He will sing the song one time and Russ will know exactly where the changes are; like he could read Kitchener mind and transcribe, make Kitchener say, 'Ah red man, you get it one time.' And the Creole will smile and tinkle the ivory.

And when you see Kitch ready to sing, he don't take long at all. He twisting his face and rolling his eye when he singing. Does be hard not to laugh, but your mouth on the reed and Mr Nurse watching you. No. One-two take and we done, then only chorus

170

to overdub. But if you ask Kitchener tomorrow what he record today he forget. So he was. Once he done with one session, he mind gone on new songs he ready to wax.

Rupert Nurse had an innovative way of arranging when it come to Kitchener; is like he mixing up jazz and Latin music inside the calypso. Plenty music. Sometimes he giving you a lil' space to solo. Nurse making a six-piece band sound like a whole orchestra, and he paying proper rates, he not cutting musician throat. But if he say play so and you can't play it how he ask, well, crapaud smoke your pipe.

The early part was at 73 New Bond Street, Levy Studios. Most of the big numbers like 'Ghana', 'Redhead', 'Saxophone', 'Be-Bop Calypso', all that record there. And then later on, we was right in Bayswater, coming down by Holland Park. Dennis Preston had a studio in the back there. When it have a session now, you line up waiting outside the studio in the morning and Mr Preston would check the budget; whether is £7 an hour or £4 an hour they paying. And you pulling Kitch or Rupert jacket for a session. And Rupert will call you, 'Alleyne, Henderson come, Coleman, Neville, Bramble,' like he picking you for football team. Preston himself would supply the boys with the first bottle of rum.

After the session, Nurse and Mr Preston would always come out to where the fellas relaxing and ask if everyone was happy with the recording. Some fellas like to listen back to the recordings, some don't. Kitch like to hear the playback, always. Me, I don't give one arse, when I blow out I done, so just pay me my money and let me go. I doh lime. I gone Soho to get drunk, gimme rum, bring scotch. Either that or I gone Chinatown, gone for the brisket of beef.

LEONARD, 1959

IT WAS A WEDNESDAY night in January when London cold like dog nose. I was working at the Riffifi in Mayfair. I get a residency there, five nights a week so I make a trio – piano, bass and guitar – and I singing, working the crowd with the big sombrero and two shac-shac. My tunic full with decal and glitter, my pants have gold embroidery down the side. I even paint Mexican moustache on my face. I used to call myself 'Mr Calypso'.

Them days my money was long. Sometimes I make fifty pound in one night. Next time, eighty, sometimes one hundred a night in tips on top of my fee. Money like peas. I always ready to extempore on white people head. I would make up song on them gentlemen head when they come in the club to eat a meal with their mistress. Before the show, the manager, Mr Corsini might show me, 'This one is a duke, this one is a shipping magnate, this one is a professor of law, that one is the Greek high commissioner, this lady from Switzerland – she's a princess.' Once I get the information, I take my microphone on the long cord and I start to walk around the room, I going all between the tables, singing on people. Well, one two liquor and money used to flow, tips in the hat.

The trio was hot. I put Neville Boucarut on bass, Fitzroy Coleman on guitar and the great Cyril Jones on piano. Now, understand, I have a band for dancing, so it's not just calypso. We playing cha-cha-cha, bolero, rumba, Frank Sinatra. I used to do things like 'Love Me Tender', 'Yellow Bird' and 'Guantanamera'. But when is time for calypso, them boys used to cause ruction in the Riffifi.

That Wednesday night the club full and we just about to start the second set. And as I stand up by the side of the stage with my scotch, I hear Neville say, 'Ai, look Kitchener.' And in walk Mr Kitchener, like a lord with the big hat and the mackintosh. He lean up by the bar, he eh see me yet, so I go in his arse.

'But a-a! Kitch, what you doing here? You in London and you eh even call me. I didn't know you coming down. You recording?'

But he can't be recording. Any recording doing in London either he or Rupert would make sure and tell me 'cause is me have to round up the boys. Kitch tip his hat back, 'Is some business I have with Mr Chilkes. Contract business with the label, boy – a quick trip. But I know you singing here and I want to hear good calypso, so I come to surprise you.' He laugh, he looking round the place.

'Who you staying with? You staying with Connor?'

'Nah, I staying in a hotel down Piccadilly.'

'But Kitch, you coulda stay by me, man; what wrong with you? Why you paying hotel? You know it have space by me.'

'But I don't like burden people.'

'Burden? Kitch? How you could burden me? Anyway, what you drinking?'

'I will take a stout,' he say.

I call for the barman, but I watching Kitchener, old time smart man. The black suit with the crisp white shirt, red paisley tie, bracers, and the big felt hat bend to one side. Mr Corsini come just so. 'Rudy, when are you starting the show? Intermission's over, I don't want people to leave, come on.'

'Yes, we starting now, two minutes. This is my friend, Lord Kitchener, he just come down from Manchester.' And Mr Corsini bend his head and look at Kitchener from over his glasses frame. He shake his hand, he grin deep. But he nod at me and I know what the nod mean. So I say, 'Kitch boy, I have to start the second set, let we talk after.' And Kitch lean up on the bar drinking his brew. But he must be see Neville big wood bass shine up on the stage like a woman backside and his eye get big. He pull Nev sleeve, 'Nev boy, gimme a lil tush on the wood nah?'

Neville laugh, 'Ah boy, no problem with me, but you have to ask Len.'

I say, 'No problem,' because I know Kitchener could handle he self on the wood, and as long as Corsini hearing music he don't care which darkie playing what. As we stand up there by the side of the stage, a white woman come from the side of the bar and touch Kitchener shoulder. Kitchener spin round. 'Ai, you reach?'

'Hello darling.' Big kiss on Kitch cheek. Is now I understand why Kitch in London. The woman short, but she well appointed. A blonde. She have she business in place, in front and behind. She wearing a red, low-neck dress, with a big pearl necklace, bangles, and even I feel I could deal with she if I get the chance to break. But Kitch rubbing the woman back while she stand up there, and she watching him, fix in his eye. He grinning sideways at me like a hairy snake. The woman say, 'You remember my friend, Anna?' And Anna step forward; she lil' taller, slimmer, black hair, and she mouth sneer and slack, like I like. She look like she wash down 'bout six cherry brandy. She watching me, but I have to work. I not on pussy.

I say, 'Kitch, we have to play, if you on the bass you have to come now.'

He say, 'Sure.' And he give the blonde mopsy his jacket to hold.

The stage is just a little raise platform, enough space for a trio. Kitch climb up, he heft the bass, he pluck up the string, he start to manhandle the damn thing. He turn to Cyril, 'What we playing?' And he roll up his sleeves.

Cyril say, 'Coconut Woman'.

Is a easy gig. The atmosphere relaxed. People just want a little light entertainment after they eat, is not a fête. Very few people does get off their seat to dance. Saturday night perhaps, when they tipsy, but not a Wednesday, not really.

But when we start to jam the vamp in truth, the crowd get active. Even Cyril, who usually quiet, bouncing on the piano stool and playing the thing like a drum. Even Corsini get excitable. He stand up by the bar clapping hand like a penguin. Kitchener behind me on the bass, sweating like a bull, he eye close, the smile spread open with teeth. All the two craft cheering. They wining on their bar stools, sipping blue Curaçao.

When we step out in Mayfair, was about 2 o'clock in the morning. The ground wet – rain fall while we in the club. The band come out – Neville, Cyril, Coleman. Each man say their farewell and go their separate way. Tomorrow night, we back again. Kitch and I stand up outside the club. I say, 'Kitch, what you for? It have a lil' after hours place in Leicester Square we could go? Tests does be playing jazz there. Russell down there tonight; you for that?'

He say, 'Rudy boy, me eh k-k-know, I have to see them Melodisc people early in the morning, if I go after-hours club now… Rudy boy.'

I know Kitch waiting on the two women to come out the club, I know. So I wondering now if Kitch and I could parry them. I don't mind parry. But the women come out with their big coat on, stepping high over water and they eh even notice me; they tipsy. The blond one lean she head on Kitch shoulder, the short one drifting behind. Kitch touch me on my arm, 'Len boy, Ah go pick up with you tomorrow. You go-go-go be home?'

I say, 'Yes, I will be home.' But all this time I grinding like a sugar mill. And I watch that man Kitchener pull he overcoat collar up and hail down a black taxi, and he and the two craft jump in. They gone Piccadilly. The thick one have arse like horse, and Kitch eh give me none.

LEONARD, 1960

KITCH HAD A NICE PLACE in Moss Side, he was doing alright. He was playing bass in nightclub, recording for Melodisc and making his living, hustling as usual. I was up there for a while, in Manchester. Nothing was really happening for me down here in London, so Kitch say, 'Leonard, boy, why you eh come up Manchester lil' bit, see what you can do here? Maybe I could get you a lil' job at the Cosmopolitan or the Orient.' But I never get nothing. Then I hear the great Trinidadian boxer Yolande Pompey coming up to Manchester to fight.

I used to stay in Yolande Pompey place in Vauxhall when I first come to England in '56, renting a room there. He was from Princess Town, down south Trinidad. Yes, a very good boxer, light-heavyweight, contender for the title; he fight Archie Moore in America, fight all around the world. He was a sweet man too, woman want him, he a saga boy, a good-looking redskin fella.

Pompey come up to England – just like we – to see what he can do. But by the time he come up Manchester to fight, he was going down in the ranks; all kinda jackass was beating him. Now, I wasn't no big boxing man eh, but Kitch like to watch boxing and he want to go. I in his house and is years since I see Yolande so I decide to go.

Pompey was fighting one Tony Dove on a Monday night at a place they calling King's Hall. I put on the one good suit I have and a pork pie hat. Kitch, he put on singlet, he put on briefs, he put on the John Collier suit with the stove-mouth pants, the black felt hat with the peacock feather in the band. Lord, he put on silk tie, he put on two-tone brogues. I say 'Kitch boy, is wedding you going? How you dress up so?' And he laugh.

'You have to be respectable among these people, you can't let them see you in rags.'

'These people?'

He laugh. 'Well yes, the white people; they very particular, and they done don't like you, so you have to be a gentleman and dress good. Show they you decent, that-that-that you have something.' I just nod my head.

We gone down to Belle Vue and as we come out the car is only, 'Kitch, Kitch.' Big white man with cigar hanging out they mouth, 'Kitch, Kitch how you doing, Kitch?' and Kitch grinning like a imps, if you see him, strolling through the foyer. I was surprise. Then he would stop and turn to call out to somebody across the floor, spin; he want people to see how sharp the suit cut. He want them see the hem roll. But when I look round at the white chaps there, I see these men dress up simple-simple with their old Burton suit, their face greasy like they get slap with mackerel, and they don't smell good.

When we go in the arena now, the place about half full. It smoky-smoky in there, tobacco you smelling, sweet pipe and perspiration. Two fellas boxing in the ring down there, the canvas lit like it glowing, and when they hit, you could feel it; it echo in the hall. We seats was right down in front, good seats, eye level to the ring.

When Pompey turn to fight, the bell ring and the announcer duck under the ropes. He have his microphone and he say, 'Ladies and gentlemen, the next fight is an eight-round bout between so and so and so and so, former light heavyweight contender and so and so on.' Tony Dove come up, the white man, he come out bouncing and he looking alright; he not tall but he stocky, he face flat and hard like pan bottom. Pompey come out in a black robe with gold trim and he moving round the ring with the cape flinging behind, face shining with vaseline, he looking good but he belly soft, he lil' flabby around the waist.

Well them men beat one another like pan. Lord, they throw some hand, but in the end Pompey win on points. After, we gone down to the dressing rooms to see if we could say hello to Pompey. But when we get by the door it have a big Englishman stand up there, hands fold across the big chest.

'What'd'you want back there, boys? Boxers' dressing rooms back there.'

I say, 'We're friends of Mr Pompey, just want to say hello to him.'

Kitch step forward, 'Tell him is L-L-Lord Kitchener.'

The bulldog laugh, 'Lord who?' and he put his hand across the door so Kitch can't pass. I see Kitch sink back and humble down in his suit. It left to me to explain to the man who Kitch was and how we know Pompey from Trinidad and so on. The fella was just doing his job, and we joke till he let we go through and see Pompey.

When we going home in the car, I making joke with Kitch. 'I thought you say you could fight. How come you didn't box down the fella by the door?'

And he mumble something 'bout how he fed up of England. That is all he say.

MARGE, 1962

AFTER WE'D BEEN MARRIED about a year, Kitch had this Jamaican carpenter, Ulric, build me a little shop called Marjorie's Milk Bar. And it were built to perfection in a place called Hulme, off the Princess Road. It used to be a corner shop, which sold newspapers and sweets and milk and things, and then the owner and his son died in a car accident and Kitch rented it from the man's wife because she couldn't stand to go near the place anymore. When Ulric were working on the place, Kitch used to provoke him, 'I didn't think Jamaicans could work so good! I heard you're even lazier than Trinidadians.' He thought it were funny, but Ulric didn't. He were a quiet man, Ulric. He couldn't be more than forty-five. He would work all day, no lunch, just a can of stout. When he were finished for the day, *then* he would eat. It took him a long time to finish the job, about three weeks to do everything in the shop. Kitch would say, 'He taking too long and charging me by the day. Marge, them Jamaicans feel they smart, you know, they worse than the Guyanese!'

The Milk Bar were hardly doing anything in the day, but in the evening, when all these young kids used to come in after school, they'd drive me potty making milk shakes and cheese on toast for them. We had a second-hand juke box in there, a few chairs around two tables, linoleum on the floor. We had ice lollies and sandwiches. We sold newspapers too, and cigarettes, and we had two dogs, big Alsatian dogs. One was pure white and Kitch called it whitey; the other was black.

The Milk Bar only lasted about a year. It was more trouble than it were worth in the end; the kids made a racket on the juke box with their rock and roll. Drunks would come in. And after a while all I could smell was milk and pretend-strawberry everywhere I went.

But I enjoyed being in the shop, because with Kitch being away

179

so often, I had to find something to do with meself. But when we had a fight, oh would he use the shop against me. He'd talk loud for people there to hear 'See, see, I put her name up in lights, "Majorie's Milk Bar", and look how she behaving.' He had a hot temper. He would throw things around.

There were a young woman who used to come into the shop, she were pregnant and having the child adopted; she already had two. I said to Kitch, 'That girl that's just been in the shop, she's getting that baby adopted.'

He said, 'Oh, what a shame.'

I said. 'Oo, I'd love that baby.'

'Do you want it? Really?'

I said, 'Yes.'

That was in 1962. I'd been to the hospital to find out why I couldn't have children. All my mates were married same as me and they were having babies. The doctor said, 'I can't see anything wrong with you; send your husband.' But Kitch wouldn't go.

He said, 'Me? Go hospital? An' let them people interfere with me?'

But this young woman used to come in the shop and I used to give her a few bits, 'cause I knew she didn't have a lot of money. I used to give her things for her kids. She was from Salford. I told her that I wished I could have the baby, but I had to speak to Kitch first. Kitch were there one day and I said to her, 'Tell Kitch what you told me.'

And she said, 'Oh, I wish you'd have this baby.'

Kitch said, 'We'll have that baby.'

He done that for me. And he must've thought, well, she won't be bothered what I get up to if she has a baby to look after. And when that girl came out of hospital, she just came to the house and gave us the baby. The social services came around when he were eight months old and said that although he were happy with us, if we wanted, they could place him elsewhere, with a white family maybe. But Kitch loved him; he said, 'Leave him right here, he looks like Edmundo Ros.'

In 1945, Lord Invader had a song, 'Rum and Coca Cola', and it was picked up by the Andrews Sisters, and Invader made so much money. Then Harry Belafonte picked up Lord Melody song, 'Mama look a Boo Boo' in 1957 and had a hit with it. So in '58, me and Melody say, 'Leh we go New York and see if we could get some money from Harry.' So after Carnival in Trinidad, we went up via the Virgin Islands, did a few shows there, and then we reach up in New York. We get to meet Belafonte and he was very pleasant. He gave Melody some money, I don't know how much, but Melody was happy, and Belafonte kept Melody to work with him as a partner up there, in New York. So I came back to Trinidad, alone. Melody was my partner eh, my good-good friend. Melo and I had a lil' rivalry going in the '50s. But that rivalry was just to get people in the tents to see if me and Melody was going to fight. So when I came back from New York I start to look around to see who I could have as a picong partner, here in Trinidad, now that Melody gone. It had a fella call Christo and we try with him for a while, but he wasn't as radical as Melody, he wasn't as debonair. So we start to look towards Kitchener who was in England at the time, because Kitchener was a big name, he was a favourite of the people.

—The Mighty Sparrow

KITCH USED TO SAY, 'Oh, I don't like to fly, I hate flying.' But after he and Pretender fell out, Preddie told me that that were a lie. He said, 'Marge, the only reason Kitch likes to travel by boat is because he can have long romances with women, not because he's afraid of flying. All those single women on the boat with nowhere to go and he will romance them, invite them to his cabin and serenade them.'

'Serenade them? You mean sleep with them?'

He said, 'What I could tell you, Margie? What you want me to say?'

'Preddie, you can't tell me anything that I don't know already,' I said.

And in 1962, when he went back to Trinidad for the first time, he went by BOAC, and that were an eight-hour flight. He wanted to take the boat. I said, 'Don't be stupid, Kitch. How do you think people in Trinidad will look at you coming off a boat – the great calypsonian, Lord Kitchener, coming home from England on a boat. They would laugh. Especially those calypsonians, you know what they're like – that Sparrow, he would laugh. Let them buy a ticket for you. You should fly.' He turned to me, 'How you mean, "Sparrow will laugh"?'

Kitch never intend to stay in England. He was a young man when he went England and young men have young ideas. He love England, yes. Is the mother country, but he didn't want to remain in England and dead like a nit and just a telegram reach Trinidad: 'Oh, Kitch dead, that one gone.' Nah, Kitch love Trinidad too much, and he wanted to go back home; nobody eh *make* Kitch go back to Trinidad.

Kitch went because he had enough of England. And when he see how Sparrow, Blakie and them young calypsonians was successful in Trinidad, that must've make him think, 'What I doing here in England then? Money not flowing like it used to; calypso like it dead in England, records not selling, is only cabaret work fellas getting, and now them Jamaican turn calypso upside down, and their thing getting popular.'

If Kitch did stay in England he woulda never become the great that he became. People knew him in England, but he wanted people in Trinidad to know how great he was, so he had to go.

— Leonard 'Young Kitch' Joseph

183

ROBERTS, Aldwin, of 48, Brooks Road, Old Trafford, Manchester, 16, Lancs, SINGER, lately residing at 23, Heywood Street, Moss Side, Manchester, 16, Lancs. – Court – HIGH COURT OF JUSTICE. Date of Filing Petition – 12th Feb., 1963. No. of Matter – 174 of 1963. Date of Receiving Order – 1st May, 1963. No. of Receiving Order – 320. Whether Debtor's or Creditor's Petition – Creditor's. Act of Bankruptcy proved in Creditor's Petition – Section 1-1 (G), Bankruptcy Act, 1914.

PART THREE: THE GRANDMASTER

Come along my boy
everything is changed
you eh got to beseech nor to bow
this is just the time, you must come back home
Trinidad is independent now.

— Lord Kitchener, 'Come Back Home my Boy'

People will tell you all kinda thing, but is me went in England and beg Kitchener to come back home. Because I want a partner, now that Lord Melody gone. He say, 'Nah boy, they-they treat me bad in Trinidad, in '46 and '47, I don't want go back there.'

I said, 'But is different now, Kitch, things not like before; the people love you there, you must come back home.' And he agreed to come back. And I get the people I was working with in Trinidad to send him a ticket. But when he come back now, and he land in Piarco, one set of people around him. They embrace him, 'Kitch! Kitch!'

And they kept me out, I couldn't get close to him. When I eventually got to him, to talk to him, I said, 'Ai, Kitch, wha' happening? Is me, Sparrow.' And he just watch me, and say, 'My people here,' and he walk away.

— The Mighty Sparrow

IN THE CALYPSO WORLD, Kitchener coming back to Trinidad is a big thing. Anybody will glad to go meet him, even people who don't like him. So when we hear that Kitchener was arriving we went straight to the airport. And when they say the plane land, we press up against the railings in the waving gallery to catch a glimpse of him. When he come down from the BOAC jet, if you see him: khaki safari suit, necktie, hat, briefcase, winter coat on his arm, walking tall across the Tarmac like the lord in truth. Somebody shout, 'Kitch!' And he look up and he flash his big teeth and we clap like we was children watching a matinee show.

Sparrow there, Lord Melody there. Melo been drinking since we leave town, so he spontaneous an' start sing 'Trouble in Arima'. Somebody have a rum bottle and a spoon, somebody have a quatro and we making noise in the people airport. Kitch come out from customs and he walk out in the open and he wave, journalists there, cameras flashing. A lil' brown-skin young girl from the *Trinidad Guardian* push in front and ask him, 'How it feel to be home, Mr Kitchener?'

And everybody waiting to hear him talk, to hear how the lord will talk, to hear if he will sound like a Englishman, now that he living in England. Is years we eh see him. We expect that. Is nothing; the man spend fifteen years in England; change bound to take place. But we want to know, we want to hear. He stop by the bureau du change to answer the girl, people in his waist, reporter on his shoulder flashing camera, he say, 'How you mean? I glad to reach home. I feeling good.'

He was staying at Hilton Hotel in Port of Spain, so we set off in a convoy behind him. He in the big Ford motorcar the Carnival Development Committee send for him, chauffeur an' thing. I was travelling with Commander and Lord Tie Head.

Tie Head driving. Hear him: 'I see fellas calling for Kitchener who don't know the man music. They know 2-3 song and say they know Kitchener. All they know is the songs he send down from London, and they bawling "Kitch, Kitch!" as if they and Kitch is friend. But they don't know half the music the man make, they don't know the man.'

Hear Commander: 'I know Kitchener when he was poncing in La Cour Harpe; he cyar play he doh know me.' And we laugh like we shy, going down the highway. When we reach Hilton, they put we in the garden, by the pool, and the waiters bring out a few drinks for Kitch and the entourage. They bring champagne, they bring rum, they bring wine, cider and soft drink. And calypsonian don't need no invitation to drink. Mr Samaroo, the promoter, get up and give a toast. Then he pass 'round pouring champagne like is water he sharing. And yes, after that, Samaroo hand Kitchener a guitar and ask him to sing a couple song. All the while he singing, I watching every part of his face. The few line in the corner of his eye when he laugh, one eyelid heavy. The big teeth. The moustache trim neat like barber shape it. I watch the gold watch on his wrist. The two gold ring, the buck teeth. How his suit back ramfle from sitting down so long, the hat how it twist at the lip where he pinch it, and when eventually he take it off to fan his scalp, how he was going bald bad from the corners and the crown.

When people come down from England or America they does look different. No matter how they try to behave like they never leave, a local will know, 'Ai, he doh live here.' Yes, no matter what they do, people does know they live abroad. How? Is they skin. It doesn't shine. And as I watching Kitchener carrying on with the boys, singing and laughing, I see him loosen himself and drink two glass of ice-water quick-quick. He grinding ice, he patting his neck with kerchief. The skin pale. I could tell he eh taste this kinda heat in a long, long time.

But he looking good. He tall, he strong, and them calypsonians eating every word that come out his mouth, like cat licking butter. The Mighty Sparrow, sitting on a couch there talking to Blakie and Duke, just so he lean forward and knock his empty glass on the table to catch everybody attention. 'So Mister Kitchener, I know you have road march material, a'mean, I hear 'The Road' and it good, it very good, but what about the big yard? You going in the big yard for Calypso King? Dimanche Gras? You have to sing for King Kaiso y'know. What you have?'

Kitch just laugh, roll his head back, and watch around as if to say, *What the arse trouble this man, lord?*

Blakie start to laugh like he kill a man and get away. He done drunk and gargling that sweet laugh he have, but he see that Kitchener don't want to answer Sparrow, so he help out the ol'man. 'Sparrow, leave the man please, you eh see the man now reach? Leave the man. Leave competition for Dimanche Gras night. Is then you will see what he carrying; now is to celebrate.'

Sparrow stand up, he stick his chest out to grand charge, he mischievous, but joke he making. 'Who talk to you, Blakie? Let the damn man talk. Kitch could talk for himself, he's a big man, he finish growing. Age before beauty, let the old man speak.' And everybody laugh, but we laugh like we frighten.

Samaroo looking 'round nervous, he don't want no bacchanal in Hilton. But Sparrow like Cassius Clay when he start and he want to picong poor Kitchener right there. He say, 'Big yard not easy y'know. You have to know your politics, what going on in the country. You away so long, boy Kitch, a bet you don't know Trinidad get independence this year.' And he laugh.

Kitchener just stretch back in his club chair, he clasp his hands behind his neck and cross his legs. He laughing with us, he laughing with Sparrow. He stutter, 'W-w-when Grenada getting independence?' Everybody bray like drake duck.

Sparrow *steups*, he turn to the boys, 'Where the Whiteways? Superior? You drink all the Whiteways? Gimme it here, man. Is only Peardrax and Champagne I drinking tonight. Kitch boy, to you, health and strength. Doh vex with the Sparrow, we go clash on the savannah stage, but the birdie have to go to the studio, now, right now.' And he raise his glass in a toast. 'Health and strength, old man, health and strength.' And the calypsonians there raise a chorus of glasses.

But Kitch not taking basket. He smile and raise his glass, bow his head slight to say thanks and then he break away from the lime and gone down to his room. Well things filter out quick after that. But I stay there drinking with Commander, Superior and Tie Head, till the last bottle of rum done, the champagne done, till the people in the hotel eh bring no more.

LORD WOODSLAVE 1963

THE PNM PARTY came to prominence in January 1956. Eric Williams was the leader, and they were starting this revolution sort of, about getting rid of England and colonial rule, looking to Independence and so forth. And that Carnival, in '56, was when The Mighty Sparrow came with 'Jean and Dinah', espousing exactly what Eric Williams was saying.

> *Doh make a row*
> *the Yankees gone*
> *and Sparrow take over now*

Now, calypso is a lyrical kind of tradition, so the voice isn't necessarily an asset. If you have it, nice, if not, well. But Sparrow came with the voice *and* a kind of vibrance, a speed, and the country was ready, and Eric Williams embrace him, of course, smart politician that Williams was, and Sparrow became, for a while, like the mouthpiece of the PNM. I don't think Sparrow fully understood that at the time, but he became very popular and powerful, and as a result everybody else, all the other calypsonians, including myself, suffered.

Eric Williams didn't want to deal with the calypso as a movement, because, remember, in the colonial days, we were the unofficial opposition, is we stick our necks out and say, 'The higher authorities must do so and so and so.' Is we who attack them. They used to jail and censor us for that, they had all kinds of laws. And Eric Williams, historian that he was, knew that.

But in 1958, when Williams had to introduce the income tax in Trinidad, Sparrow is the man who did it for him with 'Pay As You Earn'. Williams couldn't ask for better, and that was a road march as well, so imagine the whole nation singing that. Sparrow also sang things like 'Leave The Damn Doctor', 'William The

Conqueror' and many, many others. So Sparrow didn't want Kitch to come back to Trinidad.

Now, the tradition in calypso is that calypsonians should compose their own calypsos, be composers, good bad or indifferent, that was the tradition we met. So if you're not doing that, you psychologically feel less than a calypsonian. Sparrow, as we found out much, much later, used ghost writers. That was a secret he kept, and it made him insecure, because he knew he was going to look bad in the eyes of other calypsonians and the people, if he was not what he said he was supposed to be. And people start calling for Lord Kitchener, being the greatest thing that ever come out of Trinidad and Tobago, in terms of calypso, to come back from England to deal with this situation we had here with Sparrow.

It so happen that Sparrow had a falling out with Leslie Samaroo, who owned the Strand Cinema in Port of Spain, where they did a lot of the calypso recordings in Trinidad. They also had the RCA franchise. It was rumoured that Sparrow cuff the man or slap him or something. And they were powerful people. Samaroo decide to spend money and bring back Kitchener, to get even with Sparrow.

That is how Kitchener came back in December 1962. And that is how he ended up in Guyana a few days after, where he take that famous picture in the hotel room with Lord Melody and Brother Superior. These Samaroo people had the Strand Cinema in Port of Spain and they had the Strand in Georgetown. So they arrange for Kitch to perform in Guyana, to warm up before he face Sparrow, and the Carnival pressure, here in Trinidad.

THE ROAD

Somebody going to frighten bad,
because Kitchener come back to Trinidad
          — Tiny Terror, 'Tribute To Kitchener'

First Movement

THE BULL BROWN-SKIN drum beat and it blow. The beat is the blood and the heart and the road and the wood and the rhythm of people walking, so many miles in the grinning heat of Port of Spain on Carnival Monday, pushing up from Marine Square, up through Frederick Street. The beat is the Queen perspiring in her second skin of beads and sequins, the cosquelle, the dame lorraine, the glitter bands passing, the lascivious lovemaking of lovers leaning against walls that stench with urine, where some cocksman burst or some head run blood from blows and bottle – but that is Carnival: the sacred and the stink, the profane and the sin. You sit down on the culvert spewing rum frustration while the tar band, the mud mas, the oil, the burrokeets passing, or the fancy sailor in a tasselled sombrero playing real mas, so he throwing sweet talcum powder on anyone who join the band; or you pass near the midnight robber on the corner of Park and Frederick, in his black cape with the skull and crossbones, glittering with embroidered stars, with his mouth spitting convolutions of language that twist your head for coins to fall in his collection box, until you reach by Royal Jail and hear that song that Lord Kitchener sing,

I hear how they planning,
for Carnival coming

Yes, the road make to walk and so we walking behind we mother till we reach Oxford Street corner where it have people

194

living for Carnival in a wooden house there with French louvres. The house low on the ground so it taking the full strain of the Carnival vibration, and they open out the costume rooms of their tailoring shop where costumes, still to collect, hang up from the wooden beams, the smell of paint still strong on them; and the tailor still stitching mas boots for the grand Tuesday parade. I hear sound flinging from a gramophone spill out on the street like old iron and bone wood and tamboo bamboo drum, and even before Kitch reach his chorus you singing:

The road make to walk
on Carnival day
Constable I doh want to talk
but I got to say

Was so we going up Frederick Street with music and people from every street and alley side till when we reach the cenotaph at Memorial Park and see the dust rising in the savannah ahead from a steelband coming to come down from Belmont through those narrow avenues and gingerbread yards, across the mossy ravines that wash down swill from the shack hills of Laventille. The murmur of the steel getting louder as it coming, and Mammy, still a few steps ahead of us, carrying a basket of fried chicken pelau, Kool Aid and coconut drops, turns when she catch the sound of the band and says, 'Ah hearin' Kitchener tune.' So her walk is different now. In its pivot and pelt of hip it anticipates the swing of the approaching band. She is oblivious now to everything but the pan, oblivious to the small iron and spoon contingent outside the museum, to the moko jumbie's wooden feet knocking on the hard road make to walk, to the trebly speaker hissing from the Chinese restaurant. No, Mammy like nothing more than pan. Leave the ole mas, the pretty mas, the jab-jab, the oil mas, the brass bands and the mud, all Mammy want to hear is iron and only iron could make she dance like this.

And what else could the steelband from Belmont play but this song that have everybody spirit lift this Independence Carnival of red, white and black? You see, you see now how Kitchener pick his time good to come back from England? An' you hear now how the band beating hard when they reach the Barber Green in front the savannah? Is a whole lot of people that pushing the band along on racks and wheels and bunted canopies, because is their band and they from behind the bridge and they bad like yaz, so nobody could tell them nothing, and the sound ringing bright, and Mammy inside the band, and I hear somebody singing, then I realise was me.

I hear how they planning
for Carnival coming
I hear how they planning
for Carnival coming
They say they go beat people
and they doh care what happen
but tell them doh worry with me
is a different thing 1963
Because the road make to walk
on Carnival day
Constable I doh want to talk
but I got to say
any steelband man
only venture to break this band
is a long funeral from the Royal Hospital

Second Movement

The road like it really make to walk eh? Look how far I walk an' me eh even realise. A vaps take me last night. I was sitting down in my bachie up on Salvation Hill, listening to the radio. I never intend to go in their bacchanal, because once I hear pan in the savannah on Saturday night, I satisfy. But as I sit down there in the gallery, drinking my stout an' smoking my thing, I hear Bob Gittens say, 'Radio people, this is the song that everybody's talking about. Lord Kitchener is back with a Road March contender, this is "The Road".'

An' when I hear that song like I get a spirit in me, an' I put on my clothes and grab a flask of babash I was holding since

Christmas. I pass through Corbeau Town, come down by Marine Square, an' when I reach there I meet some fellas beating bottle and spoon, an' they leggo rum and is there I bounce up Rosalind – Rosie who sweet an' round like a kaisa ball, a reds from John John. I hook she an' she hook me an' is so we going through Port of Spain. When we meet up with music we take a wine. Jou'vert morning, we coming down.

We leave Marine Square an' we ease up Frederick Street. We follow pan an' brass three miles round the savannah, then we go down to New Town by Bradley, was white rum an' gouti. But Rosie say she don't wants no old man lime, so we go through the back of St Clair, down Tragarete Road an' we bounce up a ol'mas band – men with posie on their head an' rum in baby bottle. We jump with them; they leggo grog an' from there we gone down by Harvard. Is as we going over the bridge for St James, Rosie bounce up she child father, an' she gone with he, so I follow Invaders steelband through Woodbrook. Sun come up on me, an' my head twist, an' I end up back by the savannah. Lord, I really walk like a jackass all 'bout town. I had to lie down lil' bit.

Anywhere I pass, I hearing Kitchener. 'The Road'. They playing Sparrow and they playing Blakie, but you hearing Kitchener more. Is a good song for when you walking on carnival day. You take a lil' dance, then you walk again. But Kitch, like he put something else in that song. What it is? I don't know much about Africa, but if you listen you could hear like people beating big African drum with bone in there.

Well I drink till I stupid an' I lie down in the savannah like a mook, sun beatin' my back an' a watching all them tall arse woman pass.

THE MIGHTY SCAMP, 1963

1963, KITCHENER WIN THE Road March with 'The Road', nobody
come close. He come second in the Calypso King; Sparrow beat
him with 'Dan is the Man' and 'Kennedy'. But the people
welcome him; he make his money and he was in all the fetes;
anywhere you go you see Kitch. Come Panorama, the steelbands
playing his music; people offer him land, motorcar, roast duck,
wild meat, woman give him leg, but he have his house and his
wife in England, so he went back after the season. Then in '64 he
came back again – he take the Road March with 'Mama this is
Mas' kaiso. In town people singing:

> *Because the bands will be passing down Frederick Street*
> *With a ping pong beat, in the burning heat*

He bring his wife, Marge, this time. A white woman, attrac-
tive. But you know how Trini people does talk. They watch
things like that and say, 'Oh, Kitch can't find a nice black woman
to marry. So much woman in Trinidad and he gone quite England
to find this maaga white woman to say he love?' An' like the poor
woman get to know what people was saying, and even though it
had plenty English people in Trinidad at the time, I think it was
hard for her to feel like she could fit in with them. That could've
been a class thing too; the white population in Trinidad have
money, they have land – and from what I could see, Marge didn't
come from that culture.

MANGO TREE

AS HE WATCHES HER SLEEP, the mists on the mountain clear, leaving dew on the leaves of the red crotons. Here, moist heat sticks to the skin. Earth scent like rancid paraffin copper, sunlight sweeping over the Petit Valley hills, cow dung, river scent, frangipani.

The noise of the house: creak of wooden floor, electric hum of the fridge, a dying cicada buzzing in the roof. He watches her sleep, on her side, with her legs drawn up under a blue sheet. Her red hair against the pillow's white, her pale and slender arms, hands clasped under her cheek, her lips slightly open, creases in the corner of her eyes, like the timid veins of a leaf.

Yesterday, when the plane had broken through the clouds and the land below appeared, saturated with deep shades of blue and green, and the russet red of African tulip blossoms on the high ridges of the range, she had turned to him and asked, 'How big is Trinidad?

'It small,' he said.

But as he looked through the window of the plane at the hills and valleys of his island, at the geometric patterns of cane field and gardens, he realised he could not be sure of the islands' dimensions, that he had not contemplated it before, as miles to be measured, or distance across, that he was merely repeating what he had often heard: Trinidad small.

Walking tall in the hills above the house, the earth and air moist where rain had fallen during the night, a brown dog appears on the track and follows him up the incline at the rear of the house where the dirt is ochre brown, moist and slippery. Up the hillside, he sees the ground-dove nests, water sprinkling from the pommecythere tree, white lice and aphid on the Governor plum tree, the dog alongside, parting the grass for a scent.

He walks past Miss Vero's house, the last before thick mountain bush reclaims the land. There is a small path on the right, beside Miss Vero's wooden wall, the dirt there pressed smooth by feet, pebbles and random grass along it, red ant canyons. The back of Miss Vero's wooden house rests on the mountain, two tree-trunk pillars support the front. An old nutmeg tree hangs over her galvanise roof and scrapes the edge when the wind blows. Her sloping yard keeps thyme, lime, pawpaw and chataigne, and an elegant Julie mango tree with its green fruit on the lower branches. Kitchener notices one ripe, yellow-red Julie, hanging from a branch, straining the branch down, ready to fall, bound to drop, out of season.

Four Shouter Baptist flags: secret colours. He could not name them.

A man is coming down the mountain, brushing the way with a three-canal cutlass like a substitute hand, its curving-up tip blatant and churlish, the edge well grim and silver against the black iron shank. The man is old, sinewed in his arms and face. He wears a brown trilby, bent and stained smooth where fingers have pulled it over the years. Age and the hills have made outside callipers of his knees; his mouth is slack and ragged when he says, 'Morning.'

He is dressed for the bush in black Wellington boots and ragged khaki pants tucked into the top of them, stained with the milk of tubers and bleeding vines, torn at the rear pocket, the seat bruised and blackened. The calypsonian notices all this, and the grey nylon shirt open down to the navel, rolled to the elbows, one size too small. The old man does not turn his head towards Kitchener as he passes on his way down; he does not care who is who. Bush does equalise you.

At the top of the hill, where the calabash and the breadnut trees grow tall, the sky opens and the land spreads from horizon to jetty. Peninsulas, islets on the waters. Insurance offices and the fisheries. Narrow streets, warehouses and dusty yards. Anglican churches. Catholic spires. This is the babel of scents that is Port of Spain. Then to the left, grooving up the side of the mountain, shack-wood and tenements yards, government housing, water works in the hill towns of Laventille and Morvant. His eyes settle back into the familiarity of things, thinking how it look like you could just step down on these roofs to the sea.

At the airport, when the immigration officer stamped his passport and lay back in his chair to grin, he said, 'But a-a! Kitchener, you didn't bring nothin' from England for me? You come with you two hand swinging? Not even a lil' sweet biscuit self you don't bring for your boy?' He had been caught by the pungency of the officer's tone, and could not find the right words to respond quickly enough. He'd blinked and stuttered, 'Yes yes, no, is so, nothing, boy. Yes, next time,' but he knew that the officer, with his mouth slightly open and smiling, had watched him and Marge, and had noted the moment, had written the encounter into memory and opinion.

Coming out of the airport, to the Indian almond trees in the forecourt, the taxi drivers pressed their horns and shouted, 'Kitch, Kitchener, where you going?' 'Come with me man?' 'Port of Spain?' They spoke to him with their airport voices – tinged with those faux Americanisms reserved for tourists.

He turns and heads back down to the house. Taking care. The earth still slippery. And now a drizzle, gossamer light, a passing cloud. Coming down, passing through Miss Vero's land again, holding onto the knobbly branches of her cassava bushes, with the scent of chicken shit and mud, hearing the sounds of chickens in the coop, pecking at their prison wire. The Julie mango dreams gentle on the branch, glistening, heavy in the rain. This is the mango he will place next to Marge's sleeping head, the perfumed flesh that will wake her, the sticky sap of the stem oozing onto the pillow. It swings heavy there – pregnant fruit. The stem twists easily in his hand.

In them early days, people used to spread a lot of rivalry, they try to put so much ol' talk about the whole small island thing. An' like Kitchener get caught up in that and he didn't even want to share the stage with me at the Young Brigade tent. He say he prefer stand up outside, in the road with his guitar and sing, than to come inside and sing with a Grenadian.

— The Mighty Sparrow

LORD WOODSLAVE, 1964

WHEN I CAME INTO CALYPSO in the early '50s the two main bards were Lord Melody and the Mighty Spoiler. There used to be a kind of friendly rivalry between them, nothing serious. Then Spoiler died and it became Melody and Sparrow in the early 60s. They would sing on each other, who more ugly, who is a scamp. They would even sing about each other's wives; Melody sang, 'Belmont Jackass',

When your wife walking, people say she shaking,
she should get a corset for the goods she carrying.
She should wear a harness, she face like a mas.
That is why the boys does call she Belmont Jackass

Sparrow come back the following year and sang on Melody's wife with 'Madam Dracula', classic kaiso.

Then you bring the Yankee woman back to Trinidad
But none of your friends don't like she
She too old and hard
People say she husband nose perpendicular
So everybody does call she 'Madame Dracula'

But Melo and Sparrow were good-good friends and this rivalry thing was just to sell records. That is part of the historical tradition in calypso. Then, when Kitchener came back to Trinidad in '62, it became Sparrow versus Kitchener and that was the end of friendly rivalry in calypso. Their war became personal and real; it was a less palatable rivalry.

In 1964 Sparrow had a song, 'Mr Kitchener', and he record that song so it is there to document his thoughts about the man, at that time:

I cyar understand some of them old time calypsonian
It's a different era now, they come back here making row
They regret they beg me for war
I go beat them like a child, 1964
Clear the road lemme pass, Mr Kitchener
You stepping out of your class
Kitchie boy you gone too far
Old timer you're gone
I say your days done.
Clear the road lemme pass, Mr Kitchener

Sparrow actually sang that song in the Calypso King competition in Queen's Park Savannah on Dimanche Gras night in '64. Kitch sing in that same show and he was very hurt by Sparrow's lyrics. While Sparrow was on stage, Kitchener called me to his dressing room and asked me, 'But why Sparrow have to sing that song? He have nothing better to sing? Sparrow does take these things too far. He can't do better than that?'

What could I tell Kitchener? I say, 'Kitchie boy, don't worry with him. Is just a song. He don't mean those things. Is just picong he giving you; you know how Sparrow is; it don't mean nothing.'

Kitch was vex. 'You ever hear me sing anything on him like that? I feel to go right now, forget with their blasted show.' He was ready to walk out, yes, and I had to beseech him to stay. But when Sparrow sang the last verse of that song, I myself had to wonder if Sparrow was serious:

Calypso is me and I am calypso in this country
It is I does carry the load every year with a set a tunes on the road
Kitch aint got a thing to loss
He come like Mentone, once upon a time he was a good horse
But now that he old, and I am the Calypso King of the world!

And Sparrow prancing and carrying on – if you see him – he grand-charging on the stage. Eh heh? When the mark bust both he and Kitch lose to The Mighty Bomber. Bomber came first with 'Bomber's Dream' and 'Joan and James', two of the best calypso anybody ever sing. Composer run second, Sparrow come third, Kitch take fourth. But the Sparrow/Kitchener rivalry had become bigger than them and I don't know if they even realised it at the time.

Sparrow versus Kitch represent the two sides of Trinidad people. We have the jamette, the winer girl, the smutty calypso, the saga boy with the women, the village ram, the loud mouth, the bacchanal, the performance, innovation – well, that is Sparrow and that is Trinidad. Then you have the more respectable suit and tie people, the traditionalists who try to talk 'proper' English, who will try to straighten their children nose with coconut oil, who see England as the mother country, and aspire to that, to discipline and decency; they willing to work within that system. Well, that is what Kitchener represent to a lot of people, and that is Trinidad too.

In 1965, Kitchener came down from England to sing at the Revue. Jazzy Pantin was managing that tent, Samaroo was the promoter. But Kitchener fall out with Samaroo and say he not singing at the Revue, he going to sing in Sparrow tent. Now, that confuse a lot of people, because after Sparrow sing that hard picong on Kitch in '64, the last thing anybody expect is Kitchener to go behind Sparrow backside in the Young Brigade tent. But they say they make-up, they 'joining forces'; 'one hand don't clap' and all of that. And Sparrow, of course, like nothing better than to have Kitchener in *his* tent.

Well, it didn't last. They fell out, and Kitch decide he not singing in the tent. I will never forget seeing Kitchener on Carnival Friday night, across the road from the Young Brigade, on Dundonald Street, stand up under a lamp post; the jacket, the tie, the hat, the light shining down on him. A crowd of people surround him – people who going to the tent and come across the road to see what happening. And Kitch have his guitar an' he singing:

Is my pussin, she said, 'Is my pussin,' she said
'Is my pussin, it's my pussin
I feed her, mind her, raise her from small
Man, take off your hand from she
don't touch meh pussin' at all

You could imagine that? You could imagine the great Lord Kitchener, the grandmaster, my friend, to be on the street singing for the people? He wouldn't cross the road and go in Sparrow tent, no sir. People stop out their car, people stop where they going to big fête and pageant in the savannah when they see was Lord Kitchener singing there. I couldn't bring out one word to him that night. I just stand up there like everybody else and listening, and when is clap to clap I clapping. That is calypso.

That year he win the Road March again, three years in a row, with 'My Pussin''. He had another song, 'Hold On To Your Man' – the melody sweet like red sugar cane. Pan Am North Stars play it in the steel band competition and they come second; it run second in the Road March, so Kitch win first and second in the Road March; he capture the people again. Radio Guardian had him on their hit list, so every half an hour you hearing Kitch. He with his wife in high-class fête, white suit and white shoes. I hear he was building a house in Diego Martin. Things were going very well for him. But it have a zwill in the madbull tail.

MARJORIE, 1965

KITCH WERE DOING A SHOW at a night club in Manchester, and in the middle of his performance, a woman walked in. She walked in quietly by herself and stood by the bar watching him perform. But as soon as he saw this woman, it's as if he were flustered; he started acting strange. Even before the intermission, he jumped off the stage and came straight to this woman, and the two of them went outside – it was like I didn't even exist; they both passed me straight. I didn't go after them. Kitch were gone at least half and hour; the musicians were waiting. When he came back he were rough; shirt out of trousers, his tie were loose. I asked him, 'Kitch, who were that woman?'

'Oh,' he said, 'pay her no mind. She crazy, a crazy one.'

'Where did you go, where did you take her?'

Kitch had taken the woman to the train station and come back to continue his show.

Even when we got to Trinidad in 1965 and were renting a house in Diego Martin, I found a letter from an English woman on the chest of drawers in the bedroom. It were with a bunch of other papers and the woman, her name were 'Dee', was asking Kitch when he was going to send for her. She were saying she missed him and how much she wanted to come to Trinidad. He were on the veranda with Preddie, and I walked in with the letter behind my back and asked, 'Kitch, who's Dee?'

He didn't even look at me; he was peeling an orange.

'Dee? What Dee? Dee who?'

I showed him the letter and he said, 'Oh ho, *that* Dee. Well, take no notice, that stupid woman, she's some crazy woman, a crazy fan.'

I threw the letter at him. 'A fan? What kind of fan is she? Who do you think you are, bloody Adam Faith?'

He said, 'Look, I must have fans. I in music? You, you playing you don't know I have fans.'

He were acting up because Preddie were there. I asked, 'Are you bringing her here, Kitch? To Trinidad? Where is she going to live?'

'Look how you embarrassing Preddie. I tell you the woman mad. She not coming here.'

But she didn't sound crazy to me. The handwriting were neat. If anyone was crazy it were me.

KING FEARLESS, 1966

SOMETIMES HE HEAR SOMETHING; I put in a chord, what they call a passing chord – a tension chord – and he will go, 'What-what what chord is that?'

'Well, that's a G-diminished or a D augmented 7.'

And he will say, 'Oh ho, it sweet.'

Or if he don't like it he will say, 'That chord eh good. Doh put it there again.'

Kitchener didn't know to read music, he never study music. But he know when he hear it if he like it, and he was a genius when he put music together. He would start with the melody and match the words to fit, perfectly. He had a gift to do that.

In terms of performance, though, when he came back to Trinidad, Kitch was playing catch-up to Sparrow. Sparrow would dance, he would go in the audience and interfere with people. The jamette wine, the village ram, all that was Sparrow personality. Kitchener now, he come from another tradition, from the days of Growling Tiger and Invader, of Roaring Lion and Executor, when bards used to stand up in their suits in front the microphone – they wouldn't move, they wouldn't touch the mic. So he had to adapt, he had to catch up.

I used to be 'fraid for Kitchener. Kitchener was a big, forty-something-year-old man, but he would dive on the floor and roll, he would jump. Kitch had his own style; the way he would dance and kick out a leg, that was his thing. And he could dance like Joe Tex when he ready; I see Kitchener spin and drop on his knees, do splits, do boogaloo.

But still, calypso tradition didn't call for no set of dancing or jumping about, is more a theatre-type atmosphere where people come to listen to what calypsonians have to say. Even the music not that important. The musicians just there to accompany the calypsonian, so people wouldn't give one fart if the bass man could make the bass grumble, or if the guitar man hand sweet. They come to hear the words, what they not hearing on the news.

But Sparrow was one of the people that change the whole performance of calypso. We have to say, yes, we acquiesce. He raised the tempo of the music and he would put on a performance for people. Kitchener wasn't backward though, and he had a rhythm in his music, and a vocabulary that people related to, so during this time, the mid 60s, he was with Sparrow neck and neck. So, come Carnival time, nobody listening to any of the other calypsonians, is just Sparrow and Kitchener that selling records.

HARRY 'KING LINGO' PAUL, 1966

I DON'T THINK KITCH was ready for too much domestic life; he was never home. He prefer go down St James and lime with the boys lil' bit, eat souse, go in the Oval, watch cricket. At that time Kitchener in his mid forties; he feel he could still make moves, he living fast, he is a big boy in town. But when Marge left his arse and went back to England, Kitchener went up there like a mamapool behind she, and beg the poor woman to come back to Trinidad.

But Kitch wasn't no easy man to live with, because calypso life is plenty pressure; you have to be always on the fire, you have to be composing all the time, because once you make two-three song one season, you can't sing that next year, you have to come with new things every year, and the standard have to be consistent if you want to make money when Carnival come, or if you want to travel up the islands and work that circuit: St Thomas, Grenada, Grand Caricou, all have Carnival and nightclub; money to make.

But if you is a fella like your grog, like your puncheon rum, or you like plenty-plenty woman, and your standard drop or you lose your zeal, it have many mediocre calypsonian waiting to suck out your eye and take your place. And my friend, if one year your songs don't make the grade, you may find yourself scrubbing bench in the tent; the manager won't let you sing, or you footey don't make tent at all. Calypso life? You will catch your aunt, uncle and nennen before you get through.

When you get to the level of men like Kitchener and Sparrow, or a Lord Blakie, Melody or a Terror, then you make the grade, nobody could tell you you can't sing in the tent. Your songs might'n be good as last year, but people respect you as a bard and you have gambage, you know, you have charisma and a presence when you appear, and people will pay to see you.

Kitchener was a great calypsonian is true, but he wasn't a great entertainer; he kind of shy. Like he can't come out of himself. Sparrow would come out his car – he had a Opel Kapitan – an' lime on the corner. He could ol'talk with the fellas on the block about any damn thing – woman, cricket, politics, music, anything. But Kitchener was never comfortable with that kind of thing and I feel is partly because he used to stutter so bad. You having a conversation with Kitchener and you there ten, fifteen minutes, waiting for the man to done. And you can't say nothing; is Kitchener.

When Kitch was building that big house in Diego Martin, Sparrow used to come in the tyre shop where I was working and tell us Kitchener was making a mistake putting all he money in that house in Crystal Stream. Because when Sparrow build his house, he get a bar licence right away, and he used to have fête there every week, bringing down people from America, Jamaica, wrestling, boxing, fashion show. So he make enough money to pay back for his house quick-quick. But Kitchener now, Kitchener come and build his house in a middle-class area; prime real estate, one big ostentatious house. Then, when he wanted a bar licence, the neighbours kick against it. They say, 'No, we don't want no riff-raff here! If Kitchener open a bar, next thing will be gambling and loud music, prostitution, delinquency.' And no matter how Kitch try, he couldn't get a bar licence. So all he money went in that mansion and stay right there.

Kitchener was a gentleman, he was a nice chap, is true. But while he twirling cane, Sparrow making all the money. Every other month Sparrow going New York, Holland, Toronto, England. Kitchener would go Virgin Islands, he would go Curaçao, Grenada, St Kitts, he would go New York and Canada too, but he wasn't famous like Sparrow, outside of Trinidad.

Then Kitch get in big-time company; horses, he liked race horsing. He would go in Queen's Park Savannah and watch horse train, so he know how to put his money when races come. I went to his house in Diego Martin and he even had some racehorses in a pen there, and he put on Wellington boots to feed them. I say, 'Kitch, you does gamble?'

And he laugh and dash a bucket of disinfectant in the pen.

THE MIGHTY SCAMP, 1967

IF YOU GO TO ST THOMAS to play a few shows, you have to stay there for a while, you have to go to church, to market; you have to become part of the place, people have to get to know you before you could pick up with a local craft. Virgin Islands was a strict little kind of religious place – no prostitution – so it hard to catch women. As you land, everybody know that you there, they know who you is, where you staying, where you going; they have a network to monitor your movements. If you land in the morning, by the night everybody know you are there and what you doing, or trying to do. So when we went to the Virgin Islands to perform, Kitch and I used to fly across to Puerto Rico to chase women there. That was part of the whole calypso business in those days; a lot of loose women around, women chasing you. What you going to do?

PATSY USED TO KEEP his car under our house and he used to say, 'Marge, if you ever want to use my car, you can use it.' He were a calypsonian, in Kitch's calypso tent and he were building a house near Sparrow, in Petit Valley, and not far from where we lived in Semper Gardens. He said, 'Miss Margie, I'm having a big house-warming party, you gotta come.'

I told Kitch I wanted to go and he said, 'Don't go to that party, you won't like it.'

I asked, 'Why? Why won't I like it?' But he wouldn't say. Kitch were always reluctant to take me to certain places in Trinidad. I was convinced it were because he didn't want me and his mistresses to meet. But I were fond of this lad, Patsy; he were only a youngster, and we got along. He had lived in the States for a while and were used to white people. One carnival he brought a white girl from America and she were walking round in a bikini everywhere she went. I had to tell her, 'Darling, Trinidad is not that kind of place.'

Kitch didn't want to go to the party, he were never a party person, but eventually, because I moaned at him so much, he said, 'All right, you want to go, we will go.' Patsy had built a lovely little house up on a hill; you could see all the valley. I got dressed up, I didn't get to go to parties often, and my hair were all done up. But as soon as we got there, it were all, 'Oh Kitch, Kitch.' So I left him in the yard chatting and I went inside.

When Patsy saw me, he came and he put his arm round me. 'Oh Miss Marge, come, come let me show you the place.' It were all soft lighting inside; there were African carvings, masks on the walls, a little African shield, incense burning. There were a tall rubber plant in one corner, wicker chairs around the dining table where drinks were laid out – whisky, rum, cherry brandy, a bowl of ice. Another calypsonian were playing records on the gramophone – not calypso, American music, Chubby Checker, Ray Charles.

The women wouldn't talk to me. The black Trinidadian women turned their noses up at me when I walked by. They just looked me over as if to say, 'What is she doing here?' I knew a couple of them – one woman even lived a few houses from us in Semper Gardens. She kissed Kitch on both cheeks, but she pretended she didn't know me. Even the few white women there wouldn't speak to me, and when they did it were only to know if I were wealthy. They didn't have anything to say. I thought, my gosh, what have I done? The men spoke to me fine though, so I just sat on the balcony with Preddie and Bomber, smoking cigarettes and talking. Kitch came and asked me why I weren't inside and I pulled him aside by the elbow. 'These women, they won't speak to me,' I said. 'What have I done to them?'

And he laughed, 'You see, you-you, you wanted to come to party and now you see. I didn't want to bring you, now you see how Trinidadian people is, they are funny people, they does jealous you.'

I said, 'Please, take me home.' And as we were driving back I were asking myself, Why did I leave England? What's the point of living here then? To be with Kitch? Yes, but he were never home. Kitch would wake up in the morning, take a shower, drink a glass of egg nog, eat a slice of bread. He would polish the car, and then he'd be gone till the evening. I never knew where he used to go or what he were doing. I knew sometimes he were going by other calypsonians, to see Bomber or Terror, or to the studio to see Art De Coteau. Sometimes he and Pretender would go to Arima where he had horses, but mostly I'm sure he were frolicking with women all over Port of Spain. I would always find out.

Once we fell out over something and he were outside washing his car in the driveway and he were telling a neighbour, Mr Henry, a civil servant, 'Look, look how this woman is. Is me put she in house and give she luxury and she wouldn't even do the laundry!' He made such a row that I couldn't show my face in Semper Gardens for a week, I were so embarrassed.

It were a lovely house though, the house he built for us. It were split level; three bedrooms we had. A pantry, a library, a big kitchen. The newspaper came to interview him there once and they took photos of the house from the driveway, they even took photos of the three of us in the front room.

Sometimes, when Kitch were out, the neighbour, Miss Sankar, a retired headmistress, would come over and sit on the porch with me. She had just got a divorce from her husband. We'd have a coffee, some biscuits and we would talk. She used to bring *The Bomb* and *The Express* and show me pictures of Kitch in Port of Spain cavorting with all sorts of women.

Once she told me, 'Trinidadian men are all the same. They have a lot of sweet words, and they can be the nicest men in the world, the most loving, but you can't trust them when pretty women are around; their eyes are too long.' And I laughed, but she were right. She leaned forward and asked me, 'How come this man leaves you and your son alone in this house all the time? Why don't you leave his arse?'

I said, 'I don't know what to do, Miss Sankar, I'm so confused. I leave, but he begs me to come back, I just don't know. I love him.'

She said, 'Why don't you go and talk to someone? A lawyer maybe, just to get some advice. You know what, I will arrange for you to see my friend, Mr Prieto. You can't live like this.'

BENNY REID, 1969

LORD KITCHENER ACCOST ME in a Chinese Association fête. I thought Kitchener woulda beat me, no joke. I by the bar cool-cool, me and meh lady friend, Lorna. I buy two beers, a nip of scotch, and I good. I real good. One o'clock in the morning and fête hot in the yard. Mano Marcelin band blowing brass hard on a lil' stage under the big tamarind tree. They have guitar, sax man and organ pumping tempo; they hot up the place.

Whole week we advertising the fête on the radio, so Mr Fung send everybody in the radio station free tickets. Now, is bourgeois people fête eh, decent people thing. Chinese association don't have no jamette in their fête, so that is the fête to bring your woman to. Me? I like the jam-up and the ruction that the brewery fête does have, but Lorna say she eh going no more fête where man does chook one another in their waist with break bottle, and where badjohn does cut people with razor blade wipe with garlic. So she want to go Chinese Association fête. I say, 'OK.'

But if you see woman in the fête! I glad I come. Woman more than man. Woman in hot pants and strap-up heels, woman hototo! Them big-breast French Creole and them Yankee woman who cyar wine, shaking their long backside, trying to learn, an' you know how Trinidad man is? They round them like fly. Yes, the place have people for so. People all in the road and they cyar come in. Fête sell out; Chinee money overtake money.

Anyway, I there by the bar as I say, with Lorna, drinking my beer, 'cause me eh like to dance just so. Gimme a small wine on the side first. Lemme drink two, three Scotch, a couple stout, let me badden my head and *then* you will see Benny Reid wine. When I see Lord Kitchener come in the fête, I touch Lorna, 'Look Kitchener.'

'Kitchener, where?' and she stretching she neck to see. Kitch come in like the star boy in a Western. He dress all in white –

white shirt, white bell-bottom pants, white hat, pointy white shoes. People gang around him. He shaking hand, he laughing – is only teeth you could see. He talk to some white people that liming by the gate, he talk to the fella who selling salt an' fresh nuts by the palm tree. He rock back and laugh. Then he stand up in the centre listening to Mano Marcelin. I watch him walk round the side a' the fête, where they have a drain and people taking chance to smoke a little tampi in the bush against the wall, and the herb smell sweet in the air when the wind blow, and sometime a woman get brush right there against the fence overlooking the ravine and nobody don't know. I see Frankie Francis, the arranger, join Kitchener there, and they pat back and shake hand and laugh hard, like old man. Then Kitch come round by the bar where me and Lorna is. He watch me frankomen in my face, like if is me he been looking for, but surprise to see me, so he not prepared. But he come right where I lean up by the bar and want to shake my hand. 'Benny Reid, how life treating you?'

And I surprise now, because even though I meet him before in the radio station, me and Kitchener eh no friend. I hear he fuck up, how he doh eat nice. And the way he say my name, 'Ben-ny', like something sharp not far behind. But I shake the hand. 'Ai, the Lord boy, how you doing? You come for a lil' jump up?' And I grinning, because people watching and thinking, *'A-A! Benny Reid and Lord Kitchener is good friend? Benny big!'*

I suck my beer, 'You singing with Mano tonight?'

'Nah, I eh singing tonight. But I want talk to you.'

I dip my chin, *'Me?'*

'Yes, you self,' he say.

He call for a Mackeson at the bar, and I watching him – everything. I watching the veins on his hand when he take the $10 bill from his wallet, how the bill crisp. I watching the bellbottom pants, how the seam sharp, white embroidery down the side – must be stage wear, he must be now come off stage in the tent. He turn to Lorna and he smile, 'Hello, Madam, nice to m-meet you.' And he give a lil' bow and shake half of Lorna hand.

Lorna watch him up and down. 'Nice to meet you, Mr Kitchener.' And she done with that. She see a friend in the crowd so she wave she purse in the air, and is gone she gone. Mano done play and the DJ playing now, a good Lord Nelson tune. People getting on. They pack up in front the big speaker; Lorna there dancing. I want to go too, but Mr Kitchener in my arse, delaying me. He take a sip from his stout and as the bottle going up he watching me hard in my eye. Now that Lorna gone, he free to stutter. He say, 'Who-who you like for the r-r-r, for the r-r, for the Road March?'

But I cool. Benny eh no fool. I don't want to look like a mook, or like I 'fraid. My woman around, is a public place and I know how calypsonian is. I bow my head an' rub my chin. 'Well, it really have some good calypso this year, it hard to predict, but I like your one, 'Batty Mamselle'. 'The Bull' nice too. Whole album nice, Sparrow have a good song too –'

'You like Sparrow? Oh ho. But like is only Sparrow you really like in truth, because, because, you eh playing my songs much on your radio station at all.'

I laugh. I have to shout; music loud. 'NAH, MAN KITCH, HOW YOU GO SAY THAT? YOUR TUNES PLAYING. ALL THE FELLAS IN THE STATION PLAYING THEM, NOT JUST ME. THE ALBUM HOT, HIT PARADE. YOU TAKING THE ROAD AGAIN THIS YEAR, EASY.'

Kitch have a half grin on his face, like he waiting to hear more. Same time, one thick red woman come and start to wine back on him. She have open teeth and a plastic cup in she hand – it smell like rum, straight. I could smell it on her breath, cigarette in her mouth; she giving off heat. She wearing sandals and her hair straighten; she big on top and behind; her skirt tight and ride up on her leg and my prick get hard just from watching. Kitchener laughing, but he eh really wining back eh, nah, he just leaning on the bar and the bar rocking because the red woman throwing some hard waist on him. Kitchener whisper something in her ear and she bust out one scandalous laugh, then she gone, she gone in the crowd, with she drink and the cigarette in the air.

Kitchener turn back in my arse now. 'I sit down in my gallery with my radio today, Benny. Terror was there, you, you could ask him – we sit down there almost whole day ol'talking and allyuh only play 'Batti Mamselle' two time, whole day, two time. I hear Duke, I hear Sniper, Melody, I hearing plenty Sparrow, plenty, plenty Sparrow, so much Sparrow until I get so vex I dash the damn radio on the ground. Ask Terror. Allyuh have to play fair, boy, fair. I fling it down, boy, I tell you.' And he showing me how he mash up the radio; the man eye big in his head. 'Ah tell you, I fling it on the terrazzo boy, the good Rediffusion radio I buy in Huggins.'

I still smiling, tight like a puss, because I don't want people know is me get Lord Kitchener vex. He start again, 'How much Sparrow payin' allyuh eh? How much he paying? You know how much money, how much money I spend on producer and studio, me one, musicians, arranger fee, then to press the damn record, eh? Like your radio station don't want Kitchener to eat. It-it-it does baffle me boy, is a bafflement. I know Sparrow paying allyuh, I know.'

I want to laugh, because Kitchener stuttering so bad that foam coming in the corner of his mouth. And I done know – long time – since Christmas – that The Mighty Sparrow taking the Road March in '69. I like Kitch, but I not really a Kitch man. Some people is Kitch, some people is Sparrow people. I more prefer Sparrow myself, because he have that bacchanal spirit.

Last year Kitchener catch everybody with 'Miss Tourist'. All the big steelband play it in Panorama and he win Road March, easy-easy. The year before he had ''67', he mash up town with that – sweet music. But nobody could beat Sparrow this year with 'Sa Sa Yea'. Nobody. Kitch lucky if he come second. A mean, 'Sa Sa Yea' is a masterpiece in calypso. I hear they ban it in Dominica, they ban it in Guadeloupe, St Lucia too, because is patois Sparrow singing and French Creole people could understand it. My grandmother does talk fluent patois but even she refuse to translate it for me, *Sa sa yea, sa sa yea bonje, me sa oka chu eh mwe.*

Big man like Kitchener. With his English wife and the big house in Diego Martin. He win five Road March already, he have thousands of dollars and he still giving radio DJ pressure. Hear him: 'Allyuh does downpress people in this country, man. Carnival is next week; the radio should play everybody equal and let people decide which song they like best for Carnival. Is so Road March should be. Not to push one man all the time.'

The beer gone warm in my hand; I suck the dregs. 'Doh worry man, Kitch. Jou'vert morning watch, all them steel band go be playing 'Batty Mamselle'. You have it again, Kitch, you is the Road March King; everybody know that.' But the ol' bull still guffin' up.

Was Lorna had to come back and help me. She mamaguy Kitchener, she lyrics him. 'Oh I love your outfit, Kitch. You know, my cousin in Canada gets me to send up all your records for her… Oh, you know I studied nursing in England, in Middlesex.'

And is that cool Kitch down lil bit. He start to chat sweet with Lorna now, he sizing her up. He laugh, smart man laugh. Any woman that pass by Kitch mouth could get bite, mine and all. But then he put down his empty bottle on the bar. 'Benny boy, it have people waiting on me over so.' And he gone, like if was just a casual chat we had. Lorna say, 'Kitch give you ol' talk about what playing on the radio? I hear him.'

I suck my teeth. 'Steups. Let Kitchener haul he muddercunt yes! If he want more airplay, why he eh put some good English pounds in my hand, eh? Let him just pass round the station with some proper cash and then everybody go play he stupid tune.'

Later on I taking a little dance with Lorna, I see Kitchener leaning on the wall by the drain, chatting to the same red woman. He watching me, cut-eye. Same time the DJ play 'Sa Sa Yea' and the crowd break away.

I scrub bench to get a recording. When you get a recording as a calypsonian is like you suck the golden apple. Young fellas like me couldn't get no recording. The first man to record me was Kitchener, 1967. Kitchener call me one morning and tell me we going to record. Just so. Was myself, Composer and Power, and he took us to a studio to do the recording. But I can't ask Kitchener how much I getting pay. I shame. I just glad to get a recording. So he told us to prepare a song to record and he told the record man, 'Take these fellas, these fellas good', and I record a song call 'Write that down in History'. It was a big thing for us. Kitchener told us that RCA would pay us. RCA had their office by the La Basse and I went across there about once or twice and the man there said he would check how much money he have for us, but when I went back the company had dissolved. Kitchener say they rob him, too, and he would try and get some money for us, but, of course, that never happened.

— The Mighty Chalkdust

EASTER IN TRINIDAD

'YOU SEE THAT MANGO THERE? Look where I pointing, you see it? By morning that one will be ripe. That's starch mango, the best mango, mango father.'

The child angles his head, straining his eyes against the fading light to see the fruit in that gap between dusk when night falls like a swathe, chasing colour from the earth, and the hills fade from deep green to black. He hears the sound of a radio in the valley, and nearer, Miss Sylvia two pot hounds bark and rattle their chains.

Blackout.

No current in the valley. No electric light in the room. The power cut sudden. A steelband that had been playing in the distance tumbled, tinkled and stopped. Pan men cussed. Dogs barked and grumbled. The moon has no light to share tonight.

It is the second time this week that the people on this hill have to light pitch-oil lamps and candles and wait for electricity to return. It excites the boy. For him this is an adventure. Darkness like a room to hide in, the scent of candle wax, sitting on the veranda in the long cool darkness. He had been eating his dinner when the power went. His mother had suggested he go to bed, but he had cried to stay up. It was only 7.30, and he wanted to experience that magical moment when light sprang back in the house – lights no one remembered were on – when music returned to the radio, and the fridge began to hum, when he would hear voices praising the return of light all around Semper Gardens.

While they wait, his mother lights candles in the living room and the kitchen. She lights an elegant paraffin lamp and places it on the dining table, and they all sit on the veranda, the three of them watching night come to the Maraval valley. From the other side of the valley, where squatters have built their shacks amongst the immortelle trees, pitch-oil lights blink in paneless windows.

The boy sits on his father's knee, resting his head against the man's chest, smelling the rancid copper scent of his perspiration. The father puts both his hands on the boy's small shoulders and leans forward to his right ear. 'If we get up early in the morning we could get that mango. You will come with me to pick it?'

'We could pick it?'

'Yes, as long as Miss Rose don't see we. We have to be smart; you smart?

'Yes, I smart.'

'Well, you should go and sleep then, if you want to get up early.'

'But I want to see when the lights come back.'

'Current mightn't come back tonight, though; it might be morning.'

'When light come back you will wake me up, Daddy?'

'OK, if you want.'

'Promise?'

'I will wake you.'

The hill is still black with just the blink of yellow lamp-light, but the pan band start back to play again, by flambeau, gently, from a ripple to a melody.

They sit there now, the man and the woman, silence between them, with just the glow of the lamp and the sandflies around it to hum the darkness shut.

'TRUMPET', 1969

IS SO MUCH THE GRANDMASTER TEACH ME, so many things. I remember once when I was staying with him there in Semper Gardens, learning at the master foot, I went to a dance in Woodbrook and I play myself till morning. I smoke tampi, I get high, I drink babash, I get drunk, a fella had some bush meat, some quenk, I eat that. I wine on woman and woman wine back.

When I reach up in Semper Gardens was four in the morning, and as I going up the incline to the house, I see a light on in the dining room. When I reach up inside is Kitchener who there on the couch with his guitar strumming and singing. Was composing the master composing. I say, 'Morning, good morning.'

He say, 'Ai, you a'right?' and he gone back in the tune.

Ah want yuh come in town;
Don't you let me down.
Just throw on yuh morning duster,
An' pick me up by Green Corner.
We go be ragin' as it is said,
And paintin' de town in red.

And I stand up in the kitchen watching him build the song. How he tapping his foot, and sometime one kick out, and he have a little tape deck he pressing. His head rolling back and his eyes fluttering, and when he don't have the words, he humming. He was making a road march while I was playing saga boy in a four dollars fête; and I call myself a calypsonian. He was making 'Margie'. And when Margie hear that, you know she come back in truth? Is so many things the Grandmaster teach me, so much.

MARGE, 1969

IN 1969, MY MOTHER SENT ME MONEY for a ticket and I left Kitch and went back to England. It were too much, all these women, and living in Trinidad. So I took my little boy and we went home. But Kitch came all the way to Manchester to beg me to come back. He came to the house, he said, 'O gorm, Marge, *doux-doux* darling, those stupid women don't mean nothing to me. Please come back, I miss the boy.'

So I agreed to go back, but when I got to Semper Gardens, my neighbour, Miss Sankar, met me from the taxi, 'The coolie's in,' she said. 'Miss Marge, soon as you turn your back, he bring this coolie girl here.'

And it were true. When I went upstairs, there were a skinny Indian girl in the house, in my kitchen. I asked him, 'Kitch, are you mad? What are you doing with this girl? Why is she here? And you didn't even tell me?'

He said, 'No, because I know you would be vex. You didn't expect me to cook and clean for myself did you? I had to get these people in, somebody have to iron my clothes; you know I don't have time for that.'

I said, 'Well I'm not unpacking my suitcase until she goes.'

And she did, she packed her things and left. She never said a word.

KING FEARLESS, 1970

KITCH FALL OUT WITH ME in 1970 because he hear me tell a journalist that I'd like Blakie to win the Road March that year, to break the monopoly of him and Sparrow. I thought, well, give somebody else a chance; is only Sparrow and Kitch winning the Road March since 1963. And Blakie had a good song called 'A Simple Calypso' and he was hitting them hard in the tent with that song, radio was playing it, it was in the fêtes. So I tell the newspaper boy, 'Yes, I like Blakie for the road; it would be nice for Blakie to win.'

And Kitch find out I say so and he didn't much like that. He meet me backstage at the tent one night. 'I hear you was in the papers, boy.' As soon as he say that I know what coming next – was to share some licks – so I get shy now. 'You hear so? Who tell you that?'

'What, you feel I cyar read or what? I hear you like Blakie tune for the Road March.'

'Well, I think Blakie tune good, you eh find so?'

'Well, yes, the tune nice.' And he gone his way.

When the mark bust, you know Kitchener come and win the damn Road March with 'Margie'. Blakie, Sparrow, everybody get bad licks on the road. For a while it look like Blakie was leading; plenty steel band was playing his song. But when people find out that 'Margie' was really about Kitchener wife, and how he missing she, asking she to come back, the ballad touch the people heart and it run 'way with the Road March crown.

TING TANG
Carnival Monday, 1970

RENEGADES STEEL BAND coming across Keate Street beating 'Margie'. Fire in front, fire behind. The Mighty Duke, a boss calypsonian, stand up watching the band from the side of Memorial Square, right where bottle does pelt and break, and moko jumbie does wine. Scope Duke pose in a deep green bellbottom jumpsuit; gold trim, the front zip down to his hairy navel. Duke standing there like Tom Jones, hands on his hips, one leg push out in front so his totee print out long on his thigh. Afro, side-burns and moustache, the master cocksman, horse-teeth and head back, grinning in the sun. Duke, with his people buzzing 'round him like flies. They get hip by association, so they coasting plenty style, talking loud, liquor in hand; any music blow they throw a wine.

A white woman wrap her arm round Duke shoulder, her leg around his thigh, the other hand rubbing Duke belly like a harp. She see him sing and win the calypso crown in the Dimanche Gras last night and her blood take to him one time. She ready to leave her husband. But Duke see Kitchener across the street, shuffling behind Renegades, and he peel her off to call out across the sound of the iron band beating: 'Kitchener!' A wave and the gold bangle jingle; thick country gold, rings on three fingers of each hand. The band passing close, black people deep in the iron section, cowbell and hub cap ringing – ting tang – music in your pwefm. The two calypsonians embrace. Hear Duke, 'You passing the monarch straight or what?'

'I eh even see you there, boy.' Kitch say, the English tang still in his craw. 'I see you beat them bad last night. Bad licks you share. How much crown you win now, two in a row?'

Duke grin, 'Three,' and he watching Kitchener from head to toe. The long-stones man, the English man, the khaki pants, the

Hawaiian shirt, the eyes that big and seeing everything, the brain that bringing in inspiration from air. Duke watch him. And then he say, 'They thought they had me, Composer especially. But is not yesterday I start to sing calypso. I know what I doing. You will compete next year? We miss you and Sparrow in the competition this time. You must come back again.'

'We will see. If they organise proper, then maybe. Boy, I have to catch up with the band, people waiting on me.'

As Kitchener walks away, Duke, as if remembering what he had meant to say, calls out behind the band, 'The Road March is yours, Champ, is yours. Is a beautiful tune you have there, that "Margie".' And Duke spread out his stance in the middle of the government road, to watch Kitchener go. The big man going up the road, he chipping in the pan, woman in his arm, arms round his waist, they playing his song.

Carry him.

Carry him go.

Imagine that man make a ballad a road march and have people falling in love all over Port of Spain.

BLACK POWER

AUGUST. TOWN STILL TENSE with Black Power. Lord Kitchener in the white hot afternoon, on the corner of Independence Square and Chacon Street, outside the stone-washed Maritime Insurance building, leaning on the bonnet of his Jaguar, wrist across wrist, talking to Manny who sells beef pies and mauby under the shade of an oversized red and blue umbrella. Kitchener wipes his lips with his handkerchief, he wipes his fingers. 'Gimme a next one dey, Manny; the pies eating nice.'

The vendor sits on a rickety wooden stool behind his grease-stained glass display, his gold teeth glint in the sunbright. His speech is slow and casual. 'Dem fresh. Is four o'clock this morning I get up and make dem pies. I knead my dough, rise it twice, grate my cheese, season my beef.'

'You have sweet hand; is how long you making pies?'

'Kitch boy, is a long time yes. My mother – Yes man, mauby you want?'

An office worker. So Manny pours a styrofoam cup of the sweet brown drink. As he gives it to the man he grins, 'Loosen the tie lil' bit, man. Let the mauby go down, loosen it.'

The young man follows the vendor's advice, grinning, unstrapping the knot of the tie, letting the beads of sweat that were waiting on his neck run down to his chest. Ice rattles gently in the cup as he throws it back and drains it dry, sighs, wipes his lips with the back of his hand and walks away across Chacon Street, by the Treasury, upwards in the city. Kitchener and Manny watch him retightening his tie as he hurries between the traffic.

Manny wipes the metal counter top. 'How the motorcar running? Parts must be expensive, eh?'

'It expensive, yes, but nothing doh go wrong with Jaguar so – if you care it.' They both look at the car.

From where they stand, Manny and Kitchener can see the

230

tangled masts of ships in the harbour, streets that run north-south and end at the jetty, at the old colonial port and fisheries where fish gut and shrimp stalk wash up and stinking, between the buildings to the right of the square where the sky opens up above the sea.

A woman walks along the square from the east, coming down. Her afro is tall on her head, she wears dark sunglasses. Her hips swing, they dance in the stride. She is no older than twenty-five. She wears a slim white bodice and a red mini skirt that rides up higher at the back, and high-heeled, calf-high boots. Kitchener, facing her, sees her before Manny does and he leans on his bonnet with his chin cupped in the warmth of his right palm, watching the woman emerge through the crowd of faces, the scent of rotting fruit and silt in the drains, the noise of car horns, the tangible mess of the city, and he composes spontaneously, translating the image into song:

> She was walking down the street.
> Woman swing your waist,
> coming down the road.
> Brown sugar sweeter, sweeter than the white.
> – bee dip bee dam pee pam pam...

The young woman seems to be looking directly at him as she approaches. She moves past the bookshop, the Seamen's Rum Bar, the fried chicken shop, and a grin begins to spool across Kitchener's face. Manny is serving another customer. He turns to see what Kitchener is looking at and almost over-pours the customer's mauby. The woman stops on the other side of the Jaguar's long bonnet. Kitchener stays bent where he is, resting his elbows and head on the hood. He pinches the brim of his hat down to the side, Cuban style, grins, crocodile style.

> One thing I know
> brown sugar sweet
> It sweet, it sweet like –

'Are you Aldwyn Roberts?'

'Yes, that is me. What you want, darling?'

'Marjorie's husband? Mr Roberts, from Semper Gardens?'

'Yes *doux-doux*, that's right. How I could help you?'

The woman comes around to his side, shakes his hand and takes a brown manila envelope from her bag, like a fan unfolding. 'Then this is for you.'

As Kitchener takes the envelope, the smile fades from his face, slowly, like the sun edging behind a cloud. The woman steps back, as if to admire the Jaguar's bright red sheen. 'This is your car?'

'Yes, is my car.'

'Nice car.' And she gone with that.

Kitch turns the envelope over. It is addressed to him by name alone, *Aldwin Roberts*. Handwritten. There is no address.

'Wh-wh-what is this?'

But the woman is already at the corner of Frederick Street. No glance back. Manny stands behind his cabinet, wiping the glass case with a rag, admiring her curvature before she disappears. 'What she give you dey boy? Accounts? Bills? Worries?'

Kitchener does not answer, he opens the envelope and reads the first lines of the letter. He hears himself speaking. The words seem to come from some far distance within, and echoing back, collapsing on themselves. 'I get serve, boy. M-M-Manny, divorce.'

'Oh shit, pardner, you get catch,' says Manny, as flies buzz round his pies.

KITCH, TAKE IT EASY

MR PRIETO'S OFFICE was upstairs on the Saddle Road, Maraval, set back from the main road in a gravelly yard. Downstairs, there was a long-closed secretarial school. Its last tenant, Miss Arteley had defaulted on the rent and rowed back to Grenada with 4,000 Trinidad dollars in student fees she thief. On the right of the building there was a black-railed stairway to the second floor. An air condition unit hummed on the wall there, dripping cold water onto the stairs, and a vast, Africa-shaped Jack Spaniard nest hung from the eave, which Mr Prieto's clients had to negotiate in passing, or they might get bite.

To the right side of the building there was a small pharmacy, on the left, a Sissons Paint shop. On the opposite side of the road there was Ali's Rum shop, Mr Mac's One-Stop Grocery, Tasty Chicken, Stay Clean and Chex Bakery, with the scent of cinnamon, coconut drops and hops bread baking, and lower down, as the road begins to bend into Port of Span, a gas station.

Everyday for the past eight years, Ma Mable Mad-no-Arse has sat on a stool in front of the pharmacy selling lottery tickets and fanning flies from a syphilitic wound on her left shinbone. Sometimes she hummed hymns to herself, and sometimes she blew shrill songs with paper and a comb. Her face showed shallow rivers of age and longtime scars from maccoing people business and over-smiling in the blinking heat.

Ma Mable mad, but she see all that happened along that stretch of road. She saw the red Jaguar sedan swerve into the gravel yard in front of the office building, spitting stones behind. She saw the tall, long-mouth man in a seersucker shirt and a black fedora hat step out, slamming the door behind him. Mable saw him climb – two stairs at a time – up the unprimed concrete stairs to the lawyer's office. Where he grip the balustrade, silver glint. 'Oh lord,' she sighed. 'Oh Lord, look trouble reach.'

233

Ursula, the receptionist, was at her desk filing her nails. To the front of her desk were three empty chairs and a small table with dog-eared magazines and old newspapers on top.

Kitch was blowing hard from his sprint up the stairs. 'Prieto there? Where Mr Prieto? Prieto!'

'Sir, Mr Prieto is on the phone in his office at the moment. Please take a seat. I will let him know you're here.'

'I doh need no blasted sit down, I need to see Prieto. Call him for me, nah? Please. Let him come, tell him is Kitchener.'

Two week ago, Marge had sat there waiting to see Mr Prieto. It was drizzling the morning she came, yet the sun was bold in the sky. People say when you see that it mean the devil and his wife fighting for a ham bone. When Mr Prieto came up the stairs, swinging his black briefcase and wearing a navy-blue suit with gold buttons open over his gut, he had seen Marge sitting there between two women, each waiting to consult him.

The Indian woman on the left of Marge was middle-aged, with sunken cheeks and jet-black hair pinned back by clips. The woman on Marge's right wore black, square-rimmed glasses and a green gabardine dress with a mother of pearl broach pinned to the left breast. She did not smile at Mr Prieto when he walked in. She looked at her watch and sucked her teeth. '*Steups*, quarter to blasted eleven and he just reach.' The other women giggled, politely. Marge folded and unfolded her arms. Her face was pallid, around her eyes, red. She had dressed quickly that morning, yet still stylishly, in a sky-blue blouse and matching skirt with brown, patent leather court shoes. She had brushed her hair back in a band.

'Good morning ladies, sorry Ah so late,' Mr Prieto said. He was a good-looking French Creole in his early fifties, with heavy eyelids and a neatly trimmed beard; his shirt was open to his sternum. 'I had to deal with something – friend of mine in some trouble, you know how it is – wife giving him pressure. Just give me a few minutes, eh, to catch myself.' He paused over Ursula's desk to collect his mail, then went to his office.

Soon, as the three women waited, the receptionist entwined her manicured fingers on the desk and announced: 'Miss Roberts?

Mr Prieto wants to see you now.' The other women exchanged questioning looks.

Above Mr Prieto's office door there was a framed sign, written in ornate, vine-like calligraphy: *In God we trust, in man we bust*.

Marge knocked.

The lawyer was seated at his desk, leaning back in his chair, with his hands clasped behind his head. 'Marge, what are you doing here?'

'Mr Prieto, the two women out there, they been here before me.'

'I know, but I can't have Kitchener wife sit down out there with them rab. How it go look? Kitch go beat me if he find out I make you wait out there. So tell me, what you doing here?'

Outside, the Indian woman leaned forward in her chair. 'That woman reach here last and Prieto seeing she first, you eh see that?'

'Yes, he must be feel because she white she cyar wait like normal people. Is so they stop. She is Lord Kitchener wife, you know?'

'Lord Kitchener wife?' The Indian woman recoiled. 'I don't give one arse who she is. She could be Eric Williams mistress. Is five o'clock I wake up to reach here from Chaguanas this morning.' She turned to the receptionist. 'Excuse me, Miss. Miss, how come that woman getting seen first? Me and this lady was here before her.'

The receptionist raised her head and said, 'I'm sorry Madam, I'm sure Mr Prieto won't be too long.'

The Indian woman sat back in her chair. 'This not fockin' right at all-at all. She really Kitchener wife?'

'Yes child, is white woman he love, you don't know that?'

'I vex. This Mr Prieto reach a hour late and then call in the white woman first.'

The other woman adjusted her glasses. 'Is a'right,' she said. 'She sit down here weepy-weepy. Let she go first, poor thing.'

The Indian woman sucked her teeth, '*Steups*. Poor thing? Let every blasted jackass bear he own burden, yes.'

Prieto asks, 'Kitch know you here?'

'No. He's in St. Kitts.'

'So you really want to go through with this? You think about it and you sure?'

Marge's lips trembled, 'Yes.' The muscles in her stomach clenched, a heat came over her, 'I can't take it anymore, Mr Prieto. He's picked up with this young dancer girl from his tent. And she's only seventeen. What does he want with such a young girl?'

'Well, Marge, you know how some men get, when they older, y'know; they like to feel they're still young.'

'Well, it's enough, I want to go back to England. I can't do it.'

Kitchener's eyes bulge with rage. Beads of sweat build under his hat line. He walks past the receptionist's desk, oblivious to her protests. He opens the office door without a knock and finds the lawyer speaking on the phone and adjusting his tie with his free hand. Kitch puts his hands on the desk and leans forward, 'Is you give Marge divorce paper? Eh? You mad?'

Prieto rises, cupping the phone's receiver with his palm. 'Kitch please – Miss Dass, listen, I'll have to call you back… I know, OK. Kitch sit down nah; come man.'

'You give Marge divorce paper?'

'Oh gosh Kitch, why you so? You does get vex easy, eh? Oh gosh man, relax.'

'How you go-go behind my back and do such-such a thing? Is mad you mad? To break up my home? You want me strangle you?'

Mr Prieto sits back in his chair. 'The woman come here crying, Kitch; what I could do? I promise to help she out. I can't tell her, Oh I can't help you, you is Kitchener wife. Is a business I trying to run here y'know. She pay me cash. Plus I have a duty to –'

'That is my wife, boy, my wife! If she come to you asking for divorce, you have a right to call me one time. One time.'

'But how I could do that to a client, eh? Is private, confidential matters.'

Kitchener's hands form fists. Spittle foams like frog spawn at the corners of his mouth. He licks at it, makes growling guttural sounds. 'Private? You put she in house? Is me, Kitchener, put she in house, me one!'

Prieto shifts uneasily in his chair. 'Oh gorm, Kitch, take it easy. What you expect me to do?'

'You fockin' me up, man! You-you, you will have to drop the case!'

Prieto leans forward with his elbows on the desk, 'Things in motion already, pardner. I can't stop that. Listen man, Marge not stupid. She know about all those woman you friendin' with in town. I was shock; she know all your business, boy, like she have spy on you. Talk to her, man, nice she up. She footey sully your reputation. She come here crying to me, Kitch. She say how you does leave she home and go and hunt woman. She lie? People does talk. What I go do?'

'What you go do? You confuse?' Kitchener grips the protruding edge of the desk, where the laminate top meets the base, and he heaves it upwards. The desk capsizes backwards. The drawers slide out like life rafts from a shipwreck, sending the papers on the desk fluttering. The typewriter rattles to the floor with a jangle of consonants and vowels. The lawyer leaps from his chair and spreads himself against the window, lest the desk break his damn foot. Instead it falls on the chair, breaking both armrests. Prieto's mouth is open like a jug top.

Kitch swings the office door open so hard the handle punctures the partition wall. Outside, in the white-hot gravel car park he looks at his watch: 12 noon. He drives off, wheels spitting stones from the driveway. Ursula hurries down the corridor, but in her narrow skirt she can only make short steps. She leans into the office, sees the desk and the damage done, puts a palm to her mouth. 'Oh my God, Mr Prieto, are you alright? Should I call the police?'

Mr Prieto is facing the window. He can feel his thighs trembling in his slacks, his heart beating. He watches Kitchener's Jaguar shoot its red flash down the Saddle Road.

'Nah,' he says, 'doh call no police.'

MAMIE WATER

HOW LONG HAS SHE BEEN STANDING in the kitchen, looking up at the blue-green hills, and the grey clouds above?

In the last drawer of the wardrobe, where she keeps blouses and frocks she no longer wears, there is a heavy, ring-bound photo album. Several of the pages have broken away from the binding, and the corners are curling in layers. Inside, there are photos stuck neat under cellophane: Manchester, 1953, wedding photos, faded black and whites of Kitchener and her at the Cosmopolitan, or glancing back, walking towards Old Trafford, with Ras Makonnen, with Adelaide Hall and Shirley Bassey, backstage at the Manchester Hippodrome, with the Mighty Sparrow on his first trip to England, with Edric and Pearl outside the 509 club in Battersea, with Nat King Cole.

There was a time when these images were part of what kept them together, proof of what they once were. To look at them now is to enter each moment again, but also to remember the moments on either side.

She sits in the living room. The radio is always on. Birdsong in the peak of trees. Ciçadas and a cormorant in the breadfruit tree. Blackbirds on the wire she would throw rice to. She is peeling each photo of them together, out from the album's pages.

On Diego Martin Main Road the sky darkens again. She continues towards the sea, turning right into Carenage, where the sea can be glimpsed in blue fragments, like blinks between the fishermen's shacks. Here the road rises and the land falls away to her left, a plummet to stone. Lightning cracks and forks like veins over the dark ocean.

On her right, the hills rise, blue in green against the gossamer fog of clouds threatening to burst. Thunder falls from the hills like rock-stone tumbling.

238

She turns the car down a gravel road with tall bush on both sides – Bain Avenue. A man with a bucket of blue crabs is coming up the track with a cutlass swung from his waist. He wears muddy khaki trousers rolled up over Wellington boots, a dirty white sleeveless vest. He is whistling. When Marge passes, he waves his free hand.

The car tilts on the rugged terrain and then stops at the crest of the cliff. Once, one Sunday, he hired a boat and its driver, and took her cruising among the Bocas, the islets west of the mainland. As they passed each island he would name them, 'That is Carrera, is a prison… That is Gaspar Grande, people say it have pirate treasure there… That is Chacachacare, is a leper colony.'

Another Sunday they had been to Chaguaramas. She remembers walking, late in the afternoon, further out into the sea than she thought possible. The shore seemed half a mile behind, but the silky clear water still only reached her thighs. He had held her hand because the sand beneath their feet was like wet clay, sinking down. On their way back home, with the sunset so crisp and fried red, he had pulled into this same gravel road, Bain Avenue, along the coast from Carenage, to show her the true expanse of the island and the infinite breadth of the ocean, its power in death and beauty.

Now, with the sky pressing down from the weight of an impending storm, and the ocean bucking against the stone below, she walks to the edge of the cliff where a wooden barrier is all that separates this life from the next. White pine of the barrier, aged smooth and cool to the touch.

And in that sudden moment after she throws the photographs over the precipice, she regrets. She wants them back. But they flutter on the wind like birds released from an opened cage. They spiral and wing and float away on the foam.

TOO LATE, KITCH

MARGE CAME DOWN the stairs which led from the veranda to the driveway. Her walk was light and brisk. She did not wave to the neighbours. She did not say goodbye to the dogs, or stroke their heads. She sat in the front seat of the car, in dark shades of silence.

Kitchener lifted her suitcases into the trunk and said hello to the neighbour, Mr Henry, who had at that moment stepped out of his car to open the gates to his yard. Kitchener started the car, glancing across at Marge, revving the engine more times than necessary, and looking for some capricious glint in her face, some uncertainty which he could exploit. There was none. The boy sat silently in the back seat.

At the airport he decided not to watch from the waving gallery. Instead, he stood on the grassy embankment in the car park with his hands, palm within palm, behind him, watching the runway through the wire fence. He could see passengers walking across the Tarmac and up the stairs to the blue and white Boeing 707, but the noise of the engine seemed to intensify the scene. The airplane taxied and rolled, out of sight, to the edge of the world. And then it returned with a rush, lifting, straining into night. He watched its white wing-lights blink and dissolve into darkness.

In the first days after she left, the momentum of his arrogance sustained him and he would call on his calypso friends – the old one-marble-eyed test from Laventille, the tobo-foot one from Besson Street Estate, the big-eye journalist who does talk plenty-plenty – the one who never let anyone forget that he had a diploma in journalism from a correspondence school in London. They would gather in his garden to drink, lie and re-thread calypso lore. There were women who sometimes came – loud women with quick, stinging tongues and heavy thighs that made men's eyes spring water when they crossed and uncrossed them. Women who would suck beers raw from the bottle. Women who would sit on his lap and stroke the back of his neck.

On those Sunday mornings, sitting out in the red mountain soil of his back-yard with Scotch and soda, beneath the washing lines and the lime tree branch, someone would lean a ladder on the dwarf coconut tree to pick a branch of the sweetest yellow nuts. Someone else would cleave each with a cutlass and pour the water into a mug. Kitch would bring ice, cups and cutters like salt nuts and salt pork. He would lean back on an iron chair and strum random chords and parang rhythms on his guitar.

The big-eye journalist would pull his chair closer to Kitch's. 'Kitch, how you quiet so today? You sit down there, you not saying nothing. You have tabanca or what?'

'Me? No man. You think is now I know to deal with woman?'

The journalist leans back in his chair. 'I know when man get a good tabanca they does just feel to lie down on the cold ground, anywhere, and they not talking to nobody. When my wife leave me, I cry long tears. I get weak, I not shame to tell you. All the time I telling she, "Why you eh go, eh? Go your way, go!" Eh heh? One day I come back from work and the woman did really gone. I bawl like a cow. Is a process, boy. You does get over it. It does take time. But I see you with a young girl in the car the other day, so seem like you doing a'right ol' man.'

One overcast morning he went down the driveway to retrieve his mail from the box. Miss Sankar was watering her flower garden with a hose. She looked up. 'Good morning.'

'Morning, Miss Sankar.'

'Marge leave you again?' She sprayed the geraniums, the marigolds, the big aloes plant.

'I don't think she eh coming back this time. She leave me here with all this cleaning to do.' He laughed.

Miss Sankar looked over her glasses, she released her thumb from the nozzle of the hose so the water rolled, full and soft, to the earth. Then she bent to tighten the faucet shut. 'You could blame her? If it was me I left you long time. Get a maid. I hear you have a young girl; let her clean and cook for you.' And with that she left him standing on the incline, with his letters in his hand.

IT HAVE TWO FELLAS in calypso will tell you if you singing damn stupidness. Is Kitchener and Duke. And I suppose Duke get that from Kitch. Kitchener never used to put water in his mouth to talk, he will tell you plain, 'That song is shit.'

A fella call Doctor Zhivago singing. He get about three encores in the tent and when he finish sing he come backstage. Duke and Kitchener there. He ask, 'Duke, what you think of the song, boy?'

He expecting Duke to say, 'Well, wow, great, you get three encore.' But Duke say, 'That song eh good, you know. That song eh good.'

Zhivago frown, he turn to Kitchener. 'That eh good... Kitch?'

Kitch say, 'That song eh good, boy; stupidness you singing, bullshit you singing there.' Kitchener was that kind of fella. He was a straightforward critic and calypsonians respected him for that.

Another time, Allrounder singing in St Thomas – he singing in a dress. He get about nine encore. He come backstage. Kitchener and I back there talking. Well, from the time I see Allrounder, I done know what he coming for, so I bow my head. He come to me. 'Chalkie, you hear me? How I went?'

I say, 'Well, you get plenty encore, so that must mean you went good.'

He make the mistake of asking Kitchener. 'Kitch, how I went, you like it?'

Hear Kitch: 'How you went? You is a disgrace to calypso!'

It had another fella call Wonder Boy. He meet Kitchener on Henry Street and he telling Kitchener he want to sing in the tent. So Kitchener say, 'OK, sing your song, let me hear,' and they walking together.

Wonder Boy say, 'But Kitch, oh gorm, how I go sing the song just so in front all these people on the street?'

Kitch say, 'If you cyar sing in front of me and these people, you feel you could sing in front the audience in a tent?' Just so Kitchener dismiss him. After that Wonder Boy stop singing calypso, *oui*.

After Trinidad Carnival, Kitch would go to St Thomas. From St Thomas he going Miami by boat, then New York by train. He stay in New York till Labour Day Carnival, after that he come back to Trinidad to prepare for the next year Carnival. He had a routine; we used to tour together. A fella from St Kitts came to me once and tell me he trying to get Kitchener in St Kitts and Kitchener wouldn't go. But the man hear me and Kitchener close, so if I could talk to him. He say, 'Chalkie boy, I paying the man 7,000 US dollars.'

I say, 'Well yeah, I could ask him.' Because 7,000 US dollars is good money. So the guy say, 'Look, a leaving the money for Kitchener with you.'

I say, 'What? Why you don't give him yourself?'

He say, 'You give him nah, you give him for me nah, Chalkie? He will listen to you.'

I say, 'Well pardner, all I could do is talk to Kitchener. I cannot promise anything.'

He say, 'Yes Chalkie, just talk to him for me nah, man, and offer him the money. Give him the money straight away.' Cause if Kitchener in St Kitts, the fella know the whole of the island coming out.

But 7,000 US dollars in a paper bag in my car. I frighten.

I go by Kitchener; he was watching TV. 'Kitch, wha' happening? Everything all right?' So and so we ol' talk lil bit. Because I cyar go and talk to Kitchener about no show in St Kitts just so. I have to soften him up first. After a while I say, 'Well Kitch, this fella Kenny Bell, he eh talk to you? About the show in St Kitts?'

Kitch say, 'Yeah...'

I say, 'Well, he want you go St Kitts and he give me the money to give you.'

Kitch say, 'He-ee-ee he give you money to g-g-give me?'

I say, 'Yes man, he give me 7,000 dollars and I have it right here for you.'

Hear what Kitchener tell me: 'Chalkie, if I going St Kitts with you, Stalin or Sparrow I going. But he want me to go St Kitts and s-s-sing with some jackass, some Lord Jooking Board.'

Kitchener not going on a show with some reggae boy. Or some jump-up fella, or some quack calypsonian from England. If you want Kitchener to go on a show at Goldsmiths University, Kitchener not asking how much you paying him, nah, he asking you, 'Who else on the show?' And if you tell him is somebody from England or some St Kitts calypsonian, he eh going, he eh going!

HARRY 'KING LINGO' PAUL, 1971

KITCH WOULD ALWAYS remind you he live in England. He would say, 'Is sixteen years I live in England you know? Sixteen years.' And he use that like a social currency. Somebody would say, 'cow milk,' and he'd say, 'Oh, when I uses to live in England, I used to get fresh milk deliver every morning, fresh cow milk!' He ready to tell you how he met Princess Margaret, how she buy two hundred copies of a record he make, how he used to perform at the Savoy and how his salary was £100 a night plus tips.

But he don't like plenty TV or radio interview because of the stuttering, and he will eat up tape if you wait on him to finish. And sometime when they interview him he would forget he in Trinidad and say things like 'My *mate* Preddie' or how this or the other was 'brilliant' or 'excellent', and people would watch him, and talk behind his back. Vocabulary. Women would point at him with their mouths. 'A-a! You eh hear he? He feel he is a Englishman, he feel he bright.'

'Yes, once they go away little bit and marry white woman is so they does come back.'

But the Kitchener I know to work with is just a country bookie. He like country people, the smell of manure, river lime, bush meat, he like them things. He is a man like to keep money in mattress. I used to tell him, 'Kitch, if you want me to do accounts work for you, I could do that, put your money in the bank, invest it.' But he harden.

It had a time we used to lime down Wrightson Road, what used to be call the Gaza Strip in the '50s – that strip of road from Gatacre to Colville Street. It had about five nightclub along there, rum bar, brothel and frolic house. If you have a lil' money you could get action, you could gamble, drink whisky, buy pussy, do business, anything. If you want to hire a hit-man or some vagabond to bust somebody head for you, is there you go.

245

All the big boys used to lime there, all the top calypsonians. Men like Tiger, Duke, Blakie, Sparrow, even Lion with the monocle and the cane. When them movie stars come to Trini, the strip was the first hotspot they hitting. Robert Mitchum, Tyrone Power, Eli Kazan, Chubby Checker, even Sidney Poitier was down there, yes, Sidney Poitier was there one Carnival – and Belafonte too. Remember Melody was writing songs for Belafonte at one time, so he bring him down from New York.

Melo had everybody laughing that night when Belafonte was there. Melo like to show off, he was a joker and a scamp. We was sitting on the roof veranda of the Caribou Club, firing some Scotch in the moonlight, shit talking, relaxing. Now, even though we carrying on, everybody kinda nervous because Harry Belafonte there. People downstairs want to come up for autograph, to meet him, but the manager lock off the rooftop with a chain, so only VIPs up there – big men talking.

Melody had just come back from America and was leaning on the wall overlooking Wrightson Road, wearing these jackass baggy pants that he said was the latest style in New York. The crotch hanging low like Melo had donkey stones. So naturally, the fellas were making laughs at it. Kitch was the first one to say something. 'Melo, what kind of pants is that boy? How the crotch long so?'

Melody say, 'Ai, you leave my pants alone. You old timers don't know a damn thing about style.' He say *st-yle* like it have two syllables.

Kitch say, 'A'right, Crotchy, you talking fashion, but I never see you in a good suit yet. Only hot shirt and clown pants, not one good suit you have. Like is a fisherman make them pants for you.'

Well, we laugh like drake duck. And for the rest of the night we call Melo 'Crotchy'. Melo laughing too but he 'fraid the name stick. He play he vex, he start to steups. But remember, Melody is a master of picong, so his mouth not nice. He raise off the banister and he say, 'Haul allyuh mother arse. Kitchener, you playing you don't know why I have to wear these pants? You see it a'ready is a child foot I carrying here, so my ballroom must have room to move. You wearing suit with long jacket because your ballroom small and you have to hide it.' And Melo start to walk around the veranda like a duck, like if his knees so bandy from the weight he carrying down there, they couldn't straighten. The fellas laugh till they get weak.

Belafonte lean across an' hug-up Melo. 'See, see, that's what happens when you mess with Lord Melody.'

When the waitress come with a tray of drinks and cutters, Melody walking the same stupid way behind the girl; the poor girl almost drop the damn drinks. She was bulling there too. Yes, it had rooms in the back. Black girl. Black like molasses. She wasn't a pretty girl, but she was talented.

That night me and Kitch leave the club with two women. Venezuelans. We badden their heads with Scotch. Kitch driving the Jaguar he bring down from England. Leather seats, wooden steering – a good car. We head east up Wrightson Road, and cut across by the electric factory. We going round the savannah because Kitch want to eat a chicken roti from Miss Dolly before he go and bull. And he driving like a beast because it late and the road clear. When we reach Maraval Road, by Stollmeyer Castle, we hear a siren. Light flashing. Police. One of the women say, 'Go, go! No stop. No, no stop, no passport.' But the way the squad car coming up behind us was no choice but to stop. The women jump out and run down in the hollows by the botanical gardens. They gone. Good money waste.

The police drive up beside us and an Indian officer lean out the window, 'Where allyuh going so quick? Switch off the engine.' Kitch switch off and come out the car. He step out broad, he not 'fraid, he tall, the look on his face fix like the police delaying him from some important business. The officer come out the squad car. Is he one alone, a black Indian. He build tough, stocky, thick moustache, muscular. Before he could open his mouth, Kitchener was on him,

'Yes officer, what you want with m-m-me? What I do? I do something?'

The officer explain to Kitch that he was driving without headlights on, and speeding too.

'Speeding? Nah, I wasn't driving fast, you mad or what? You stop me for shit.'

The officer watch Kitch. 'I mad? You driving without headlights on, with two prostitute in your car and you calling me mad? You want to spend the night in jail? What your name is?'

'My name? You want my name? You don't know who I is?'

'No sir, I don't know you. What name you have?'

Kitch laugh. 'Man, you making joke. You… how you mean you don't know me? You don't recognise me? Where you come out from? You come from the bush or what?'

The officer rest his hand on his holster.

Kitch say, 'Aldwyn Roberts, Lord Kitchener.'

'Let me see your licence. This is your car?'

Kitch didn't bother to answer him. He just reach behind the sun shade and take out his papers. The fella turn in my arse now, flashing his torchlight in my face where I sit down in the front seat. He ask me my name, I tell him. He write it down. He check Kitch documents. 'Yes, Mr Roberts, how much you drink tonight?'

All this time people passing on Cipriani Boulevard and slowing down to see. Kitch grinding one set of malice. He don't want people recognise him so he pull his hat right down over his eyes; he cussing and mumbling, and when he vex so he does stutter bad-bad. 'Officer, look 'ere, let me go my way please, let me go my way. Is one blasted stout I drink. One s-s-stout and a nip of rum. I look drunk to you? Eh? A big man like me, you s-stop me for nonsense. I doh even drink. Is these things does m-make me want to go back England. Look, look, I going my way,' and he go to open the car door. The officer get belligerent, he say, 'Boss, move from the car, I eh finish with you yet. You feel you could guff up on me? You don't know I could carry you down to the cells right now for solicitation and obstruction of justice. You feel because you have big car…?' And he put a hand on he holster. Revolver there, the handle peel back like dog prick.

When I see that I talk. 'Look now, look, Mr Officer, Kitch, all yuh ease up nah man. Let we live in peace. Officer, this is Lord Kitchener, you must know is Kitchener; it eh no criminal.'

The officer laugh and shake his head, he taking his notes. 'You could be Lord Byron or Doctor Kildare, you can't drive so in Port of Spain again.'

Kitch vex. He feel insulted because the officer treat him like a stepchild. When the man satisfy with we he give Kitch back his documents. He say, 'Allyuh best go from here now, go now before I lock up allyuh arse. Turn on your headlights. Go, go from here now.' And we just pull out, and go.

So much years I know Kitchener I never see him get vex so, except one time in '66 when he kick off a sink backstage at the calypso tent because the MC make a joke on how he tongue tie. And Marge tell me how sometimes they used to be home cool-cool and he get vex for the slightest thing, like how the house looking untidy, or how his soup too hot to eat, so Marge have to blow it, or he will capsize table and fling plate. He wasn't easy, you know. It take him a lil' while to settle back in Trinidad and for a while it seem like he was vex with everything.

EUGENE WARREN, 1973

YOU KNOW WHEN you playing mas you does get some good vibes? Well, I could remember how in 1972 they put off Carnival till May because of the polio epidemic. And up to when they announce that, Kitchener was leading the Road March race with a tune call 'Mrs Harriman'. Kitch release that the previous December, as usual, in time for Carnival. He don't know Carnival getting postpone. And smart-man Sparrow come late in the season – in late January, an leggo 'Drunk and Disorderly'. Lord, well that mash up everybody, including Kitchener, an' Sparrow take the crown.

The next year now, 1973, Kitchener write on that; how Carnival get put off till May, and how rain wash it out. The song was 'Rain-O-Rama'.

An' they start to jump around, and they start to tumble down,
and they fall down on the ground, if you see how they gay.
But what was so comical, in the midst of bacchanal,
rain come and wash out mas in May.

Ice in your ice, boy, that was tune! Town went mad, and Kitchener take back the Road March crown. Nobody, not even Sparrow coulda compete with that one. Was eight bars in the verse, sixteen in the chorus.

I was playing guitar pan with Marubunta Steel Band, and that year we come out in fancy sailor outfit – white bell-bottom suits, shirt-jac with the glittering green trim, and we throwing powder and we blowing whistle. We beat 'Rain-O-Rama' all through Port of Spain – Adam Smith Square, Tragarete Road, St James.

That was a Carnival, them days was sweet, sweet mas.

FOUR ROADS. I was walking up Four Roads, Diego Martin. I was seventeen and working at Fernandes in Laventille, and every day I used to have to pass through Four Roads to go home. One afternoon I minding my own business, walking. When a-a! I hear a car horn blow behind me. Then the car slow down on the road next to me, so people have to drive around it. Is a fancy car. When I look inside: two old man, both of them in hat and suit. The one driving I recognise; was Lord Kitchener, the calypsonian. The next man just sit down there grinning. Kitchener lean across, 'Darling, were you going? You want a drop?'

I say, 'Well no, I going home. No thank you.'

'You going home? Where you living? Let me drop you nah? What is your name?'

I say, 'Valerie, but is OK. I will walk.' And I keep walking, because I not going in no man car just so.

'A nice girl like you, Valerie, you shouldn't be walking this dangerous road on your own. You could get bounce – these drivers so careless. You want iron bounce you?'

I laugh. So he stop the engine and ask me one set of question. Where I coming from, if I have boyfriend, where I working? When I tell him I working Fernandes, he say, 'Oh ho, you working Fernandes? OK, well tomorrow I have to drop somebody in the airport and if, if I passing by Fernandes, I might, if, if I have time, I might come and pick you up, and bring you home, because I not living far from here. But you have to give me your phone number.'

I say 'Well… OK, no problem.' But I confuse and I watching him. What Kitchener want with me? He ask me how old I was; I tell him eighteen.

You know the next day when I come out from the factory I see the car park up outside the gate. I get frighten. I was with some friends and I go amongst them and hide to pass. But Kitchener see me and he know I see him, so he call, 'Valerie', but I run.

By the time I reach home the telephone ringing. My father say, 'A man on the phone for you.' It was Kitchener, but I couldn't tell my father that. Kitchener was vex. Oh, how I leave him there like a fool and embarrass him. How he is a big man and he was only being kind, and how he went out of his way to pick me up. He want to know who is the fellas I was with, he want to know why I treat him so.

The next day he was there again. I get in the car this time, and is so things start. But it take a long, long time; it take about two years before I really let my family know, before I say, 'OK, Kitchener is my man.' Because I didn't want no old man, I wanted to meet boys my age. But he was very charming and polite, he was a gentleman.

He told me he was married to an English woman. But he tell me he and his wife was having problems and that he was going to leave her. I never meet her. Those evenings I was doing a course in Port of Spain, and he used to come and pick me up every night – if he was in the country – and bring me home. One night he pick me up and say he left his wife. He said she was going back to England and that they were selling the house. But he could see that I didn't believe him so he took me outside and opened the car trunk and showed me he had one plastic bag of clothes in there; a couple shirt, socks, some drawers. I say, 'That is all the clothes you take with you?'

'Yes, I will go back for the rest.'

'So where you will live?'

And he close the trunk and say, 'Doh worry.'

I know for a while he was staying with Pretender; maybe Errol Peru help him, and then the government give him one of the new houses they were building in Mt Hope, and I went to live there with him. But when I got there, the walls not paint; was bare cement, no furniture, no stove, just a bed. I thought, *Lord, I leave my parents house for this?* But we bought some chairs and a couch, a chest of drawers, I fixed up the kitchen, and we made it a home the best we could.

Next thing coming now is tour. He have to go to Aruba, St

Thomas, New York, Montreal and he want me to come. I say, 'All right.' He carry me town to take out my passport, get visa, injection. I remember when we hit New York we was on a boat on the Hudson River, and there was a calypso party on the boat. And that year, 1973, the dance was 'the bump', so people disco dancing an' bumping on the deck. I hear Kitch start to hum, and anytime I hear that, I know, he get a melody, he composing.

He said, 'When I get back to Trinidad I going to write a tune for this dance. I go write a bump.' And as soon as we land back in Trinidad that August, he gone in the studio. Was to start recording next year Carnival album. Art De Coteau produce and arrange. The Sparks sing the chorus. That album was, 'Tourist in Trinidad' and the last song on that album was '1-2-3-4-5-6-7-8 Bump'.

Then he start to organise the tent. 1974, the Calypso Revue was in Princess Building, right by the savannah. He had a dancer there to dance the bump, but like she wasn't able. One night he ask me if I could dance it, and if I would consider dancing in the tent. So I told him I would think about it. Because even though I could wine, I don't know nothing 'bout dancing on stage. But I see it was worrying him, eh. Carnival coming and he have this big 'bump' tune but nobody to dance it. So I said I would give it a try.

He took me to the seamstress in Belmont to get a gold hot pants outfit make. He carry me to the newspapers, on T.V., the radio, advertising the tune and the tent, and when the tent open, it sell out. People all down Wrightson Road waiting to get in. When it was my turn to dance, the crowd went crazy. Next day, the pictures was in all the papers.

EPILOGUE

So for this Carnival
when you're jumping up take a break
Try and take in this song I make
To remember for old times sake
        — The Mighty Sparrow, 'Memories'

When you get to know well its gonna
break your heart.
        — Lord Kitchener, 'Tribute to Spree'

'YOUNG KITCH', 1999

THE CARNIVAL BEFORE, I was in Trinidad, and I went to look for him at his house in Diego Martin. He was so glad to see me; he say, 'Let's take a drive.' And we went up by Fitzroy Coleman in Laventille. Coleman had some chickens there in a coop, and he gave us some eggs, and then the three of us sit down in the gallery talking, sun going down; we looking out over Port of Spain and we could hear a steel band practising.

The talk turn to reminiscing on England. I ask Kitchener if he miss England and he lean forward so I could hear. 'Sometimes, boy, I does miss the life we used to live up there, fellas I used to lime with. I had a ball in England, but I don't miss the cold, couldn't take the cold. That weather bound to make anybody run back home.' He turn in my tail now, 'And you, you eh think is time you-you-you come back home? You don't miss Trinidad? A good sea bath, a good wild meat. Since the 50s you up there. Why you don't come back? You want to dead in England?' And I watch him. But is how he say, 'You want to dead in England?' That stay with me.

When I hear my good friend Kitchener sick, I catch the first flight to Trinidad. When I reach in the hospital I see him lying there. He seeing me, he hearing, but he couldn't even talk. His madam there, sopping his head. I never know a woman love a man so, will suck out cold from his nose hole.

Time I reach back in London, is dead he dead.

I used to always think he would outlive me. He is a fella never smoke, never was a big drinker, he eat good, he care himself. I always thought I woulda go before him. But every year the Grandmaster consistent, since 1940-something he making kaiso, and that is over sixty years. And every year he coming good, up until the last. But the old bull was breaking down, and people was talking. He was weak. He must've known he was sick, but that scamp never tell nobody.

257

THE INCONSOLABLE

IS REAL TEARS that rolling there; that man really crying.
Surround him with fifty calypsonians,
with cush-cush musk and lily of the valley.
Wipe the tears from his funeral suit. Steady him
before the microphone, so he can sing; hold him.
He can't bear to face the Grandmaster casket.
The chorus, help him sing it:
>   *Grandmaster, wherever you are, compé,*
>   *just for you, we coming*
>   *with real fire this year*

Because he did love the man. Loved him madly,
with a vengeance, a fire, with the sweetest verse
of picong in his throat. *Mauvais langue.*
'Small island, Grenadian, nowherian,
go from here with yuh calypsong,
that ain't calypso – only Trinidadian
could sing true calypso,
come better than that.'
Road March Champion, Calypso King,
help him. He can't open his mouth.
The muscles of his jaw are turning to stone,
to keep his water from running out.

He was there, *compé,* December 1962,
when the Grandmaster land at Piarco Airport
and couldn't step a stride without camera flashing
and calypsonian swarming like wood lice
to touch the master hand.
Who don't know him want to hear him,
they want to see how cold weather brutalise his skin.

Well, is so they surround the Grandmaster casket
at noon at The Trinity Cathedral.
And is so they surround the master great rival,
with heat and dust suffocating him
in the pew. Sing with him, sing the minor
with the Sparrow,
prop his sorrow, wipe his face.

Sugary, peppery –
Kitch was never one for class.
Grandmaster, where ever you are, compé,
just for you,
we come with real fire this year.

WE NOW REACH TOWN and taking that legendary walk up Frederick Street, through mas and muscle and every junction blazing. We pass through Raoul Garib band by Park Street. Woman in silver bikini wining by the Royal Jail, jumbie peeping over the wall, and all about is horn you hearing and bass rattling the road. Round by Memorial Square, we see Peter Minshall band coming up Keate Street with masqueraders a thousand deep. And when you see Minshall that mean David Rudder and Charlie's Roots on a truck somewhere near behind.

The great King David was there in truth, hanging out the side of the band truck with a towel round his neck, bringing in the chorus:

This is not a fête in here, this is madness!
This is not the kinda jam where you stand up like a moomoo,
de riddim go jam you.

Is so we end up crossing the big yard stage with Minshall and Roots, to find ourselves chipping through the savannah dust on the other side, in the trample out, still dancing, hip flinging, sweet in the paradiddle of the moment. Is there we was – dust kick and coming across the green to Queens Park West where the snow cone stands and beer and roti stalls line along the road. Smoke and scent of roast corn and sunburnt grass, wind blowing down sweet from the St Ann's Hills, sunlight glancing on sequins and glittering breast plates, Olmec helmets and spears, scattered and gleaming in pieces and beads on the asphalt where we walking, among the debris of Carnival Tuesday afternoon, looking to see where the bacchanal would lead us. That is where we was.

Now, across from the savannah was Marli Street, where the

US Embassy was, and where black people would line up from dark foreday dawn, everyday, to catch hope in visas to escape this island. But on that burning day we was walking cool round there, not begging them white people for nothing. In fact we was wining, praising our birthright to mas and pissing on those white walls. Tomorrow, Ash Wednesday, the line would come back long.

Well, is in front there he was. Standing between the dust, and the green haze, and the grass-flies buzzing, and the savannah's burning ground swirling around him on all sides. But where he stood, calm savannah ghost, with his hands clasped behind him and his trouser legs billowing in the breeze, like fish still flapping, his yellow shirt striped with blue and starch, his canvas trilby tilt to the right, against the sun, so that it cover at least one eye. But even from the back we knew it was him. I turned to Noel. 'That look like Kitchener.' And we side up alongside him, 'Mr Kitchener?' He shook both our hands, he blinked. Then he swung his hands back behind and rocked back and forth on the balls of his feet, grinning in the dust.

We knew that this private meeting with the master was both precious and impossible, and so Noel and I slowed our vibration to bask in the glare and presence of his myth. And so as not to let any awkward silence seep in and give him reason to walk the few yards to the street and be lost among the blam and the flutter of Carnival, I strained to engage the master; impromtu, extempore. I asked him, 'What you think of the calypsos this year? I mean, who you like for Road March?'

His big teeth were brown at the roots in the recessed gullies of his gum. His impediment was folklore. We expected it. 'S-S-Stalin have a good song. D-Duke song good too… T-T-Thunder.'

Noel, awkward in his limbs, blinked hard in the sun. He asked, 'What you think of Iwer George song?' Because Iwer was fresh and in serious contention for the Road March title, and it was curious that the Grandmaster had not mentioned this, nor any of the other jump an' wave anthems of that season. Well, is this debate what make Kitchener engage and explain what was real calypso and what was not, how Stalin does sing good. Duke and

Relator too. How he not sure about the Tambu and the Blue Boy and the Iwer and the jump and wine calypso, but he like David Rudder tunes. He speak on ray minor and sans humanité, on true-true kaisonians that used to sing in the golden age – bards like Growler and Invader, Roaring Lion and Beginner. He sang a few lines. Teach us how to know the difference between major and minor.

'*Ja No!*
That is the major.
Jah
   no…
That is the minor.'

All these mysteries get unravel down till we left him standing there in the grainy field, with mas and gladness all around. He said he was watching the parade of the bands. He fixed his hat and leaned back in the heat. The master there, coasting a role.

We rejoined the multitude behind Roots and they start back to jam down Cipriani Boulevard, Tragarete Road and cut across to Ariapita, until they settle beside the Mas Camp Pub on French Street corner. Was a blood and rebellious mas that year, like the history of a people was exploding in the full bright and glitter, buzzing heights, bass to rock foundations, cuss words to burst fire like carbide.

See we in St James that night, seeking the last beating heart of the Carnival. Is bitter-sweet sadness to let it go, but the spirit must go back up to the hills. Then we hear a steel band – far, like it far, far in the distance. But it coming to come and when it reach we start to jump with them, jump because this might be the last proper dance we have before the spirit gone. Invaders. They had a flag man leading, clearing the way – let the damn band pass. Further more, tell the DJ in the bar to stop spinning them kiss-me-arse record so the people can hear the sweetness of the pan.

As the steel band passing through the back roads of Woodbrook it taking people with it. Till what at first was a trickling crowd become a mighty gang of las' lap revellers, all seeking that last sweet lagniappe.

Invaders tired but they beating sweet. We tired too but we

carrying a joy. As we rounds by the Oval they start to play 'Pan in A Minor', by the Grandmaster Kitchener, his big pan tune for that year. That was the minor so melancholy, that was the zwill in the mad bull tail. Chip we chippin' behind Invaders, following them into the mystery of darkness, into the heart of the damn thing self.

All this get write in my copybook that night, as I write this down here now. Same way. Yes. Is there we was.

This is how we know they used to play mas in Trinidad.
— Lord Kitchener 'Play Mas'

KITCH: A LIMINAL LIFE, A COMMUNITY OF VOICES

As a 'fictional biography' *Kitch* occupies a deliberate position between the two genres. In a conventional biography, the claims and assertions of the narrative have to bear the burden of truth. In its fictional counterpart, however, the reader is led away from facticity, and invited to understand the work, not necessarily as a historical document, but through its construction, the way it is put together.

Kitch is a work based explicitly on a historical figure, but one which utilises the narrative methods and devices of fiction. It is distinct from the kind of fiction which presents a quasi-biographical rendering of an imagined life.

Like Michael Ondaatje's 1976 novel, *Coming Through Slaughter*, a fictionalised account of the life of the pioneering jazz cornetist Buddy Bolden, *Kitch* makes use of discontinuous and dislocated narrative voices alongside a range of ancillary devices, such as newspaper clippings, historical documents and interviews. Both novels are experiments in literary collage and both challenge ideas about what is authentic. The 'facts' of Kitchener's life, like Bolden's to Ondaatje, came to me in fragments or 'splinters', and this is how the text is presented; as a series of shifting styles, perspectives, devices and voices.

As a Caribbean author, I have a political investment in a polyvocal narrative, in which the voices of the characters – fictitious or otherwise – who surround a protagonist contribute non-hierarchically to the narrative being told. This is in contrast to the 'traditional' method in which there is generally a single narrator and a protagonist who is the sole focus of the narrative.

At a workshop at the Bocas Literature Festival in Trinidad, in 2014, the novelist Earl Lovelace explained that his focus is never solely on the central figure or narrator in a story, but equally on who or what lies on the periphery. In this way, Lovelace gives voice to a community rather than just to an individual. As Heather Russell has rightly suggested in her *Legba's Crossing: Narratology in the African Atlantic*, this decentering approach is part of a wider de-colonising strategy in Lovelace's work which emerges as 'a metonym for the nation-building project.'

The focal character of *Kitch*, Lord Kitchener, is decentred and he provides no first person commentary on his own life. Instead, his story is witnessed – and carried – by a community of voices. While he remains at the centre of their stories, the community which reflects and constructs him also reveal themselves in the telling. The reader is offered a glimpse of the socio-political and cultural background to Kitchener's life, and of the lives of those within the milieu in which he lived, loved and worked. It is in this liminal place in the text, at the interstice of fiction and biography, at the point where community and individual meet, that we all, writer and reader, create Lord Kitchener.

In the iconic Pathé footage of the *Windrush's* arrival, Kitchener occupies a liminal border, a physical threshold – not yet in Britain but no longer in the Caribbean. In his symbolic role of griot – both messenger and entertainer, artist and public figure – Kitchener was able to enter the colonial centre, and return, in the mid 1960s, to the postcolonial sphere of newly independent Trinidad. He is like Legba at the crossroads, suggesting both horizontal migratory movement to the metropolis, and the vertical retention of ancestral memory through time.

Kitch is divided into three sections that correspond to temporal and geographical locations, tracing Kitchener's story within a wider political narrative which comments on the Caribbean experience in colonial Trinidad, postwar Britain, and finally, in postcolonial, independent Trinidad.

Kitch does not strive to offer a comprehensive biography. A biography can suggest one point of entry, but can never tell the whole story. What I have tried to do in *Kitch,* is to suggest one version of the many lives Kitchener might have lived.

Central to my research were the numerous interviews I conducted. I interviewed several colleagues and contemporaries of Lord Kitchener. I spoke to calypsonians, to Brother Superior, Calypso Rose, The Mighty Chalkdust, to Black Stalin, and the Mighty Sparrow. I visited La Cour Harpe, now Harpe Place, 'behind de bridge' in east Port of Spain where Kitchener had lived in the early 1940s to speak to Beryl Baptiste, an octogenarian matriarch of the enclave, who remembered the young calypsonian's arrival in the barrack yard in 1942. The steel pan player and masquerade artist, Eugene Manwarren, who had lived in a barrack yard on Henry Street, provided important, detailed, first-hand descriptions of his and Kitchener's shared community, and of the steelpan movement in Port of Spain during the 1940s and '50s.

In Manchester, I interviewed Marjorie Moss, Kitchener's first wife whom he married in 1953, and returned to Trinidad with in the mid 1960s. Retired calypso and cabaret artist Leonard 'Young Kitch' Joseph had been a close friend and protégé of Kitchener for almost sixty years. From him I learned much about Kitchener's creative process, as composer, performer and recording artist.

In London I spoke extensively with Russell Henderson, a Trinidadian pianist and steelband pioneer who had recorded with Kitchener throughout the 1950s and '60s. I also interviewed family members in Trinidad, forming an honest, composite and critical representation of Kitchener, beyond his sobriquet. Some interviews led to those monologues which can be found in the text. At other times one sentence, one memory recalled at the end of a conversation became an entire chapter, fictionalised or imagined into reality.

My research began at Kitchener's death in 2000. His death felt personal, as if a relative had died. It symbolised the end of an era, the closing movement of a generation which included my grand-parents, people born into the heart of the colonial project. I saw loose parallels between his life and mine: we both migrated, as musicians, to the UK in our 20s. I was concerned, too, that after a six-decade career not much was known about Kitchener's life beyond his musical achievements. There was no book I could consult. As Pearl Connor once commented on the contributions of Caribbean artists in Britain, 'There is a hole in the ground and we fall into it.' With *Kitch*, I have tried to address one of these omissions.

Anthony Joseph
May 2018
London

Anthony Joseph was born in Trinidad. He lectures in creative writing and literature at Birkbeck College and at The University of Liverpool where he is the Colm Tóibín Fellow in Creative Writing. He holds a PhD in Creative and Life writing from Goldsmiths College, for which he completed a fictional biography of the Calypsonian Lord Kitchener. In 2015 he presented *Kitch*, a documentary for BBC Radio 4. Anthony is the author of four poetry collections: *Desafinado, Teragaton, Bird Head Son* and *Rubber Orchestras*, and a novel, *The African Origins of UFOs*. As a musician and bandleader he has released seven critically acclaimed albums. He lives in London.

ALSO FROM PEEPAL TREE PRESS

Kevin Le Gendre
Don't Stop the Carnival: Black Music in Britain, Volume 1.
ISBN: 9781845233617; pp. 374; pub. 2018; £19.99

From Tudor times to the mid 1960s, this is a story framed by slavery, empire, colonialism and the flow of music around the Black Atlantic of Africa, the Caribbean, the USA and Great Britain. It is about temporary but influential visitors such as the Fisk Jubilee Singers, the Southern Syncopated Orchestra and Paul Robeson; about the post-1945 migration of people from the colonial empire to Britain; about the new energies released by independence in the ex-colonies that created new musical forms such as ska, rocksteady and West African high life.

It is the story of a struggle against racism, but also of institutions like the military that provided spaces for black musicians from the middle ages to the mid-20th century. It is the story of John Blanke in the court of Henry VIII, Ignatius Sancho writing minuets in the 18th century, Billy Waters scraping the catgut on the streets, the violinist George Bridgewater and his falling-out with Beethoven, the composer Samuel Coleridge-Taylor whose music is still played today, and popular 1930's entertainers such as "Hutch" and Ken "Snakehips" Johnson. Above all, it is the story of those who changed the face of British music in the post-war period in ways that continue to evolve in the present.

It is the story of actual Windrush arrivals such as the calypsonian, Lord Kitchener, and singer, Mona Baptiste; of Edric Connor, Cy Grant and Winifred Atwell who made inroads into the BBC and British hearts; of those who brought calypso and steel band to Britain's streets; of Caribbean jazz musicians such as Leslie Thompson, Joe Harriott, Dizzy Reece and Andy Hamilton; of great West African high lifers such as Ambrose Campbell and Ginger Johnson; of escapees from apartheid South Africa who brought the sounds of Soweto to British jazz; and of that great worker across steelband, jazz and African music, Russell Henderson.

Based on extensive research and many first-hand interviews, Kevin Le Gendre's book recognises that much important development took place in cities such as Manchester, Leeds, Liverpool, Cardiff and Bristol, as well as London. He brings together a keen sense of history and the ability to describe music in both vivid and meaningful ways.

"A meticulous, sweeping and vivid history of black British music."
Diana Evans, *The Financial Times*